X + 9
our

CA

CONTEMPORARY
AMERICAN PLAYWRIGHTS

EDITED BY

BURNS MANTLE

CONTEMPORARY AMERICAN PLAYWRIGHTS

by

BURNS MANTLE

DODD, MEAD & COMPANY

NEW YORK   1938

PRINTED IN THE UNITED STATES OF AMERICA

INTRODUCTION

AN earlier volume, "American Playwrights of Today," published in 1929, was confined to the achievements of those writers of plays who had had two or more samples of their work produced since the season of 1919-20. This limitation was placed arbitrarily against the one-play dramatists because it was feared a more liberal inclusion would result in a volume of the approximate thickness of a city directory. There are, in the history of the American theatre, hundreds of men and women who have had a single play produced and who have then disappeared from the record. It does not follow that each wrote only a single play. A majority, in fact, have, or had, either trunks or attics stuffed with rejected manuscripts. But one production each was their sole contribution to the theatre and the inference was natural that they had nothing more to say, or at least nothing more to sell, in the theatre. There was little chance of their careers being of interest to theatre followers.

The situation since 1929 has changed perceptibly. The motion picture market has changed it. Nowadays, immediately following the production of a single play of promise, the lucky author is besieged with offers of such generous sums of money to devote his next few years to scenario writing that almost without exception he succumbs to the temptation. Meaning, usually, that he is lost to the theatre, it may be for years and it may be forever, forcing play producers to hunt out other playwrights to take his place.

In compiling the material for this new book, I was soon impressed with the unfairness of the two-play restriction against authors. At least against the more promising of the one-play authors, many of whom have already sold second plays to Broadway and are even now awaiting their production. In fact, since beginning work on "Contemporary American Playwrights," four or five of the one-play authors selected for this chapter have had their second plays produced. Lillian Hellman, for example; Katharine Dayton, Irwin Shaw, Leopold Atlas and Lawrence Riley among others.

Therefore, I quickly decided that any book devoted to American playwrights that did not include some reference to these promising beginners among the playwrights of the future would not only be doing a great injustice to these writers, but would be a pretty poor excuse as a comprehensive and useful record of playwrighting in America.

Immediately there arose the problem of space. If I added the records of fifty or a hundred beginners, what should I do with the records of such important dramatists as appeared in the other book and are still actually, or threateningly, of importance in the prevailing scene? Cut them down, obviously. And this I did. So, if it happens that the reader finds the careers of former favorites noticeably curtailed in this volume he will have to turn back to the earlier book to have his search for detailed intimate facts properly satisfied.

Otherwise this new record of American playwrights follows the general form which I used before. It is more expansive. It includes the names and records of a great many promisingly young and youthfully eager writers for a changing theatre—a theatre that is being definitely builded on new foundations. Through these records, it expresses a new and constantly expanding hope for the future of a living theatre, considerably changed from any we of the last two generations of playgoers have known.

The theatre of today is a theatre in which a poetic drama of high quality is being developed; a theatre in which even the conventional prose drama is being definitely influenced by the inspiration of poets newly attracted to the stage. The winning of one prize this season (1938) by a drama expressing the acute realism of John Steinbeck's "Of Mice and Men" is balanced by the winning of another prize by the sensitive and spiritually inspired "Our Town," written by the poet, Thornton Wilder.

"Unless I am greatly mistaken many members of the theatre audience . . . are not only ready but impatient for plays which will take up again the consideration of man's place and destiny in prophetic rather than prosaic terms," Maxwell Anderson wrote in his preface to "Winterset." "It is incumbent on the dramatist to be a poet, and incumbent on the poet to be a prophet, dreamer and interpreter of the racial dream. Men have come a long way from the salt water in the millions of years that lie behind them, and have a long way to go in the millions of years that lie ahead. We shall not always be as we are—but what we are to become depends upon what we dream and desire. The theatre, more than any other art, has the power to weld and determine what the race dreams into what the race will become. All this may sound rather far-fetched in the face of our present Broadway, and Broadway may laugh at it unconscionably, but Broadway is itself as transient as the real estate values under its feet."

The theatre of today is also a theatre in which experiments are common—experiments with sceneryless plays; experiments with plays that reproduce with startling exactness the physical settings in which they revolve; experiments with dramatic recitals employing the equivalents of the Chinese property man and the Greek chorus. And experiments with the writing and ideas of young playwrights who have been emboldened by these other experiments.

In the preparation of the book I am still indebted to those who helped me in the collection and confirmation of data used in the earlier volume, particularly to John Byram and Barrett H. Clark. To which names I should like to add that of an industrious co-worker on this volume, Clara Sears Taylor, who has been indefatigable in running down the elusive data and hunting out those mossy stones behind which shrinking and modest violets love to hide.

B. M.

Forest Hills, L. I.

CONTENTS

PRIZE WINNERS

A chapter in which are grouped those dramatists who have received one or the other of two major prize awards given annually to the writers of American plays. Nineteen of these have been given the Pulitzer prize, two the award established three years ago by the New York Drama Critics' Circle. In the order and arrangement of their presentation we have begun with 1938 and worked backward.

JOHN STEINBECK
"Of Mice and Men" (1938)

It is reported of John Ernest Steinbeck, whose "Of Mice and Men" was awarded the New York Drama Critics' silver plaque as the best play of American authorship to be produced in a New York theatre the season of 1937-38, that he wrote the novel from which he made the play for the exact purpose to which it was afterward dedicated—that of being an acted drama.

Intrigued by the thought of trying his hand at playwriting he thought an interesting approach to stage technique would be to write a book that would be as much like a play as possible. Which would mean writing it as a sort of skeletonized novel, the body mostly dialogue, the trimmings (which would be the scenic background) reduced to the ultimate minimum.

Since the report comes from one of Mr. Steinbeck's most intimate biographers, the same being Joseph Henry Jackson, book reviewer of the San Francisco *Chronicle*, and was printed in the September, 1937, issue of the *Saturday Review of Literature*, it may reasonably be accepted as a true statement. But if it should need confirmation the fact that the book does read like a play, and that it appears to have been literally lifted from the printed pages and put upon the stage, under the supervising eye of George S. Kaufman, is more than proof enough.

The Steinbeck urge originally was for the novel. He is, in a way, a Eugene O'Neill of the high roads and the

3

ranches. The youth and lust for adventure that O'Neill devoted to the sea Steinbeck gave to the bunkhouses and the life of the itinerant ranch workers. The two are, apparently, also much alike in their attitude toward life and in their hatred of pretense and intellectual snobbishness. They are both shy men and refuse to be drawn into those accepted formalities of living adopted by their socially grooved and conforming fellows. To hell with them, says John as lustily as Gene.

Salinas, California, which is in the center of the lettuce industry, was the scene of Steinbeck's birth. His ancestry is German and Irish. He is thirty-six years old now, and during his early school years he worked with the itinerants in the field and lived with them in the bunkhouses during his vacation periods. It is a custom with California youths, reports Mr. Jackson, to help pay for their educations in this fashion.

"Young Steinbeck was running cultivators, bucking grain bags, doing odd jobs around cattle all through his Salinas high school days. Later, when he had learned enough chemistry, he worked for a while in the laboratory of the big Spreckels sugar refinery near by. Once he was a straw-boss on a valley ranch."

He took two or three stabs at a college education at Stanford University, boldly assuring the Palo Alto deans that he had no intention of acquiring a degree. He simply wanted to learn as much as he could about those things that interested him most. He was true to his intention not to work for a degree and when he quit college in 1920 he headed for New York on a freight boat. In New York he tried a variety of things—reporting for one thing, carrying bricks during the building of Madison Square Garden in

Eighth avenue for another. He was a free-lance writer for a while, but finally he headed home for California.

He got a Winter job as watchman for a Lake Tahoe camp when he got back to California. That was the Winter he wrote his first novel, "Cup of Gold." When this was published he acquired sufficient courage to ask Carol Henning of San Jose to marry him, which she did. He wrote "Pictures of Heaven" and "To a God Unknown" after that, and finally "Tortilla Flat." It was "Tortilla Flat" that, as the commercialists say, put him in the money. The book sale was big and there was active bidding for the motion picture rights. "Tortilla Flat" was a pretty sad failure as a play last Winter, as dramatized by John Kirkland, but it still is a good seller as a novel.

The Steinbecks went up into the hills at Los Gatos and built themselves a small house with the profits from "Tortilla Flat." Later came "Of Mice and Men" and an ascending fame. George Kaufman, thrilled by the book and the possibility of its easy transferal to the stage, turned adviser and consultant. The play, in New York, was a resounding success, many of the reviews being fairly rhapsodic. Produced in November it ran through to April, when it was given the Critics' Circle prize before mentioned.

True to form, Mr. Steinbeck could not be lured East to see his work on the stage. Such a visit, he said, would just be a waste of time. He did let Mrs. Steinbeck come on, however, and she made a family report that added to his satisfaction with staying home. All was well, Kaufman had done a perfect job, so why bother?

In reply to those who have read subtle meanings into "Of Mice and Men" Mr. Steinbeck is quick to deny their implications. No particular significance attaches to the play.

"All I tried to write was the story of two Salinas Valley vagrants," he says. "It hasn't any meaning or special significance outside of what appears on the surface. It's just a story. I don't know what it means, if anything, and I'm damned if I care. My business is story telling—only that and nothing more."

THORNTON WILDER
"Our Town" (1938)

WITH a persistence worthy of the cause it has endured to benefit, Thornton Niven Wilder has clung to his love of the drama. His first and greatest literary success was won with the novel, culminating in his receiving the Pulitzer award for having written the best novel of the year in 1927. That was "The Bridge of San Luis Rey." Before that he had written "The Cabala," which many people still insist, a little perversely, Mr. Wilder thinks, is his best work. Following the popular success of "The Bridge of San Luis Rey" he wrote "The Woman of Andros" and "Heaven Is My Destination."

However, as said, it is success in the theatre that has for the last several years most deeply interested the novelist. He wrote his first play as far back as 1926. It was called "The Trumpet Shall Sound," was given a production by Richard Boleslavsky, who was conducting the Laboratory theatre of New York, and attracted very little attention. The author has since intimated that he would be just as well pleased if this adventure should be entirely forgotten and, so far as we know, his wish has practically been granted.

In 1932 Mr. Wilder made a beautiful adaptation of André Obey's "Lucrece," which Katharine Cornell as beautifully realized, but for which there was only a restricted sale—restricted, that is, to the more devoted Cornell admirers.

The successful "Our Town," Pulitzer prize winner for 1937-38, is the dramatist's first full-length original work to reach the stage and appears to stem from a comparatively recent contact with the New England from which his parents moved to Wisconsin just prior to his birth. His father, Amos Porter Wilder, had taken over the editorship of a newspaper in Madison, Wisc., but was shortly appointed to an American Consul Generalship in China. As a result of this appointment much of the dramatist's childhood was spent in the Far East.

As he approached college years he was sent back to California and attended high school in Berkeley and the Thacher school at Ojai, which is near Ventura in Southern California. Later he had two years at Oberlin College in Ohio, continued on to Yale, where he was given his A.B., took up graduate study at the American Academy in Rome and came back to America to earn an A.M. at Princeton in 1925. He has been a member of the faculty of the University of Chicago since 1930, previous to which assignment he taught in the Lawrenceville School in New Jersey. For six summers he was a tutor at a boys' camp in New Hampshire, and this experience, in addition to one he enjoyed at the McDowell colony at Peterborough, N. H. where for several additional summers he sought seclusion and a chance to write, account for the sympathetic interest in and authentic detail of New England village life and character that are so definite a part of "Our Town."

Mr. Wilder has said that he does most of his creative work while walking, an exercise of which he is extremely fond. "Whole pages are created during my walks. When I return I put them down, and I seldom change a word. I rewrite very little."

His knowledge of the theatre was greatly expanded by his attendance upon the rehearsals of "Lucrece," when Guthrie McClintic was directing Miss Cornell and her associates in that play. In this experience he followed the Bernard Shaw custom of non-interference at rehearsals, but immediately after rehearsal Mr. McClintic would receive voluminous notes containing pertinent suggestions and possibly a few gentle protests.

GEORGE KAUFMAN, MOSS HART
"You Can't Take It with You" (1937)

EIGHT years ago George S. Kaufman was one of the three prominent playwrights who worked to the best advantage, for themselves and for the theatre, as collaborateurs. The leader of the three at that time was George Abbott. Kaufman came second and Marc Connelly was the third. Since then Mr. Abbott has become a producer, seldom seeking further fame or credit as part-author of the plays he presents, and Mr. Connelly has devoted his time either to solo writing or to direction.

This leaves Mr. Kaufman as the Great Collaborateur of his time. He has continued consistently to work with other playwrights. He frankly confesses that he works best and most happily when he, so to speak, furnishes the steel for another's flint, or the flint for another's steel. The general assumption is that in a majority of instances his collaborating associates, having an idea for a play, seek the Kaufman judgment and aid in developing it. Mr. Kaufman, however, has been quick to insist that any play resulting from collaborative effort is as definitely the work of one author as it is of the other. Thus he and Moss Hart split the Pulitzer prize for 1937, as well as a couple of theatre club medals, when their "You Can't Take It with You" was selected as the prize-winning play of that year.

Katharine Dayton, with whom Mr. Kaufman wrote "First Lady" in 1935, was very frank in admitting that she had jokingly told her literary agent, who had suggested a play on Washington life, that she would not even consider writing a play unless she could be assured of George Kaufman's help in fashioning and finishing it. Being approached, the idea of such a play appealed to Mr. Kaufman and a meeting was arranged. Miss Dayton was terribly surprised, as she hereinafter admits.

In the previous edition of this record of native playwrights we had come as far forward with Mr. Kaufman as "The Royal Family," which he wrote with Edna Ferber. This play was produced in December, 1927, and was a great Broadway success. The year following the playwright was inactive, save for a patchwork job with Morrie Ryskind on a musical show for the Marx Brothers called "Animal Crackers." The season of 1929-30, however, he returned to comedy writing with the late Ring Lardner. Together they evolved the immensely amusing satire of Tin Pan Alley called "June Moon."

That same season Mr. Kaufman also worked with Alexander Woollcott, who used to be a writing person himself, with a drama called "The Channel Road" (1929). This was a dramatization of a Guy de Maupassant story, "Boule de Suif," detailing the adventure of a sometime noble courtesan who was expected to save a party of French aristocrats during the Franco-Prussian war by surrendering herself to a particularly brutal German lieutenant.

A 1930-31 Kaufman success was "Once in a Lifetime," written with Moss Hart and with the intent of putting the highly fantastic life of Hollywood under a succession of clarifying microscopes; an exposé that would not only expose but riddle with satire in the operation. "Once in a Lifetime" completely achieved the playwright's intent. No more devastating picture of life among the movie artists and their exploiters had been staged up to that time, nor has been staged since. The piece ran a year and still serves as an inspiration for most of the Hollywood satires that are either written or played.

The next two Kaufman collaborations were musical. He shared honors again with Howard Dietz in the writing of "The Band Wagon," which, as Frank Morgan confessed before the curtain at each performance, was really a purposeful production in that it "was designed solely for the purpose of making a little money." He worked again with Mr. Ryskind on the book of "Of Thee I Sing" (1931), accepted as the greatest political satire of all time. George Gershwin furnished the music and Ira Gershwin the lyrics for this exhilirating and hilarious cartoon. It was played for the better part of two seasons, after winning the Pulitzer award in 1931-32. A sequel, called "Let 'Em Eat Cake" (1933), also written with Ryskind, which tried to make sport of the anticipated social revolution, failed as quickly as most sequels do.

Miss Ferber was drawn into the Kaufman picture again

in 1932 with the novel and interesting "Dinner at Eight,"
also outstanding among the successes of its season. This, it
may be recalled, was the drama that began with Mrs. Oliver
Jordan's telephoning invitations for a formal dinner at
which Lord and Lady Ferncliff were to be guests of honor.
In multiple scenes the drama thereafter revealed the reactions of the invited guests, exposing the tragedy and the
tragi-comedy afflicting each of the persons summoned.

"The Dark Tower," a murder melodrama concerned
with the beautiful Jessica Wells, actress, who was cast
under a hypnotic spell by an evil husband and saved when
her brother, impersonating a foreign manager, stabbed the
husband to death, was a second Alexander Woollcott collaboration, and not quite as successful as the first. "Merrily
We Roll Along" (1934) brought Moss Hart back into the
list. This was also a dramatic novelty in that the story was
told backward—catching the hero in his middle years of
failure and tracing his deterioration step by step back
through his early manhood to his youth and ending on the
day he spoke as the valedictorian of his class, laying elo-
quent stress upon the ideals of youth and the loyalties of
friendship born of a college experience. "Merrily We Roll
Along" ran for 155 performances in New York but, because of the cost of transporting it, was withdrawn in
Philadelphia when the playgoing citizens of that city did
not react favorably to its message in reverse.

"First Lady," written, as recorded, with Katharine Dayton, was an outstanding success of the 1935-36 season, with
Jane Cowl playing the role of Lucy Chase Wayne, the
grand-daughter of a former president of the United States
and the wife of a current Secretary of State. Lucy, alertly
minded, socially popular, craftily tactful but not one to be

put upon by her rivals, seeks the advancement of her husband and suffers a temporary setback when her deepest laid plan goes wrong. She is able in the end, however, to recover literally acres of the lost ground. Finishing the season in New York, Miss Cowl took the play on the road and scored a succession of triumphs in the drama-starved theatre centers of the country.

Last season, which would be that of 1936-37, there were two outstanding Kaufman-and-collaborator successes. With Edna Ferber he wrote the comedy-drama, "Stage Door," and with Moss Hart the comedy-farce, "You Can't Take It with You."

"Stage Door" had an interesting career, both in New York and in Hollywood. Produced first on Broadway, with Margaret Sullavan playing the leading role of Terry Randall, it posed the problem of a discouraged but ever so brave ingénue who refused to sell her soul and her attractive youth to the cinema. She had rather clerk in Macy's, she said (and did) than give up her hunt for a real acting part. She is rewarded in the end by getting her big Broadway chance, and it quite nobly the legitimate stage's defiant advocate.

The comedy was a success on Broadway, running the season through. When Miss Sullavan married Leland Heyward and later decided not to return to the drama the following season, being more interested in the arrival and early upbringing of a baby daughter, "Stage Door" was sent touring with Joan Bennett in the name part.

Meantime the Metro-Goldwyn-Mayer motion picture company paid a handsome price for the screen rights, something like $200,000 by published report, and rewrote Miss Ferber's and Mr. Kaufman's story for the screen. Morrie

Ryskind, a familiar Kaufman collaborator, and Anthony Veiller, Bayard Veiller's and Margaret Wycherley's son, fashioned the screen version and with great impertinence but considerable success turned the tables on both the original authors and the defenders of the legitimate stage. In place of Hollywood and its pots of gold, Broadway and its varied pitfalls of sin became the old debbil menace threatening the heroine's happiness. Katherine Hepburn played the Sullavan role, supported principally by Ginger Rogers. There was, so far as we heard, nothing in the way of a statement in rebuttal issued by Miss Ferber and Mr. Kaufman.

"You Can't Take It with You," which had been scheduled for production at Thanksgiving time, did not reach Broadway until December 14. Its success was nothing less than sensational, and within the first month of its playing seats were selling as far as four months ahead. It ran out the season, continued on through the next season and at this writing has passed the 500-continuous-performances record. In the Spring of 1937 as previously recorded, this comedy was awarded the Pulitzer prize given annually to the best American play of the year.

There was, as usual, some little questioning of the Pulitzer committee's judgment by the experts, both lay and professional (the New York Drama Critics' prize having gone to Maxwell Anderson's "High Tor" the same season), but in the matter of general popularity the Hart-Kaufman comedy was an easy winner.

"Mr. Kaufman is a Pennsylvanian, born in Pittsburgh," reads the earlier edition. "Out of High School he devoted a few months to studying law and gave it up, he says, because he found it too hard. He floated about after that, worked first as a chainman and later as a transit man on a surveying corps: was a window clerk in the Allegheny county tax office, and finally took up stenography seriously. He was, as he remembers it, a good stenographer but a bad traveling salesman, which he also tried.

"He was 19 when he left Pittsburgh and came to New York. Here he became a volunteer contributor to the F. P. A. column, at that time running in the *Evening Mail*. Through Adams he later acquired a column of his own in Mr. Munsey's Washington paper. Many subscribers thought it a funny column but Mr. Munsey, whose sense of humor was what it was, was not so sure. So George came back to New York. When Mr. Adams went over to the New York *Tribune* Kaufman was one of those who tried out as his successor on the *Mail*. His success was moderate, but he found little satisfaction in it and drifted into theatre news reporting on the *Times*."

Through all the years of his early playwriting success, even when his annual income was approaching six figures, Mr. Kaufman continued as the *Times*' drama editor. Having a job, he used to say, kept him out of such mischief as idle hours might suggest, especially with bridge and poker pals. Even after he gave up newspaper work Mr. Kaufman continued a routine that embraced a good many of his journalistic habits. He still does. For one thing, he is convinced that he works better when he works against a deadline. Consequently when he actually starts work on a play he prefers to have a theatre engaged and an opening date set for the première performance. Now that he is virtually a partner with Sam H. Harris in most of the latter's productions it is easy for him to stipulate his own working conditions.

MOSS HART

As the Moss Hart story runs (and my, how it runs!) this young New Yorker as perfectly realizes the bright-young-man-makes-good legend of Broadway as any other of whom we have record. A theatrical office boy in 1923, he sold his first play to his employer, Augustus Pitou, without the employer's suspecting that his office boy had written it. A well-to-do young author ten years later, with three hits to his credit ("Once in a Lifetime" (1930), with George Kaufman, "Face the Music" (1932) and "As Thousands Cheer" (1933) with Irving Berlin, his income caused communists to weep and income tax collectors to chortle. From obscurity, without rags, to riches in a decade —that's traveling. It has, it is true, been accomplished in less time, but never with a steadier consistency or with more lasting promise.

Mr. Hart, born in New York in 1904, selected writing as a vocation and playwriting as an objective while he was still in high school. He did festival sketches and school plays then. Later he studied short story writing at Columbia, though he never got far with that. He was in cloaks and suits briefly, which was long enough for him to write an annual show for the other employees. He tried selling for a time, but his best job in this line was selling himself to Mr. Pitou as a typist and secretary. Pitou was at that time manager for Fiske O'Hara, Irish tenor and melodramatic hero. It was for O'Hara that young Hart started to write "The Hold-Up Man," which eventually ran for nearly five weeks in Chicago, even without O'Hara.

The springboard from which Mr. Hart was really tossed into the arena, however, was his "Once in a Lifetime," which he wrote and submitted to several managers in 1930. He had four acceptances, as he remembers, and chose Sam H. Harris because Harris suggested having George Kaufman work with the script and stage the show. This was the beginning of a happy collaboration, but before it jelled Mr. Hart worked with Irving Berlin on two other successes, "Face the Music" and "As Thousands Cheer." He came back to Kaufman in 1934, when they did the backward-turn-backward drama called "Merrily We Roll Along." (See Kaufman.)

In 1934 Mr. Hart went it alone, just for the exercise, and turned out what was spoken of then as the very best original musical comedy libretto that had been written up to that time. This was called "Jubilee" and lightly satirized a social situation similar to one which was then developing at the Court of St. James, and which later resulted in a king's abdication and his marriage with a commoner he loved. In Mr. Hart's story the Royal Family was ordered to a distant and gloomy castle as the result of a playful communistic threat perpetrated by one of the more mischievous Princes. King and Queen, Heir Apparent and Princess Royal individually and severally rebel and, escaping from the castle, go on a bust of their own devising. The King thus has a chance to circulate incognito among his subjects and incidentally develop his parlor tricks. The Queen is given a long-desired chance to meet Mowgli, the ape man of the movies. The Heir Apparent is able to keep a date with a charming night club divinity and the Princess Royal meets and charms a romantic novelist. In the end,

however, the royal escapists are rounded up and returned
to the castle in time to prepare for the celebration of a
golden jubilee. Mary Boland, playing the Queen, and a personality of supreme importance to the success of the entertainment, was forced out of the cast by a motion picture contract after something like a hundred and sixty performances, and "Jubilee" was withdrawn shortly after. It
was too heavy a production to tour, even with a perfect
cast.

The two greatest Kaufman-Hart collaborations were
soon to follow. In 1936 they brought back from California
the slightly insane but broadly amusing, "You Can't Take
It with You," and in 1937 they produced a frankly satirical
criticism of the New Deal, naming names and peopling the
stage with actual characters from real life in Washington.
Headed by George M. Cohan as President Franklin D.
Roosevelt, this piece laid by the ears the cities of its trial
performances, including Boston and Philadelphia, and
practically floored New York. No such box-office success
had previously been recorded in all Broadway history.
Seats for the opening performance of "I'd Rather Be
Right" sold as high as $100 the pair, with even more out-
rageous prices frequently quoted.

"I'd Rather Be Right" is an excessively timely political
satire fitted with velvet-tipped barbs in which a nice young
American boy and girl, eager to get married, are denied
that happiness because the boy has lost his job. Not until
the budget is balanced, the boy's employer has said, can
there be a return of prosperity which will give him back
the job. Falling asleep in a park the boy dreams that he
meets the President of the United States and tells him his
story. The President, entirely sympathetic, agrees to do

what he can toward setting things straight.

Mr. Hart has a simple system of keeping busy. He works, he says, until he is exhausted and then spends considerable playtime recovering. His homelife he finds "a glamorous mixture of New York, Hollywood, insomnia, nervous indigestion and a child-like passion for the theatre." It is this last that will probably keep him writing. Which is to be catalogued under the head of good news for theatre followers.

Beginning with the first of the Kaufman-Connelly collaborations, in 1921, and continuing on through the season of 1937-38, Mr. Kaufman has been associated as author or co-author with the following plays:

"Dulcy" (Kaufman and Connelly). Produced by George C. Tyler and H. H. Frazee. Frazee Theatre, New York, August 13, 1921.

"To the Ladies" (Kaufman and Connelly). Produced by George C. Tyler and A. L. Erlanger. Liberty Theatre, New York, February 20, 1922.

"Merton of the Movies" (Kaufman and Connelly). Produced by George C. Tyler and Hugh Ford. Cort Theatre, New York, November 13, 1922.

"Helen of Troy, N. Y." (Book by Kaufman and Connelly). Produced by Rufus LeMaire and George Jessel. Selwyn Theatre, New York, June 19, 1923.

"The Deep Tangled Wildwood" (Kaufman and Connelly). Produced by George C. Tyler and Hugh Ford. Frazee Theatre, New York, November 5, 1923.

"Beggar on Horseback" (Kaufman and Connelly). Produced by Winthrop Ames. Broadhurst Theatre, New York, February 12, 1924.

"Be Yourself" (Book by Kaufman and Connelly). Produced by Wilmer and Vincent. Sam H. Harris Theatre, New York, September 3, 1924.

"Minick" (Edna Ferber and George Kaufman). Produced by Winthrop Ames, Booth Theatre, New York, September 24, 1924.

"The Butter and Egg Man" (George S. Kaufman). Produced by Crosby Gaige. Longacre Theatre, New York, September 23, 1925.

"The Cocoanuts" (Book by George S. Kaufman). Produced by Sam H. Harris. Lyric Theatre, New York, December 8, 1925.

"The Good Fellow" (Kaufman and Manckiewicz). Produced by Crosby Gaige. Playhouse, New York, October 5, 1926.

"The Royal Family" (Kaufman and Ferber). Produced by Jed Harris. Selwyn Theatre, New York, December 28, 1928.

"Animal Crackers" (with Morrie Ryskind). Produced by Sam H. Harris. 44th Street Theatre, New York, October 23, 1928.

"June Moon" (with Ring Lardner). Produced by Sam H. Harris. Broadhurst Theatre, New York, October 9, 1929.

"The Channel Road" (with Alexander Woollcott). Produced by Arthur Hopkins. Plymouth Theatre, New York, October 17, 1929.

"Strike Up the Band" (musical comedy by Morrie Ryskind based on libretto by Kaufman). Produced by Edgar Selwyn. Times Square Theatre, New York, January 14, 1930.

"Once in a Lifetime" (with Moss Hart). Produced by Sam H. Harris. Music Box, New York, September 24, 1930.

"The Band Wagon" (with Howard Dietz). Produced by Max Gordon. New Amsterdam Theatre, New York, June 3, 1931.

"Of Thee I Sing" (with Morrie Ryskind). Produced by Sam H. Harris. Music Box, New York, December 26, 1931.

"Dinner at Eight" (with Edna Ferber). Produced by Sam H. Harris. Music Box, New York, October 22, 1932.

"Let 'Em Eat Cake" (with Morrie Ryskind). Produced by Sam H. Harris. Imperial Theatre, New York, October 21, 1933.

"The Dark Tower" (with Alexander Woollcott). Produced by Sam H. Harris. Morosco Theatre, New York, November 25, 1933.

"Merrily We Roll Along" (with Moss Hart). Produced by Sam H. Harris. Music Box, New York, September 29, 1934.

"First Lady" (with Katherine Dayton). Produced by Sam H. Harris. Music Box, New York, November 26, 1935.

"Stage Door" (with Edna Ferber). Produced by Sam H. Harris. Music Box, New York, October 22, 1936.

"You Can't Take It with You" (with Moss Hart). Produced by Sam H. Harris. Booth Theatre, New York, December 14, 1936.

"I'd Rather Be Right" (with Moss Hart). Produced by Sam H. Harris. Alvin Theatre, New York, November 2, 1937.

Mr. Hart's plays produced in New York follow:

"Jonica" (with Dorothy Heyward). Produced by William B. Friedlander. Craig Theatre, New York, April 7, 1930.

"Once in a Lifetime" (with George Kaufman). Produced by Sam H. Harris. Music Box, New York, September 24, 1930.

"Face the Music" (with Irving Berlin). Produced by Sam H. Harris. New Amsterdam Theatre, New York, February 17, 1932.

"As Thousands Cheer" (with Irving Berlin). Produced by Sam H. Harris. Music Box, New York, September 30, 1933.

"The Great Waltz" (adapted). Produced by Max Gordon. Center Theatre, New York, September 22, 1934.

"Merrily We Roll Along" (with George Kaufman). Produced by Sam H. Harris. Music Box, New York, September 29, 1934.

"Jubilee" (music and lyrics by Cole Porter). Produced by Sam H. Harris. Imperial Theatre, New York, October 12, 1935.

"You Can't Take It with You" (with George Kaufman). Produced by Sam H. Harris. Booth Theatre, New York, December 14, 1936.

"The Show Is On" (sketches). Produced by Messrs. Shubert. The Winter Garden, New York, December 25, 1936.

"I'd Rather Be Right" (with George Kaufman). Produced by Sam H. Harris. Alvin Theatre, New York, November 2, 1937.

ROBERT SHERWOOD
"Idiot's Delight" (1936)

ROBERT EMMET SHERWOOD, who has of late seasons dropped the Emmet and signed himself plain Robert Sherwood, was just emerging from the after effects of a first hit when last we were expatiating upon his playwriting promise in "American Playwrights." His first play, "The Road to Rome," with Jane Cowl and Philip Merivale playing Hannibal and the lovely Amytis, had played out its season to a succession of capacity audiences. His second play was "The Love Nest," a dramatization of a Ring Lardner story about a movie director's wife who filled up on liquor and told the world what she thought of her husband. It was a failure. His third play, "The Queen's Husband," had Roland Young as the husband of a ruler of an island kingdom who, while his wife was absent raising money in America, ran things with a high hand and a wise head at home. It swung between success and failure, but continued for a hundred and twenty-five performances.

After that Mr. Sherwood, a little discouraged, rested until 1930, in England mostly. He is extremely fond of England. Has a place in Surrey and hurries back there the first chance he gets when he has completed his writing commitments in America. In January, 1930, a new Sherwood melodrama called "Waterloo Bridge" was produced. This was the story of an American chorus girl who had gone on the streets in London and was later picked up by an idealistic young American doughboy whom she refused to disillusion in respect to his belief and faith in "good women." It did rather better in London than it did on this side. Then in November of that year Arthur Hopkins produced another Sherwood melodrama called "This Is New York." It just missed being as good a melodrama as it was exciting. It brought Lois Moran back from Hollywood to play opposite Geoffrey Kerr in a story that involved a pompous Senator from South Dakota, his daughter Emma and a New York playboy. Emma wanted to marry the playboy. Her Senator father demanded that she give him up. The playboy's mistress threatened blackmail. While Emma was boldly conferring with the mistress a suspicious suicide occurred in the same building and everybody in the building was held as a material witness. A scandal broke and the Senator couldn't stop it, but it helped clear the situation. The blackmail scheme was scotched. The playboy was frightened into a sort of reform and the Senator was largely deflated. "This Is New York" was too florid a picture for New Yorkers to accept, being filled with true talk they did not relish. It was withdrawn after fifty-nine performances.

But now the Sherwood trail had reached its nadir. Thereafter it described a sharply ascending curve that began with the Theatre Guild's production of "Reunion in Vienna" in 1931 and is still rising. Alfred Lunt and Lynn Fontanne, playing the leads, were undoubtedly a factor in this comedy's success, extending a run that would normally have been completed within the season to cover the better part of two seasons. "Reunion in Vienna" was written in the Continental manner and spirit of Molnar. It relates an adventure of Prince Rudolph Maximilian the time he returned to Vienna from driving a taxi in Nice to join other assembling Hapsburgs in a family anniversary. He meets and is charmed again by Elena, who was once his favorite mistress, and though Elena is now happily married to a psychoanalyst of international fame, the enthusiastic assaults of the somewhat wild young Hapsburg eventually break down her defenses. "Reunion in Vienna" was played for nearly three hundred performances before its popularity waned.

For the next three or four years Mr. Sherwood collected the rewards of success and did little writing for the stage, though he did put in a good deal of time in Hollywood fussing with scenarios. The living theatre was at a low ebb. There was little inspiration to put aside huge Hollywood fees to risk uncertain stage productions in New York. But by 1935 the old enthusiasms were again stirring. From the Sherwood workshop now came "The Petrified Forest." This, too, was an overnight success. In it the engaging and extremely popular Leslie Howard played the frustrated representative of a dying civilization who was thrust back into life in the raw when he ran into gunplay and romance at an Arizona filling station. The romance, covering the hero's sudden understanding love for a frustrated daughter of the desert, resulted in his making his life insurance over to her and engaging a bandit leader to wipe him out as an incident of his (the bandit's) escape from the law.

"The real origin of 'The Petrified Forest,' " the author told Lucius Beebe the day following the production, "was an attempt to show the passing of an epoch in the terms of melodrama and assembled characters. But do the great run of theatregoers peel off banknotes to see an Indian fighter, a gunman, a millionaire and an American Legionnaire symbolizing the passing of a world order? They do not. They come to see two parts of highly improbable and sentimentalized romance stirred, like a Martini, with one part gunplay. The trouble with me is that I start with a big message and end with nothing but good entertainment."

Which is a typical Sherwood belittlement of a rare talent. No other native dramatist has so successfully combined sane thinking with exciting writing, and no one has put honest melodrama to such good use as he. An editorial conviction that was strengthened a year later when Mr. Sherwood's "Idiot's Delight" not only established another long-run record for the Lunts, but won him a Pulitzer award as the author of the best play written by an American that year.

The message that broke through a fascinating combination of high comedy and tense drama in "Idiot's Delight" was an anti-war message. A troupe of cabaret dancers, piloted by an ex-vaudeville promoter, ran into the beginning of the next world war at a tourist resort in the Italian Alps. There was a munitions merchant there, and a German scientist; a French communist, a variety of Italian

Fascists, and a group of would-be passive non-combatants. Between them they represent about every facet of the war problem, and through them it is very stirringly and thoroughly analyzed. In a postscript to the play as published by Scribner's Mr. Sherwood added these words:

". . . If decent people will continue to be intoxicated by the synthetic spirit of patriotism, pumped into them by megalomaniac leaders, and will continue to have faith in the 'security' provided by those lethal weapons sold to them by the armaments industry, then war *is* inevitable; and the world will soon resolve itself into the semblance of an anthill, governed by commissars who owe their power to the profundity of their contempt for the individual members of their species.

"But I don't believe this will be so. I believe that a sufficient number of people are aware of the persistent validity of the Sermon on the Mount, and they remember that, between 1914 and 1918, twelve million men died in violence to make safe for democracy the world which we see about us today. That awareness and remembrance can be strong enough to resist the forces which would drive us back into the confusion and the darkness and the filth of No Man's Land."

Thus truthfully spake a melodramatist who, in place of pretending to despise the hokum of our theatre, frankly embraces it with noble purpose and to fine effect.

Mr. Sherwood's last job in the theatre was one inspired, I assume, by expediency and commercial wisdom. For his friend Gilbert Miller he made an English adaptation of a comedy by Jacques Deval called "Tovarich." This happens to be a typical theatre piece that was dashed off by M. Deval a few years back and which, to the surprise of many, including the author, immediately bounded into a popularity that swept Europe and the Continent. Done into English it ran over a year in London, and, reaching America belatedly, repeated its world success over here, both in New York during its first season, with Marta Abba and John Halliday, and later on tour, where it was played by the New York Company, headed by Miss Abba and Rodolf Forster, and a second company featuring Eugenie Leontovich and McKay Morris. Miss Leontovich created the role of the Grand Duchess in the London production, playing opposite Sir Cedric Hardwicke.

"Tovarich" is builded upon one of the oldest and safest of comedy forms, that in which the aristocracy, in this instance represented by the Grand Duchess Tatiana Petrovna and her husband, Prince Mikail Ouratieff of the Russian nobility, is humbled by being forced into service with honest but simple folk below stairs.

The Russians are living in exile in Paris, the custodians of four billion francs entrusted to Prince Mikail by the late Czar. Though they are penniless and often hungry they refuse to draw upon the fund held in sacred trust, and are forced into service as a means of self-support. Engaged as butler and maid in the home of a French banker their embarrassment is greatly increased when they are discovered by agents of the Soviet government and eventually forced to surrender the Czar's funds. After which they continue happily in service.

With "Tovarich," a tremendous money-making success, returning weekly royalty checks Mr. Sherwood again retired to his English estate, making occasional trips to Hollywood when the wage and bonus pressure became too insistent to be contentedly denied.

You will find, by consulting our earlier record, that Mr. Sherwood is a very tall and a rather shy person who does not enjoy talking about himself. His next birthday will be his forty-second. He was born in New Rochelle, N. Y., and was moved into New York proper at the age of two.

"His literary tendencies developed comparatively early," continues that account. "He was, a modest family pride permits his sisters to confess, the editor of a magazine called *The Children's Life* at 7, but gave it up a year later to re-write 'A Tale of Two Cities' because he found himself in disagreement with Charles Dickens as to the ending of that tale.

"His schooling followed conventional lines until he was sent to Milton Academy from which he was graduated in 1914. In 1918 they gave him an A.B. at Harvard, after which he took up with the war, joining the Black Watch in Canada, performing creditably therein and sustaining honorable wounds that eventually necessitated his discharge from the army.

"In college he had edited the *Vanity Fair* number of the *Harvard Lampoon* and, it being a good number, Frank Crowninshield, editor of *Vanity Fair*, gave him a job. He was the motion picture critic and, as I recall it, Dorothy Parker and Robert Benchley were at the same time writing pieces about the drama for the same magazine. One of Miss Parker's criticisms gave offense to a Broadway manager, who protested to Mr. Crowninshield, who spoke to Miss Parker, who answered with spirit and was fired.

"Thereupon Mr. Benchley and Mr. Sherwood, rising manfully to the defense of the freedom of the critic and the rights of woman to speak her own mind, quit their jobs in protest. As a sympathetic strike their action did not make the first pages of the press, but it gave the strikers vast satisfaction and was a lot of fun."

From *Vanity Fair* Mr. Sherwood went to *Life*, of which he later became editor, and from *Life* to *Scribner's Magazine*, for which he did a job of editing as well as serving as book reviewer. It was his playwriting success that took him out of the magazine field, probably for good.

The Sherwood dramas so far produced have included:

"The Road to Rome." Produced by William A. Brady, Jr., and Dwight Deere Wiman. Playhouse, New York, January 31, 1927.

"The Love Nest." Produced by The Actor-Managers, Inc. Comedy Theatre, New York, December 22, 1927.

"The Queen's Husband." Produced by William A. Brady, Jr., and Dwight Deere Wiman. Playhouse, New York, January 25, 1928.

"Waterloo Bridge." Produced by Charles Dillingham. Fulton Theatre, New York, January 6, 1930.

"This Is New York." Produced by Arthur Hopkins. Plymouth Theatre, New York, November 28, 1930.

"Reunion in Vienna." Produced by The Theatre Guild. Martin Beck Theatre, New York, November 16, 1931.

"The Petrified Forest." Produced by Gilbert Miller and Leslie Howard in association with Arthur Hopkins. Broadhurst Theatre, New York, January 7, 1935.

"Idiot's Delight." Produced by The Theatre Guild. Shubert Theatre, New York, March 24, 1936.

"Tovarich" (adapted from comedy by Jacques Deval). Produced by Gilbert Miller. Plymouth Theatre, New York, October 15, 1936.

ZOE AKINS
"The Old Maid" (1935)

IN 1929 we left Zoe Akins sitting on a limb, as it were. Comfortably rather than precariously seated, but still on a limb. "When Miss Akins came East she was welcomed with the hopeful prediction that she would make her mark as a playwright," ran the introduction to her achievements up to that date. "And she did. But the hope has lingered that she is yet to do her best work and may, any season now, burst forth suddenly with what we shall be pleased to call her greatest play."

Miss Akins' last production at that time was a modernistic melodrama called "The Furies," played in March, 1928, by Laurette Taylor. It was the hope of a large number of people that this play would serve to bring Miss Taylor, still remembered for her "Peg-o'-my-Heart," back to a deserved Broadway prominence following a protracted absence. It did serve to introduce her to the younger reviewers who had not known her and they were pleased. But the play did not appeal to the crowd and was withdrawn by John Tuerk, its producer, after forty-five performances.

In the Spring of 1929 a play which Miss Akins had adapted from the original of Lili Hatvany called "The Love Duel," was played with some success by Ethel Barrymore, who had, in 1919, scored one of her greatest successes in Miss Akins' "Declassé." But "The Love Duel," being an adaptation, was more a Barrymore success than an Akins success.

The year following that, however, in September, 1930, William Harris, Jr., produced a new comedy by Miss Akins cleverly and craftily entitled "The Greeks Had a Word for It," and this brought the playwright back to her full stature as a popular dramatist. This was the lightly satirical and amusing story of three young women of great loyalty (to each other) who sentimentally pool their love affairs, each promising not to invade the other's territory.

There is some slight confusion of interests when two favor the same catch, but in the end, and at the wedding of the first of the trio to take on a promised respectability, the flow of wine and the presence of her old pals so affects the bride-to-be that she decides to leave the aging groom waiting at the altar and fly with her pals to Paris with a party of high-flying aviators. "The Greeks Had a Word for It" achieved a total of 253 performances in New York and her royalties built a handsome home for its happy authoress in Pasadena.

Miss Akins then returned to the cinema studios and continued writing for the screen until she came on Edith Wharton's story of "The Old Maid." This so intrigued her that she sought and obtained Miss Wharton's permission to make a drama of it. The play, viewed with distrust by those managerial minds that fear a frank, not to say obvious, display of sentiment in the theatre, was bought by Harry Moses and brought to production finally in Baltimore the first week in January, 1935, and brought to New York the week following.

The early reception was doubtful, the critical acclaim muffled, but soon large numbers of women discovered the maternal love theme and the matinees were crowded. From then on the play's success was assured. It ran for 305 performances, was given the Pulitzer award in the Spring and continued a huge success on tour the season following. The familiar story of Delia and Charlotte Lovell, cousins, and the tragedy that grew out of their both loving the same man, caught playgoers in a receptive mood the country over. Delia, tired of waiting for Clem Spender, married one of the Ralston boys. Charlotte, seeking to assuage the pain in Clem's heart by giving him her love, later bore him a child she could not acknowledge. Delia adopted Charlotte's child, and Charlotte, forced to pose as an old maid aunt, was denied the mother love she so desperately craved. Judith Anderson and Helen Menken were jointly starred in "The Old Maid" and also shared in the profits of the tour.

Again Miss Akins returned to her California home and her interest in pictures. But not for long. Another dramatic idea assailed her. She had seen any number of once-popular older actresses come to Hollywood from the East, their legitimate careers apparently finished, their finances low, their hopes trailing in the dust. And she had seen several of them, starting again from scratch, as it were, pick up the shreds of their careers and carry on to a new victory in pictures. There was drama in that, she thought, and there was her friend of many years, the late Jobyna Howland, who should be ideal for the part.

So Miss Akins wrote a play called "O, Evening Star," which told the story of an aging down-and-out actress who, called suddenly to take over a leading role in a Western picture, elected to burlesque the part instead of playing it straight and so convulsed the picture's director, as well as its producer, that she was immediately engaged as a star at a salary of $2,000 a week.

Mr. Moses, grateful to Miss Akins for the success of "The Old Maid," agreed to produce "O, Evening Star." Miss Akins, grateful to Miss Howland for a friendship that had blossomed when Miss Howland played a part in Miss Akins' first play, "Papa," asked that she be engaged as star. The play was produced in January, 1936. It was roughly treated by the reviewers, ignored by playgoers and withdrawn after five performances. Misfortune followed after.

Within the year both Miss Howland and Mr. Moses were dead.

To go back to the record and the essential facts, Miss Akins was born in Humansville, Mo., in 1886. She lived for many years in St. Louis and did much of her first writing there, principally for a weekly publication known as William Marion Reedy's *Mirror*. She wrote a good deal of poetry as a younger woman. Her first try at playwriting resulted in "Papa," a sophisticated comedy which caused quite a stir in liberal literary circles because of its alleged boldness. The story covered the discussions between a father and two daughters of their individual affairs and their frank reactions to them. That was in 1914, and the liberal drama was not particularly well cushioned.

Two years later Miss Akins brought "The Magical City" East and it was included in an early bill of short plays organized by the Washington Square Players, from which the present Theatre Guild was later to grow. Following the success of "Declassé" Miss Akins was active but not often encouraged. Arthur Hopkins produced her "Daddy's Gone A-Hunting," the story of an artist who studied in Paris and came home eager to be free of all family responsibility. Sam H. Harris followed six months later with "The Varying Shore" in which Elsie Ferguson, reappearing as the ghost of a Mme. Leland the day after her death in Monte Carlo, related the story of her life and the previous deaths she had died in the sacrifices she had made —at 40, at 30 and as a young girl. Neither play was popular.

A year later Miss Akins wrote "A Texas Nightingale," also in the hope that its leading character would give Jobyna Howland a lift toward stardom. It didn't. There were a number of not-quite-good-enough plays after that, leading up to the success of "The Greeks Had a Word for It" previously noted.

The Akins plays have included:

"Declassé." Produced by Charles Frohman. Empire Theatre, New York, October 6, 1919.

"Footloose." Produced by George C. Tyler. Greenwich Village Theatre, New York, May 10, 1919.

"Daddy's Gone A-Hunting." Produced by Arthur Hopkins. Plymouth Theatre, New York, August 31, 1921.

"The Varying Shore." Produced by Sam H. Harris. Hudson Theatre, New York, December 5, 1921.

"The Texas Nightingale." Produced by Charles Frohman. Empire Theatre, New York, November 20, 1922.

"A Royal Fandango." Produced by Arthur Hopkins. Plymouth Theatre, New York, November 12, 1923.

"The Moon-Flower" (adapted from Hungarian). Produced by Charles L. Wagner. Astor Theatre, New York, February 25, 1924.

"First Love." Produced by Messrs. Shubert. Booth Theatre, New York, November 8, 1926.

"The Crown Prince" (adapted from Hungarian). Produced by L. Lawrence Weber. Forrest Theatre, New York, March 23, 1927.

"The Furies." Produced by John Tuerk. Shubert Theatre, New York, March 7, 1928.

"The Love Duel" (adapted from play by Lili Hatvany). Produced by Lee Shubert in association with Gilbert Miller. Ethel Barrymore Theatre, New York, April 15, 1929.

"The Greeks Had a Word for It." Produced by William Harris, Jr. Sam H. Harris Theatre, New York, September 25, 1930.

"The Old Maid" (adapted from story by Edith Wharton). Produced by Harry Moses. Empire Theatre, New York, January 7, 1935.

"O, Evening Star." Produced by Harry Moses. Empire Theatre, New York, January 8, 1936.

SIDNEY KINGSLEY
"Men in White" (1934)

AN INTERESTING newcomer among the Pulitzer prize-winning and playwriting immortals is Sidney Kingsley. Interesting and promising, I'd say, were he not, like his brilliant contemporary, Elmer Rice, given to such nursing of temperamental moods there is no definite assurance he will deign to keep at the playwriting trade.

Young Mr. Kingsley (he celebrates his 32nd birth anniversary in October of this year) approached the Broadway theatre stealthily through his school years, notably through the four years he spent at Cornell (1924-28). Stealthily, and I am sure, with a twinkle in his eye. He had, on finishing high school, won a State scholarship for Cornell and one of the first things he was asked to do was to write a play for the Dramatic Club. He wrote several and began his prize winning with them.

Graduated in 1928, and with his eye still on Broadway, he went in for a bit of self-conditioning by taking a place in a Bronx stock company playing at the Tremont Theatre. He had done some acting in college, but never was what you might call stage struck. The season following he continued stalking Broadway by accepting a small part in a piece called "Subway Express," which had some success.

Meantime he had been writing and had finished a play he called "Crisis." It was about a fine though not too noble young hospital interne who was willing, if pushed, to sacrifice love and a girl for his Hippocratic oath. Mr. Kingsley sold the play in 1930 to Louis Cline, Mr. Cline paying the customary $500 for a six-months' option. At the end of six months Mr. Cline reluctantly brought the script back, regretting that promised backing had failed him and he could not negotiate a production of "Crisis."

That same day Mr. Kingsley sold the play to a second hopeful producer named Sidney Phillips, who also thought he had backing for its production. Those early-thirty years, you may recall, were bad years for money-raising. Mr. Phillips paid $1,000 for the privilege of holding on to "Crisis" for a year and then he gave it up.

When Phillips released the script it went to a third Broadway optimist who had read it while serving as adviser to the Columbia Motion Picture Company, another Sidney named Harmon. Making the third Sidney to have to do with the play, and a total of $2,000 Mr. Kingsley had collected. It was Mr. Harmon who came through a year later with a production, though he had to split the cost of it with two others—the Group Theatre, Inc., and James Ullman. The title was changed to "Men in White," and the play, it may be recalled, was an overnight success when it was produced September 26, 1933, under the direct sponsorship of the Group Theatre. Alexander Kirkland, J. Edward Bromberg, Morris Carnovsky and Margaret Barker were prominently cast and am ambitious young fellow named Clifford Odets played a small part.

This, then, was Mr. Kingsley's Broadway debut. He had put a first foot on a low rung of the ladder and then skipped lightly past the next dozen rungs with the agility of a rookie fireman. This was his first play, his first production and, when Spring came, there he sat smiling at joy, the winner of the Pulitzer's $1,000, with laurel as well. "Men in White" was played for 351 performances in New

York and afterward was as popular on tour.

Mr. Kingsley, being wise and also less avaricious than some, waited two years before he offered a second play for sale. This he called "Dead End." It was sold to Norman Bel Geddes with the understanding that Mr. Kingsley should both cast and stage it. "Dead End" came to production the night of Oct. 28, 1935, in perhaps the most solid, the most striking setting Mr. Bel Geddes had ever devised for the theatre—a scene at the dead end of a New York City street that runs into the East River. The orchestra pit represents the river, the footlight trough is flanked with the abutments of a wharf. Back of these, at one side of the stage, rises a swanky apartment house, with high posted gate and elaborately uniformed hall man. Just back of the apartment house a lowly tenement, fire escape and bits of drying wash. In the center of the street a steam shovel is parked for the day. At the river end stands a towering sand hopper.

In the early days of the engagement of "Dead End" the setting was as freely discussed as the play, and the play was received with enthusiasm. Its story might have been sub-captioned "The Birth of Crime," seeing that it detailed with both incisive logic and literal realism the evolution of a gangster of the killer type from those street corner gangs of young boys driven to play where they can and to drift naturally into such hoodlum organizations as are a common result. "Dead End" represents a police and social service problem of every large city.

The second Kingsley play was a more sensational and even a more substantial success than "Men in White," and again Mr. Kingsley found himself sitting extremely pretty, reading such flowery encomiums as pleased him and depositing liberal royalty checks regularly. He did not win a second Pulitzer prize with "Dead End," but he did win one or two lesser awards, notably that of The Theatre Club, an organization of playgoers that had also decorated him with a medal for his first play.

Mr. Kingsley did not wait two years before he produced a third play. A year after the "Dead End" success he came forward with a drama entitled "Ten Million Ghosts" which he not alone wrote, cast and staged but also financed. He leased the St. James Theatre and became, for a little while at least, a one-man producing unit. "Ten Million Ghosts," however, failed him. His production was huge and handsome. His cast was carefully selected and as carefully trained. But his story of the vicious munitions makers who are frequently accepted as heartless merchants of death who promote wars, although it was carefully documented, was one of those stage protests that play patrons just refuse to accept in the theatre. Honest liberals, honest pacifists, honest haters of war in all divisions of society agreed with every line of the Kingsley argument, but few of them bought seats for the play.

It might be a provable truth that some sort of agreement kept the military forces of both France and Germany from either bombing or attempting to bomb the respective iron basins which were the sources of supply of their cannon material in the Great War, but in the staging it seemed at least highly incredible and only the more excited proletarians rose to it.

Mr. Kingsley was greatly disappointed at the attitude of both newspaper reviewers and the playgoing public toward "Ten Million Ghosts." After eleven performances he sent it to the storehouse. With the same gesture he put the

Sidney Kingsley independent producing unit out of business and called it a season.

Mr. Kingsley is a native New Yorker. Besides his experience as an actor he has been a play reader and a writer of picture scenarios. He remains, however he may feel about it at the moment, one of the brighter hopes of the native drama's future. He has already been hailed abroad, notably in Hungary, where "Men in White" broke records in Budapest, as an American dramatist of international stature.

Mr. Kingsley's plays produced in New York include:

"Men in White." Produced by The Group Theatre, Sidney Harmon and James R. Ullman. Broadhurst Theatre, New York, September 26, 1933.

"Dead End." Produced by Normal Bel Geddes. Belasco Theatre, New York, October 28, 1935.

"Ten Million Ghosts." Produced by the author. St. James Theatre, October 23, 1936.

MAXWELL ANDERSON
"High Tor" (1937), "Winterset" (1936), "Both Your Houses" (1933)

MAXWELL ANDERSON was a prophet's choice in the first edition of "American Playwrights of Today." He had not at that time been included in the Honor Group confined to the Pulitzer prize winners. But he had given every indication that he was most notably eligible and there was little doubt that he would one day be so honored. As it happens, he won his first Pulitzer distinction four years after the publication of that first issue, taking the prize for his political satire, "Both Your Houses," the season of 1932-33. In the author's opinion "Both Your Houses" is the least worthy of his playwrighting efforts and the Pulitzer honor did not greatly impress him. In 1936 he won the first New York Drama Critics' Circle award with his "Winterset" and in 1937 took the same award again with "High Tor." He has said he was pleased with these.

It is the conviction of this reasonably observant playgoer that Maxwell Anderson has, within the last five or six years, advanced with giant strides to the head of our list of native dramatists. The temporary absence of Eugene O'Neill may or may not be counted as a factor. O'Neill, health and creative urges being normal, might have delivered such dramas as would have equaled the works of Anderson in importance and outshone them in literary brilliance. The question is debatable. But however it may be settled, the fact is patent that the Anderson output since 1930 has been of a standard and has sustained a consistency in quality that no other American dramatist of our time has matched within a like period.

This list of plays includes "Elizabeth the Queen" (1930), "Night over Taos" (1932), "Both Your Houses" (1933), "Mary of Scotland" (1933), "Valley Forge" (1934), "Winterset" (1935), "The Wingless Victory" (1936), "High Tor" (1937), "The Masque of Kings" (1937) and "The Star Wagon" (1937).

With the exception of "Both Your Houses" which exposed with ruthless logic and fine humor the weaknesses of a corruption-ridden, if not grafter-controlled, republic, all the Anderson plays have been written in a combination of blank verse and poetic prose that has given them a particular appeal to receptive and sensitively minded playgoers. It is a style, however, that many have complained gets definitely in the way of their enjoyment. The verse form Mr. Anderson has defended with characteristic eloquence in his preface to the published "Winterset."

"When I wrote my first play, 'White Desert,' I wrote it in verse because I was weary of plays in prose that never lifted from the ground," says he. "It failed and I did not come back to verse again until I discovered that poetic tragedy had never been successfully written about its own place and time. There is not one tragedy by Aeschylus, Sophocles, Euripides, Shakespeare, Corneille or Racine which did not have the advantage of a setting either far away or long ago. . . . 'Winterset' is largely in verse and treats a contemporary tragic theme, which makes it more of an experiment than I could wish, for the great masters themselves never tried to make tragic poetry out of the stuff of their own times. To do so is to attempt to establish a new convention, one that may prove impossible of acceptance, but to which I was driven by the lively historical sense of our day. . . . Whether or not I have solved the problem in 'Winterset' is probably of little moment. But it must be solved if we are to have a great theatre in America."

"He has brought verse and the form of verse back to the American stage," Stephen Vincent Benét wrote in the *Stage* magazine in a tribute to the dramatist captioned "New Grandeur," "not as an experiment, not as an oddity, but as an essential of the later plays he has written. And because of it he has opened a shut door."

There were no more Pulitzer awards for Dramatist Anderson after the award to "Both Your Houses." "Elizabeth the Queen," an eloquently and dramatically expanded retelling of the Elizabeth-Essex romance, was reported to have been a strong candidate, but was voted down because it was not, in a strict, or Columbia college sense, "an original American play." "Mary of Scotland," which did as much for Mary and Bothwell as "Elizabeth" had done for Elizabeth and Essex, was apparently similarly classified.

But what of "Valley Forge," "Winterset" and "High Tor?" Here are three fine plays that are definite reflections of the American scene. "Valley Forge" recites a vigorously humanized biography of the Father of His Country. It may be that the Anderson humanizing is entirely too complete, inasmuch as it emphasizes a romance lightly hinted at in Washington biographies involving Mary Philipse, and takes good, round thumps at the Tory interest which influenced the Continental Congress and reflected none too creditably upon such wavering centers as the little old New York of that day. Still it is also a vigorously patriotic drama in that it pictures this country's greatest military hero as a man of strong character and great courage, and brings him through a succession of supreme tests to rewards honestly earned.

"Winterset" was doubtless frowned upon by the solons of Cathedral Heights because it is tinged with a sympathetic radicalism, being a reflection of emotions stirred by the Sacco-Vanzetti case and the part played therein by a great American commonwealth. This is the story of such a son as either of these condemned men might have borne and relates his search for justice in the name of a wronged father. His quest is successful, but his triumph is halted in the end by his love for the sister of one of his father's betrayers.

"High Tor" was most decidedly related to the American scene, being a fantasy compounded of legends having to do with the coming to these shores of Hendrick Hudson. When the *Onrust*, which was a Hudson ship, foundered in the Tappan Zee its crew sought the heights of the Hudson and lived their lives out there waiting for the return of Hendrick to take them back across the sea. Even now, the "High Tor" legend goes, their spirits haunt the Catskills and are to be heard in the winds when storms rage and seen in the mists that circle the hilltops. In this atmosphere the hero of the play, a young descendant of the Dutch, fights to retain his ownership of High Tor mountain and save it from the traprock trust that would gouge out its innards to construct crushed rock roadways. The practical American sweetheart who would have him sell, and the shade of the pretty young wife of the captain of the *Onrust*, are parties to the hero's conflict. "High Tor" was also voted down by the Pulitzer prize givers.

In 1935, however, a new-prize-awarding organization came into the field. This was the New York Drama Critics' Circle. The critics, selecting the play that in their estimation was the best play of that year written by an American author, proceeded promptly to give their first prize to "Winterset" and to follow it, the second year of their voting, by again selecting "High Tor" as their idea of the best play of American authorship in 1936. Thus, in the critical mind, at least, was justice belatedly done an onrushing contender for first honors in the American field.

Going back to the Anderson playwriting beginnings I quote again from the earlier edition of this expanding record:

"As playgoers we met Mr. Anderson first in 1923, when a drama of his called 'White Desert' was produced by Brock Pemberton at the Comedy Theatre. We learned then that he was an editorial writer on the staff of the New

York *Morning World* and we feared—those of us who have seen many newspaper playwrights come quickly into prominence and fade almost as quickly out again—that here was one more one-play man likely to become too quickly discouraged with failure and return embittered to Mr. Pulitzer's editorial conferences and what is known in newspaper dramas as the grind.

"However discouraged Mr. Anderson may have been—(he has written that he was 'much depressed over it, if you really want to know')—and whatever his state of mind, he did not give up the drama.

"Laurence Stallings was working with Anderson on the *World* at the time, and had been greatly interested in the sale and production of 'White Desert.' Also, having had adventurous and tragic experiences in the war, and having acquired, as most of the young warriors of that day did acquire, a complete disgust of the shallow and trumpery war play of commerce, Stallings was eager to write from out his own experiences and reactions and those of his fellow soldiers a real war drama. He confessed the desire to Anderson. They consulted together concerning such a play, its development and dramatic treatment, and finding themselves in accord they finished the play together.

"That play was 'What Price Glory?' It was produced by Arthur Hopkins in September, 1924, and so electrified theatrical New York that it definitely marks an epoch in the play producing history of the theatre capital. In addition to performing the great service of debunking the essentially untrue and no more than prettily patriotic war play, it served to crystallize a growing rebellion of young moderns who were protesting the conventional limitations of artificial stage dialogue. It tore down old puritan barriers that had for many generations stood as a protection against the use of any and all profanity on the stage. It established the license if not the rights of soldiers in stage trenches to talk as much like soldiers in real trenches as a liberal interpretation of what constitutes decency and good taste would permit.

"We probably will have to wait a generation before we shall be able to approximate fairly the good that has resulted from this newer freedom of expression in the theatre. At the moment, as is the case with prohibition, the evidence is confusing. Playwrights and producers, following the Anderson-Stallings-Hopkins lead, have rent the air with familiar oaths and made a kind of blasphemy common. Whether it makes for a better as well as a stronger drama remains to be proved."

There was, as previously recorded, the first Anderson play, "White Desert" (1923), in which George Abbott was an actor and which was beautifully produced by Brock Pemberton. Playgoers, however, did not support it. After "What Price Glory?" there were two other collaborations with Laurence Stallings—"First Flight" (1925), founded on an episode in the early life of Andrew Jackson, and "The Buccaneer," a romantic and lightly historical drama of Captain Henry Morgan the time he sacked the city of Panama. Anderson made a colorful and slightly verminous drama out of Jim Tully's "Beggars of Life," calling it "Outside Looking In" (1925), and in this James Cagney, now of Hollywood, and Charles Bickford played the leads.

In 1927 the dramatist took a long step forward, in popularity, at least, as a writer of incisive character drama based on a keen observation of his native American neighbors. This was "Saturday's Children," which had to do with the struggle of a young pair trying to prove that two who are married and in love can, in fact, live as cheaply as one. It ran the better part of a season with Ruth Gordon playing the heroine. This was followed, in 1929, by "Gypsy," another of the few Anderson failures.

"The Anderson background is in no sense theatrical," to quote again the earlier edition: "His father was a Baptist minister, the Rev. William Lincoln Anderson, with a pastorate in Atlantic, Pa., at the time of Maxwell's arrival. Later there were pastorates in other Pennsylvania towns, as well as a few in Ohio, Iowa and North Dakota. The son of the family acquired some part of his schooling in each of them.

"He was 19 when the family finally settled in North Dakota and he went to the University of that state, graduating in 1911. He taught school his first two years out of college, was at one time on the faculty of Leland Stanford University and again that of Whittier College in Southern California.

"Tiring of the academic life and having a natural writing gift, Mr. Anderson quit teaching and became an editorial writer on the San Francisco *Bulletin*. He made the change, he has said, because he needed more money than teaching jobs pay. Some time after this his employers decided that he was too outspoken and suggested that he better be looking around for another job. He went over to the San Francisco *Chronicle*. Happy or unhappy there, he did not stay long, but came east and became a contributor to the *New Republic* in New York. Later he tried newspaper work again, going to the New York *Globe* and later to the *Morning World*."

Mr. Anderson's plays include several not yet produced

on Broadway. "Sea Wife," written largely in verse and highly imaginative, was presented at the University of Minnesota in December of 1932. Its theme is taken from Matthew Arnold's "Forsaken Merman." An earlier one, "The Feud" (also called "Holy Terror"), written in collaboration with George Abbott, was sold to John Golden in 1925. The next year he wrote one called "Forfeits." The radio has presented two of his microphone plays: "The Feast of Ortolans" and "Second Overture."

Anderson plays so far produced in New York include the following:

"White Desert." Produced by Brock Pemberton. Princess Theatre, New York, October 18, 1923.

"What Price Glory?" (with Laurence Stallings). Produced by Arthur Hopkins. Plymouth Theatre, New York, September 3, 1924.

"First Flight" (with Laurence Stallings). Produced by Arthur Hopkins. Plymouth Theatre, New York, September 17, 1925.

"Outside Looking In." Produced by Macgowan, Jones and O'Neill. Greenwich Village Theatre, New York, September 7, 1925.

"The Buccaneer" (with Laurence Stallings). Produced by Arthur Hopkins. Plymouth Theatre, New York, October 2, 1925.

"Saturday's Children." Produced by Actor's Theatre, Inc. Booth Theatre, New York, January 26, 1927.

"Gods of the Lightning" (with Harold Hickerson). Produced by Hamilton MacFadden and Kellogg Gary. Little Theatre, New York, October 24, 1928.

"Gypsy." Produced by Richard Herndon. Klaw Theatre, New York, January 14, 1929.

"Elizabeth the Queen." Produced by Theatre Guild, Inc. Guild Theatre, New York, November 3, 1930.

"Night over Taos." Produced by Group Theatre, Inc. 48th Street Theatre, New York, March 9, 1932.

"Both Your Houses." Produced by Theatre Guild, Inc. Royale Theatre, New York, March 6, 1933.

"Mary of Scotland." Produced by Theatre Guild, Inc. Alvin Theatre, New York, November 27, 1933.

"Valley Forge." Produced by Theatre Guild, Inc. Guild Theatre, New
   York, December 10, 1934.
"Winterset." Produced by Guthrie McClintic. Martin Beck Theatre,
   New York, September 25, 1935.
"The Wingless Victory." Produced by Katharine Cornell. Empire Thea-
   tre, New York, December 23, 1936.
"High Tor." Produced by Guthrie McClintic. Martin Beck Theatre,
   New York, January 9, 1937.
"The Masque of Kings." Produced by Theatre Guild, Inc. Shubert
   Theatre, New York, February 8, 1937.
"The Star Wagon." Produced by Guthrie McClintic. Empire Theatre,
   New York, September 29, 1937.

MORRIS RYSKIND, GEORGE AND IRA GERSHWIN
"Of Thee I Sing" (with George Kaufman, 1932)

MORRIS (MORRIE) RYSKIND deserves a place in any book
concerned with the lives and activities of American playwrights. He has not been in many of them because his
work has been mostly confined to the writing of librettos
for musical shows. What work he has done in the dramatic
field has been that of a doctor called in as a consultant just
before the baby play is born, or just after it had been born
and was threatening to die.

As a George Kaufman collaborator, however, Ryskind
has had a hand in (1) that outstanding sensation among
musical comedies, "Of Thee I Sing," (2) a piece called
"Strike Up the Band" which he salvaged after Kaufman
had given it up and retired, (3) "Animal Crackers,"
through which the Marx Brothers romped to an accompani-
ment of wild laughter and (4) "Let 'Em Eat Cake," which
the writing pals had hoped would prove a popular sequel
to "Of Thee I Sing." It didn't.

The Ryskind inclusion in this particular work is justi-
fied, I feel, by his connection with the prize-winning "Of
Thee I Sing." He has been fooling around the theatre since
the middle twenties. He would have graduated from Columbia if he had not put Nicholas Murray Butler into
verse just about the time they were applying the seal to his
(Morrie's) B.Litt. diploma. Reading the verse, the college
board tore up the diploma and expelled the writer, insist-
ing the action was due to his anti-war editorials written
for the college paper.

"Morrie," who had been a consistent and successful contributor to the Franklin P. Adams columns, took immediately to newspaper work on the *Morning World*, but soon
went over to the stage and screen and was long with Paramount as both scenarist and publicity consultant. It was
the Kaufman collaborations that brought him back to the
theatre. Ryskind was born in 1895, the son of a cigar-
maker on New York's East Side. A lot of his Columbia
friends are still hoping the college will one day forget the
Butler lampoon and give him his degree. As a successful
alumnus, Morrie is one of their outstanding credits.

George and Ira Gershwin, who shared the "Of Thee I
Sing" success, have also enjoyed close touch with stage
success the last twelve or fourteen years. George Gershwin, who died last year in Hollywood, was widely honored and greatly beloved as the creator of a form and
style in composition that brought something like dignity
and higher musical value to jazz. Ira Gershwin, working
for the most part with his brother, supplied a superior type
of literate lyrics for George's compositions.

The Gershwins were born on New York's East Side,
Ira, the elder, in 1896, George in 1898. They were edu-

cated in the New York public schools. As a composer George first attracted attention with a piece called "La, La Lucille" in 1919. His climb upward was steady, culminating so far as the stage is concerned, in his score for Heyward's "Porgy and Bess" (1935). His "Rhapsody in Blue" which took him into Carnegie Hall and a variety of other symphonic temples, will always be named as his greatest orchestral achievement.

Ira Gershwin, not wanting to trade on his more famous brother's reputation, adopted the pen name of Arthur Francis (the given names of a younger brother and sister) when he wrote the lyrics for "Ladies First" in 1918, and those for "Dangerous Maid" and "Two Little Girls" in 1921. Proving that he could stand alone, he resumed his own name and worked almost exclusively with his brother until the latter's untimely and widely mourned death.

SUSAN GLASPELL
"Alison's House" (1931)

SUSAN GLASPELL joined the honor list of prize-winning dramatists in the Spring of 1931 when the Pulitzer committee selected her "Alison's House" as the best play of that season written by an American author. The award came as a surprise to playgoers and as something of a shock to most of the professional play reviewers.

"Alison's House" was founded on episodes from the life of the belatedly acknowledged American poet, Emily Dickinson, who won a place among the immortals eighteen years after she died. It was produced modestly but competently by Eva Le Gallienne at the Civic Repertory

theatre in Fourteenth Street, which at that time was proceeding steadily but uncertainly under power provided by
a good deal of experimental theatre enthusiasm and a small
subsidy in cash raised by popular subscription.

Miss Le Gallienne and her company had given Miss
Glaspell's play a total of twenty-five performances, repeat-
ing it once or twice a week in her repertory. When the
prize was awarded in May it was decided to move the winning play into the Broadway sector. Miss Le Gallienne,
playing the title role, had announced the close of her season, but agreed to go on until "Alison's House" had been
given a chance in the competitive market. The first week
at the Ritz theatre was entirely successful. But the second
week, with Gale Sondergaard taking over the Le Gallienne part, suffered an additional handicap of hot weather
and the play was withdrawn. The critics were quite correct in their contention that "Alison's House" was a literary
drama of limited popular appeal.

With one more try at the Broadway drama, the production of a comedy called "The Comic Artist," written with
Norman Matson, Miss Glaspell withdrew and returned to
the writing of novels and short stories which was the first
choice of her literary career. Her experiments with playwriting, in fact, were largely accidental from the first. She,
with the late George Cram Cook, was one of the forward-
looking writers who organized the Provincetown Players'
group and brought the original Wharf Theatre at the tip
of Cape Cod, in Provincetown to life. She wrote one-act
plays for the Provincetowners because they needed them.
Most of her output proved successful. One play, "Trifles,"
became a favorite with the producers of short plays all
over the world. She later tried the long-play form as a

means of satisfying both a newly awakened interest and a lively curiosity as to what she could do with it. "The Inheritors" was a noteworthy result. "Suppressed Desires," which she wrote with Mr. Cook was also highly regarded by everybody excepting the larger and more fickle paying public.

Miss Glaspell is a native of Davenport, Iowa. In her early writing years, after she left Chicago University, she contributed to all the better magazines and did good work as a journalist on several of the better newspapers.

Her produced plays from 1919 to date include:

"The Verge." Produced by the Provincetown Players at the Provincetown Playhouse, New York, November 4, 1921.
"Chains of Dew." Produced by the Provincetown Players at the Provincetown Playhouse, New York, April 27, 1922.
"The Inheritors." Produced by the Civic Repertory Theatre at the Civic Repertory Theatre, New York, March 15, 1927.
"Alison's House." Produced by the Civic Repertory Theatre at the Civic Repertory Theatre, New York, December 1, 1930.
"The Comic Artist" (with Norman Matson). Produced by Comic Artist Inc. at the Morosco Theatre, New York, April 19, 1933.

MARC CONNELLY
"The Green Pastures" (1930)

EIGHT years ago, when we were last writing of the achievements of Marc Connelly as a playwright, he was still a collaborator. He and George Kaufman, with whose career his own was definitely joined when first they came to the theatre as writing men, had separated and both had achieved independent productions—Mr. Kaufman with "The Butter and Egg Man" and Mr. Connelly with "The Wisdom

Tooth." But their names were still linked and the sum of their joint achievements was much greater than anything they had done individually.

A year later, in February, 1930, this set-up was changed completely so far as Mr. Connelly was concerned. Rowland Stebbins (Laurence Rivers, Inc.) produced "The Green Pastures" and a new bit of stage history was made. Mr. Connelly, who, though he worked with Roark Bradford's "Ol' Man Adam an' His Chillun" as a story base, was alone responsible for the adaptation and rearrangement of scenes, as well as the creation of new scenes to fit the material to the drama's demands. He also cast and staged the play, which made its success pretty much a Connelly success.

Following that triumph, however, Mr. Connelly settled back comfortably upon his laurels and was content. "The Green Pastures" ran on and on, for 640 performances in New York, which took it well into its second year, and for three additional years on tour. During this period Mr. Connelly, always threatening to return actively to the theatre, gave some time to motion pictures and more time to consultations concerned with promising ventures that did not come to production. He traveled a good deal. He got married—and unmarried—and married again. But he wrote practically no new plays. Not for four years. Then he agreed to a collaboration with the late Frank B. Elser on a dramatization of Walter Edmond's novel, "Rome Haul." Together they made it into a play called "The Farmer Takes a Wife" which was moderately successful with Henry Fonda and June Walker in the leading roles.

Another rest spell for Mr. Connelly. For the better part of three years this time. Then he became interested in a play written by Arthur Kober called "Having Wonderful Time"; so interested, in fact, that he decided to turn producer. He cast and staged the Kober comedy in the Spring of 1937 and produced it, in association with Bela Blau. It ran through the Summer and Fall, being withdrawn finally in January, 1938, with a record of 372 performances to its credit. The following June Mr. Connelly, again in association with Mr. Blau, imported a Victorian operetta, "The Two Bouquets," which had had a year's success in London. "The Two Bouquets" was variously received by the professional reviewers, and with no better than a restrained enthusiasm by early Summer playgoers. It was written by Eleanor and Herbert Farjeon, brother and sister, the grandchildren of the American comedian, Joseph Jefferson, and writers of distinction in English literary circles. The musical score was assembled from the compositions of some twenty Victorian composers.

In the records this favored playwright was born in McKeesport, Pa., in 1891. He went through the public schools of his native town, and from there to Trinity Hall in Washington, Pa. In Pittsburgh later he became a newspaper man. Writing quips and columns turned his thought toward the theatre. He did the lyrics for a piece called "The Amber Princess" and came to New York to see it produced. That was in 1916. The "Princess" failed him, but he never went back to Pennsylvania. His signature then was Marcus C. Connelly. He wrote for newspapers and magazines, submitted sketches for revues and tried play doctoring. It was in 1921 that he and George Kaufman got together on a comedy built around the character of Franklin Pierce Adams' column heroine, the queen of the bromides, Dulcinea of the *Morning World*. "Dulcy"

was the result. It was produced by George C. Tyler and
H. H. Frazee at the Frazee Theatre in 1921 and ran for
246 performances. The Kaufman-Connelly writing firm
was established. For the next three or four years it flour-
ished and then, as reported, was dissolved by mutual agreement and with mutual respect.

The Kaufman-Connelly collaborations included:

"Dulcy" (Kaufman and Connelly). Produced by George C. Tyler and
H. H. Frazee. Frazee Theatre, New York, August 13, 1921.

"To the Ladies" (Kaufman and Connelly). Produced by George C.
Tyler and A. L. Erlanger. Liberty Theatre, New York, February 20,
1922.

"Merton of the Movies" (Kaufman and Connelly). Produced by George
C. Tyler and Hugh Ford. Cort Theatre, New York, November 13,
1922.

"Helen of Troy, N. Y." (Book by Kaufman and Connelly). Produced
by Rufus LeMaire and George Jessel. Selwyn Theatre, New York,
June 19, 1923.

"The Deep Tangled Wildwood" (Kaufman and Connelly). Produced
by George C. Tyler and Hugh Ford. Frazee Theatre, New York,
November 5, 1923.

"Beggar on Horseback" (Kaufman and Connelly). Produced by Winthrop Ames. Broadhurst Theatre, New York, February 12, 1924.

"Be Yourself" (Book by Kaufman and Connelly). Produced by Wilmer
and Vincent. Sam H. Harris Theatre, New York, September 3, 1924.

Mr. Connelly's other playwriting ventures follow:

"Wisdom Tooth." Produced by John Golden. Little Theatre, New
York, February 15, 1926.

"The Wild Man of Borneo" (with Herman J. Mankiewiez). Produced
by Philip Goodman. Bijou Theatre, New York, September 13, 1927.

"The Green Pastures." Produced by Laurence Rivers, Inc. Mansfield
Theatre, New York, February 20, 1930.

"The Farmer Takes a Wife" (with Frank B. Elser). Produced by Max
Gordon. 46th Street Theatre, New York, October 30, 1934.

ELMER RICE
"Street Scene" (1929)

"ELMER RICE is also one of the retiring moderns," I wrote in the first edition of "American Playwrights." "Ask him to tell you anything he has done in or for the theatre and he will meet the query with a deprecatory shrug intimating that his contributions are quite unimportant. He sees himself, I think, as a kind of victim of a playwriting passion he cannot successfully resist nor conscientiously approve.

" 'I enjoy writing plays, but I don't like the theatre,' insistently proclaims Mr. Rice. 'I shall probably go on writing plays until stopped by an act of God or of the public enemy.' "

And it came to pass that Mr. Rice did, in fact, go on writing plays until stopped—not by an act of God, nor yet by a public enemy, but by hurt pride and an outraged sense of justice.

After he had written, staged and cast "Street Scene," which was the Pulitzer Prize winner of the 1928-29 season, Mr. Rice continued as his own director through the production of "See Naples and Die" (1929), his own director and producer as well through "The Left Bank" (1931), "Counsellor-at-Law" (1931), "Black Sheep" (1932), and "We, the People" (1933). "The Left Bank" and "Counsellor-at-Law" were popular successes; "See Naples and Die" and "Black Sheep" were failures and "We, the People" might be called a fighting success, inasmuch as it did attract a series of enthused audiences but was withdrawn because of the high cost of its upkeep and maintenance.

Mr. Rice's enthusiasm for playwriting had grown apace. His progress, despite his failures, was marked by a growing assurance and a developing technique and his interest in the theatre had expanded to such an extent that he was now determined not only to continue as an independent creator and producer of plays but to acquire a theatre of his own in which he could set the prices of admission and dictate the length of the run of any particular drama produced. The playwright had spent the better part of a year in Europe, much of the time in Russia, and had returned with a vivid impression of the Soviet drama and a crystallized conviction that a people's theatre conducted on general Soviet lines was the need of the hour.

Shortly thereafter announcement was made that the Elmer Rices (Mrs. Rice figuring in this instance as the party of the first or paper-signing part) had bought the Belasco Theatre from the executors of the late David Belasco's estate. This theatre would thereafter be the home of the Rice drama, with a promising chance of one day becoming the long-cherished people's repertory theatre of its lessee's dream (Mrs. Rice assuming the obligations of owner and Mr. Rice those of lessee of the newly acquired house).

On the 12th of September, 1934, twenty years after the production of his first success in the theatre, which was "On Trial," Mr. Rice offered the first of his individually produced and controlled dramas in the new theatre. This was called "Judgment Day." The story was inspired by the burning of the German Reich and the prosecution (or persecution) of the unfortunate anti-Nazis accused of the crime.

It was a court-room drama, of which this playwright is an acknowledged master, and a ringing preachment against intolerance that contained many dramatically inspired moments. But it also suffered, or so it was charged, from the emotional bias of its author and director, as so many propaganda dramas do. It was desperately one-sided. The framing of the unhappy culprits who were its heroic victims was a shade too deliberate to seem credible to audiences as far removed from the German scene as those of Broadway. This fact, plus the normal handicap faced by an unpleasant play, held the financial receipts of "Judgment Day" far below its producer's expectations. It was withdrawn after ninety-three performances.

Mr. Rice was disheartened but still hopeful. He had a second play in readiness and put it into immediate rehearsal. This was "Between Two Worlds." A month later it was produced, and again the reception was mildly discouraging. A divided press and a lukewarm reception from the public. "Between Two Worlds" relates the adventure of a junior leaguer who meets a ruthless Bolshevik on an Atlantic crossing. She succumbs, a little defiantly, to his physical lure and his charge that she is a coward, and comes to rue the experience but to acknowledge herself awakened to Life's deeper significance. He goes on to Russia and she into social service. "Between Two Worlds" was withdrawn after thirty-two performances. Mr. Rice was now not only discouraged but pretty mad as well. He was, he declared, through with the theatre and certainly through with Broadway.

Since then, except for "Not for Children" presented by the Stage Society in London (1935) and by the Pasadena

Art Theatre in the Spring of 1936, he has made but one contribution to the theatre. When the Federal Theatre Project was organized in 1935 Mr. Rice was induced by Hallie Flanagan, the National Director, to take the post of Administrator for New York. He worked on the project with some enthusiasm until the executives in Washington saw fit to interfere with the production of a "Living Newspaper" feature that made a few allegedly undiplomatic references to several European dictators, and particularly to Il Duce Benito Mussolini in regard to his taking over Ethiopia. The Government's interference, declared Mr. Rice, was a direct violation of his agreement with the directors of WPA. If he couldn't enjoy a reasonable freedom of thought and action he did not wish to continue as an administrator. His resignation was accepted.

Thereafter the playwright lived in comparative peace until he happened inadvertently, during an hour's talk on the commercial theatre at Columbia College, to give voice and emphasis to his opinion of the New York dramatic critics, to wit:

"Taking them by and large, and making due allowance for honorable exceptions, they are the bulwarks of the commercial theatre. For the most part men without intellect, sensitivity, perception or background, they pander to the tastes of the empty-headed, the bored, the insensitive, the complacent who constitute the bulk of the agency trade and supply the golden stream upon which the Broadway theatre feeds."

Mr. Rice had no thought that his remarks would ever be made public, but when they were he stood stanchly back of them. A few of the critics replied in kind. The majority preserved as discreet and diplomatic a silence as do most playwrights when their productions have been similarly torn apart.

After having thus more or less unwittingly found himself the center of a minor whirlpool in the Broadway current, Mr. Rice again struck out for the shore, determined to lose himself in the sheltering woods of retirement. Broadway has missed him, and will continue to miss him, until he returns, for his is the type of alert intelligence, the sincerity and earnestness of conviction, of which the theatre stands always in greatest need.

Elmer Rice's first play, written in 1914, sold to Arthur Hopkins, and produced by Cohan and Harris in association with Mr. Hopkins, was "On Trial," and "On Trial," as reported in our previous volume, served to bring into focus one of the most important modifications of the art of the dramatist that had been developed in a hundred years.

"He helped to wipe out several set and accepted rules of dramaturgy and establish, or at least re-create, an acceptable new constructural form," reads the account of the dramatist's early activity in the theatre. "He wrote 'On Trial' and brought over the flashback of the screen to the stage.

"Later he wrote 'The Adding Machine,' the first and most frequently quoted of impressionistic dramas with a native background and of native authorship.

"Mr. Rice acknowledges, again without boasting, that New York was the scene of his birth (in 1892) and that for twenty-six years following that event he continued to live within two miles of his birthplace. Which fact, if it prove nothing else, proves that the Rices are not as restless as most New Yorkers.

"Through the public schools and half-way through high school without, he says, having learned anything that he has found of the slightest value to him, young Mr. Rice was pointed for a business career—'the highest goal of American manhood.'

" 'It took less than a year to demonstrate my ineptitude for business,' he wrote to those who were eager to learn something about the author of 'The Adding Machine,' 'so I went in for law. (A step down, but still respectable: if one can't be a business man one can, at least, be a satellite to business men).'

"He had five years and a half of law and hated all of them. But he passed his bar examinations and could even now, if he wanted to, stand for appointment to the district attorney's staff or the Federal prohibition enforcement squad.

"Having tried business and the law and, to his own mind, having failed in both, Mr. Rice decided that he would become an author. He might have become a bricklayer, he admits, given the requisite mechanical skill, or a policeman if he had been six inches taller and built, as the saying goes, in proportion. He might have become almost anything with a little urging and a little more equipment. But he decided to become a playwright."

The first night success of "On Trial" was talked of for months along Broadway. Mr. Rice, his face only a few tints less red than his hair, bowed nervously from a stage box as the audience stood to applaud him. He wrote several plays after that, but, it being war time, and he, hating war, being completely out of sympathy with the excitement of the day, suffered failure with both "The Iron Cross" and "The Home of the Free." His first post-war play, "For the Defense," produced in 1919 with Richard Bennett heading the cast, was a near-success.

Rice collaborated with Hatcher Hughes on "Wake Up, Jonathan," which Mrs. Minnie Maddern Fiske helped to some popularity. He did a play with Hayden Talbot called "It Is the Law" and then came the Theatre Guild's production of "The Adding Machine." By this time the playwright was set for his first rebellion. Not much had happened as he thought it should have happened in relation to the acceptance and understanding of his plays, and when he tried another collaboration, this time with the brilliant Dorothy Parker, their comedy being called "Close Harmony" (afterward "The Lady Next Door") and that failed, he just couldn't stand any more.

He took steamer for Europe, which is his favorite avenue of escape. He was in Europe nearly three years. Over there he met Philip Barry, also a playwright with opinions concerning the theatre and its ruling influences. Together, largely, I suspect, in a spirit of fun inspired by a contempt for playgoers' taste, they decided to write "one of those mystery things" which were having something of a vogue. Collaborating by correspondence they turned out "Cock Robin" and promptly sold it. Guthrie McClintic produced it in New York in January, 1928, and much to their amused surprise it ran for 100 performances.

Mr. Rice, hating clubs, is not a joiner. "I do not vote or play golf," he wrote some years ago. "I am violently opposed to censorship, prohibition and, in fact, almost everything." He has done a good deal of work for the movies, but he does not care much for them, either. Yet, for all his disclaimers, he is a dramatist of both the present and the future upon whom, I believe, an assured dependence can be placed.

The Elmer Rice plays produced in New York since the season of 1919-20 include:

"For the Defense." Produced by John D. Williams, at the Playhouse, New York, December 19, 1919.

"Wake Up, Jonathan" (with Hatcher Hughes). Produced by Sam H. Harris, at the Henry Miller Theatre, New York, January 17, 1921.

"It Is the Law." Produced by Samuel Wallach, at the Ritz Theatre, New York, November 29, 1922.

"The Adding Machine." Produced by the Theatre Guild at the Garrick Theatre, New York, March 19, 1923.

"Close Harmony" (with Dorothy Parker). Produced by Arthur Hopkins, at the Gaiety Theatre, New York, December 1, 1924.

"The Mongrel" (an adaptation). Produced by Warren P. Munsell, at Longacre Theatre, New York, December 15, 1924.

"Cock Robin" (with Philip Barry). Produced by Guthrie McClintic, at the 48th Street Theatre, New York, January 12, 1928.

"Street Scene." Produced by Wm. A. Brady, at the Playhouse, New York, January 10, 1929.

"The Subway." Produced by Lenox Hill Players. Cherry Lane Theatre, New York, January 25, 1929.

"See Naples and Die." Produced by Lewis E. Gensler. Vanderbilt Theatre, New York, September 26, 1929.

"The Left Bank." Produced by the author. Little Theatre, New York, October 5, 1931.

"Counsellor-at-Law." Produced by the author. Plymouth Theatre, New York, November 6, 1931.

"Black Sheep." Produced by the author. Morosco Theatre, New York, October 13, 1932.

"We, the People." Produced by the author. Empire Theatre, New York, January 21, 1933.

"Judgment Day." Produced by the author. Belasco Theatre, New York, September 12, 1934.

"Between Two Worlds." Produced by the author. Belasco Theatre, New York, October 25, 1934.

EUGENE O'NEILL

"Strange Interlude" (1928), "Anna Christie" (1922), "Beyond
the Horizon" (1921)

THE most exciting—certainly the most important—event to
touch closely the life of Eugene O'Neill these last few
years, since last we were writing of his varied career as
America's No. 1 dramatist in the first edition of "American Playwrights of Today," was his selection as winner
of the Nobel Prize for Literature for 1935, he being the
second American writer to be so honored. Sinclair Lewis,
the novelist, was awarded a similar distinction in 1930.

The Nobel prize, which adds up to a neat $40,000 in
addition to the honor bestowed, caught up with Mr.
O'Neill in Seattle, Wash. He had but recently arrived
there from his formerly beloved Sea Island, Ga., because
he wished to be in closer touch with the Oregon country
while at work upon his next major dramatic composition,
a cycle of eight plays that will carry an American family
through successive generations from 1806 to 1932. He will,
I assume, move back to the Eastern seaboard as these plays
develop.

The First Playwright has been inactive in the theatre
the last few years, having made no contribution thereto
since 1934, when one of his few failures, a drama of religious background called "Days Without End," was produced in New York. Previous to that he had scored two
major successes since 1929—one with "Mourning Becomes
Electra," a New England tragedy erected on a Greek base,
and "Ah, Wilderness," a native folk drama having to do

with adolescence, also with a New England background.

It was reported at the time of its production that "Ah, Wilderness," which was one of the greatest popular successes the playwright has scored, was written out of a dream. Twice Mr. O'Neill has had the experience of awaking from a night's sleep to find that his subconscious had deposited a full-length drama in his conscious mind and that there could be no rest for him until it was transferred to paper. The other one was "Desire Under the Elms."

Following the success of "Mourning Becomes Electra" in 1931 O'Neill started work on "Days Without End." This was a serious drama peopled with exceedingly complex characters and writing it was laborious. It is the O'Neill custom to write his first drafts in long hand, to have the first draft copied and then to correct it for a second draft. Frequently, fearing he may have gone stale on a subject, he will put a second or third draft aside for days or weeks before taking it up again. By August, 1932, he had finished a second draft of "Days Without End" and voted himself a fortnight's rest. He had no more than started upon his rest, however, than he awoke one morning with the full plot and all the characters of "Ah, Wilderness" in his mind and clamoring to be put on paper. Before he was out of bed, and while he lay for minutes in a semi-doze, the whole play, from opening to closing scene, came to him. To his further surprise it was a play of so simple a type that he was a little resentful of it. His intimates, too, have been trying ever since to explain the playwright's interest in a form of drama that previously had seemed completely foreign to his theatre interests. Still, at the time, there seemed nothing to do but to write it. So easy a task did this prove that within fifteen days the completed first draft was ready to be set aside.

O'Neill then returned to the writing of "Days Without End." In due time this play was finished, and before starting for New York and the Theatre Guild with the manuscript O'Neill thought to have a casual look at the "Ah, Wilderness" script to make sure that he wanted to go on with it. Again he was vastly surprised to find it about as finished as any of his plays. Such changes as suggested themselves were made within two days and the playwright started for New York with the two plays in his bag. Arriving here he turned the important "Days Without End" over to the Guild readers and called their attention incidentally to "Ah, Wilderness." Practically with its first reading the directors were prepared to put "Ah, Wilderness" into rehearsal, while they took their time with "Days Without End." The casting also became absurdly simple. George Cohan was suggested for the principal role. Cohan had never starred in any part not of his own writing. It was thought highly improbable that he would agree to play one by O'Neill. But he did, and with considerable enthusiasm. Five or six weeks later "Ah, Wilderness" was produced. It proved one of the biggest hits in Guild history and was played to huge profits for two years.

When it came time for "Days Without End" to make its bid, however, there was no such welcome awaiting it. That play barely ran through the Guild's subscription list, a matter of some fifty-seven performances.

Yet this was one of the author's plays in which he took greatest personal interest, and to which he gave probably more of himself than any other. In its pattern he had employed two of the aids to character clarification he had used before, combining the thought-directed soliloquies of "Strange Interlude" with the dual personality masks of "The Great God Brown." The hero of "Days Without End" is one person played by two men. The name is John Loving. In the presentation John, the real man, was played by Earl Larimore, and Loving, his weaker, baser self, by Stanley Ridges.

John, his prayers for the lives of his father and mother unanswered by the God to whom he prayed so faithfully, turns from religion and becomes an atheist. Loving, his baser self, approves the decision and is constantly at John's side urging his further rebellion. John, having married Elsa and being devotedly in love with her, is nonetheless led into a betrayal of that love by the false Loving. Elsa, hearing a confession of John's faithlessness, falls into an illness from which only John's agonized return to prayer reclaims her. This results in the restoration of his faith.

The Catholic Clergy was strong in praise of "Days Without End." Patrons of that faith were numerous and enthusiastic, even though they found theme and performance depressing. Protestant, Jew and the irreligious multitude, however, were frankly bored and the play failed.

The reception of "Mourning Becomes Electra" was much more generous. Here again the theme was somewhat forbidding and the physical bulk of the drama undoubtedly acted as a deterrent when considered in terms of an evening's entertainment. Originally "Electra" was written as a trilogy, three full-length plays covering the tragedies of the House of Atreus as they were duplicated in the history of the Mannons of New England. The three plays were first produced as a sort of telescoped trilogy, starting with the first, called "Homecoming," at 4 in the afternoon. The second, "The Hunted," followed a supper interlude, and ran until 9 o'clock. The third division, "The Haunted," began at 9:15 and was completed before 11. Afterward Mr. O'Neill approved necessary cuts and the three plays were brought within an evening's playing time, beginning at 8 and continuing to sometime after 11 as a formal three-act tragedy.

In the O'Neill adaptation of the Atreus legend Christine Mannon (Klytemnestra) is in love with a sailor man, Capt. Adam Brandt (Aegisthus) while her husband, Brigadier General Ezra Mannon (Agamemnon) is at the front in the Civil War. This affair inspires the complete disgust of Christine's daughter, Lavinia Mannon (Electra) who follows her mother and Brandt to New York and there confirms her suspicions of their intimacy. Lavinia extracts a promise from Christine to break off with Brandt, but Christine secretly plots with Brandt for the murder of General Mannon. When the General and Lavinia's brother, Orin (Orestes), return from the war Christine carries out her plan to be rid of the General by exciting him emotionally until he suffers a heart attack. When he calls for medicine Christine substitutes a poison provided by Brandt and the General dies. Orin, acquainted with the facts of the murder by Lavinia, later discovers his mother in Brandt's arms and kills the sailor. Christine, hearing of her lover's fate, kills herself. Orin, haunted by ghosts of the dead, also commits suicide, leaving Lavinia to shut herself up in the Mannon mansion with the shutters nailed up. She swears to spend the rest of her life in atonement for the sins of her family.

O'Neill, who has little sympathy with the Broadway scene or the galloping and gossiping shadows that people it, prefers to write in comparative seclusion. He has done much work in Bermuda, went to the south of France to write "Mourning Becomes Electra" and is now living in the West while he draws together such history and persons as will go into the first of the contemplated new cycle of plays with which, as said, he hopes to cover the domestic, dramatic and psychological record of an American family that took root in the soil of the new land in 1806 and spread to cover succeeding generations up to and including, according to his tentative draft, the year 1932.

Going back to the facts of birth as reported in the first edition of "American Playwrights of Today," Eugene Gladstone O'Neill was born October 16, 1888, at the Barrett House, New York, a hotel at the corner of Forty-third Street and Broadway, that afterward became the Hotel Cadillac. His mother was Ella Quinlan O'Neill, a devout Catholic, who had no direct touch with the stage save that of having greatly loved his father, James O'Neill, actor.

The playwright lived through a rather tempestuous youth until he was 27, when he was ordered to a sanatorium. His lungs were touched. It was while he was in the sanatorium that he first felt a definite urge to write. It was there that he did his first one-act plays, concerned mostly with stories of the sea, for which he has a passionate fondness and with which he has had a good deal to do.

"I think the O'Neill who first fascinated me was the author of 'Beyond the Horizon,'" I quote from the first edition of "American Playwrights of Today." "As a reviewer of plays I had come through the experiences of his approach toward this production with him: had seen most of his one-act plays, found them vital and dramatically sound and was eager to see this first full-length effort. For me a new playwright was born the afternoon of that special matinee.

"Before that he had been James O'Neill's rather wild young son possessed of a feeling for drama and a promising sense of the theatre, but no more. I had pictured him as a rebellious boy being dragged from town to town as an exacting responsibility attached to the entourage of his discouraged father's 'Count of Monte Cristo' company: probably loved as other children are loved but despaired of periodically as a mischievous and thoroughly exasperating nuisance: a bit of human excess baggage as hard to keep track of as the hotel trunks and a lot less useful.

"As soon as he was old enough to be left anywhere, which was when he was seven, he was sent to a Catholic boarding school. Then to the De La Salle institute. When he was fourteen he was entered in the Betts Academy at Stamford. Four years later he became a freshman at Princeton in the fall and was suspended for a year the following Spring.

"His misdemeanor at Princeton is generally passed over as a boyish prank. And so it was. A generous impulse born of the heavenly nights, according to one of his friends, inspired Eugene with an urge to present the president of the college (it was during Woodrow Wilson's regime, I believe) with a cooling bottle of beer. Being in doubt as to how the gift would be received, and, naturally, not wishing to embarrass Prexy, he tossed the bottle nonchalantly in at the latter's study window and immediately went away from there.

"The college authorities felt obliged to discourage this practice of gift-bearing for fear similarly generous impulses might become common with the undergraduates. And so young O'Neill was invited to spend a year at home.

"At the end of the year Eugene did not go back to Princeton. He went rather in search of a job. And thus began the second or adventurous phase of his exciting life."

Soon he was prospecting for gold in Central America with a friend who was a mining engineer. A few months of this and he was down with malarial fever. Six months later he was shipped home. Back on his feet in New York he was given a job as the assistant manager of a touring theatrical company and hated that. Off to sea for one more escape he worked his way to Buenos Aires on a Norwegian barque. In the South American city he held various jobs. One in the draughting room of the Westinghouse company. Another in a wool packing plant. A third as a clerk in the Singer Sewing Machine Company, South American branch.

But soon there was no job at all and the sea urge was on him again. He shipped as a mule tender for Durban, South Africa. He wanted to stay in Durban, but the authorities would not let him land with his scant capital and he came right back to Buenos Aires in the same mule ship. Another period of job finding and job losing; a month "on the beach" and the adventurous spirit of our roving hero was temporarily whipped. He shipped for home on the first boat that promised a New York landing.

At home the family again set him up, and would again have taken charge of his life. To escape this O'Neill shipped as an able seaman on the American Line and made the crossing to Southampton and back. Now he tried the settling down process in earnest. He took a job as a reporter and columnist, though they did not call them columnists in those days, on the New London, Conn., *Telegraph*.

It was while he was working in New London that the break in his health occurred. The year at Gaylord Farm Sanatorium and the urge to write followed. Out of the sanatorium with a healed body and a freshened mind O'Neill continued his outdoor life and exercise, and also his writing of one-act plays. Inspired now by thoughts of a new theatre that was in process of creation he studied for several months with Prof. George Pierce Baker at Harvard. He later lived for a year with the radicals and the Bohemians of Greenwich Village. In the Summer he went to Provincetown, Cape Cod. It was the Summer that George Cram Cook, Susan Glaspell, Mary Heaton Vorse, Frank Shay, Hutchins Hapgood, Harry Kemp and others organized the Provincetown Players. O'Neill was invited to read a play for them. He timidly obliged with "Bound East for Cardiff." It was the beginning of a beautiful and profitable friendship.

"Naturally there has been some dispute as to just how much O'Neill owes to the Provincetown group and how much they owe to him," I quote from that earlier O'Neill chapter. "It probably is fair to say that they could never have progressed as far as they did without him, and that he would never have made his entry into New York and the commercial theatre as successfully nor as quickly as he did if he had not had their help." Thus honors are easy.

When the Provincetowners moved back to Greenwich Village in the Winter O'Neill came with them. He was already accepted as potentially their most promising writer of plays. All his early short dramas, "The Long Voyage Home," "The Moon of the Caribbees," "'Ile," "The

Dreamy Kid," etc., had their first showing at the Province-town theatre, a converted stable with benches and a tiny stage in Macdougal Street. But these were the war years of 1917 and 1918 and there was not as much attention being paid new plays and new playwrights as there would have been had times been more normal.

The emergence of O'Neill, begun with the production of "Beyond the Horizon" in 1919, continued through the early 1920s, gaining momentum and distinction with each new theatre victory. He won the Pulitzer prize with "Beyond the Horizon," and repeated two years later with "Anna Christie." He brought the professional play reviewers to their knees, figuratively, with his "Emperor Jones." He co-operated with Robert Edmond Jones and Kenneth Macgowan in the formation of an independent company that staged "The Fountain" and "The Great God Brown." And, as a result of this steadily ascending climb, he entered into an agreement with the Theatre Guild by the terms of which that organization was to have first refusal of all his major works.

His first two seasons with the Guild saw the production of "Marco Millions," "Strange Interlude" and "Dynamo." "Marco Millions," proved the playwright's earliest approach to comedy in detailing the adventures of the world's greatest traveling salesman on his visit to the court of Kubla Khan. "Strange Interlude" was the sensation of its season, an incisive and intimately revealing history of thirty eventful years in the lives of unhappy mortals seeking happiness and satisfaction in living. "Dynamo" was the first of three dramas that the playwright had outlined in the hope of probing human reactions in the universal quest for a completely satisfying religious faith. "Dynamo" failed and the trilogy was never completed although it is a natural assumption that "Days Without End" represented some part of it.

Between 1916 and 1918 Mr. O'Neill had ten short plays produced by the Provincetown Players, two at the Wharf Theatre in Provincetown and eight at the Playwrights' Theatre, Macdougal Street, New York. These were "Bound East for Cardiff," "Thirst," "Before Breakfast," which was his first New York production; "Fog," "The Sniper," "The Long Voyage Home," " 'Ile," "The Rope," "Where the Cross Is Made" and "The Moon of the Caribbees." In 1917 the Washington Square Players produced "In the Zone" at the Comedy Theatre, New York.

Since 1919, the O'Neill productions have included:

"The Dreamy Kid." Produced by the Provincetown Players. The Playwrights' Theatre, New York, Oct. 31, 1919.

"Beyond the Horizon." Produced by John D. Williams, Morosco Theatre, New York, Feb. 2, 1920.

"Chris Christopherson." Produced by George C. Tyler. Atlantic City, March 8, 1920.

"Exorcism." Produced by Provincetown Players. The Playwrights' Theatre, New York, March 26, 1920.

"The Emperor Jones." Produced by Provincetown Players. The Playwrights' Theatre, New York, Nov. 3, 1920.

"Diff'rent." Produced by Provincetown Players. The Playwrights' Theatre, New York, Dec. 27, 1920.

"Gold." Produced by John D. Williams. Frazee Theatre, New York, June 1, 1921.

"Anna Christie." Produced by Arthur Hopkins. Vanderbilt Theatre, New York, Nov. 2, 1921.

"The Straw." Produced by George C. Tyler. Greenwich Village Theatre, New York, Nov. 10, 1921.

"The First Man." Produced by Neighborhood Playhouse, New York, March 4, 1922.

"The Hairy Ape." Produced by Provincetown Players. The Playwrights' Theatre, New York, March 9, 1922.

"Welded." Produced by Macgowan, Jones and O'Neill in association with the Selwyns. 39th Street Theatre, New York, March 17, 1924.

"The Ancient Mariner." Produced by Provincetown Playhouse Inc. Provincetown Playhouse, New York, April 6, 1924.

"All God's Chillun Got Wings." Produced by Provincetown Playhouse Inc. Provincetown Playhouse, New York, May 15, 1924.

"S.S. Glencairn." Produced by The Barnstormers. Provincetown, Mass., Aug. 14, 1924.

"Desire Under the Elms." Produced by Provincetown Playhouse Inc. Greenwich Village Theatre, New York, Nov. 11, 1924.

"The Fountain." Produced by Macgowan, Jones, and O'Neill in association with A. L. Jones and Morris Green. Greenwich Village Theatre, New York, Dec. 10, 1925.

"The Great God Brown." Produced by Macgowan, Jones, and O'Neill. Greenwich Village Theatre, New York, Jan. 23, 1926.

"Marco Millions." Produced by Theatre Guild. Guild Theatre, New York, January 9, 1928.

"Strange Interlude." Produced by Theatre Guild. Guild Theatre, New York, Jan. 30, 1928.

"Dynamo." Produced by the Theatre Guild at the Martin Beck Theatre, New York, Feb. 11, 1929.

"Mourning Becomes Electra." Produced by the Theatre Guild. Guild Theatre, New York, Oct. 26, 1931.

"Ah, Wilderness!" Produced by the Theatre Guild. Guild Theatre, New York, Oct. 2, 1933.

"Days Without End." Produced by the Theatre Guild. Henry Miller Theatre, New York, Jan. 8, 1934.

PAUL GREEN
"In Abraham's Bosom" (1927)

PAUL GREEN has clung with characteristic consistency—a disappointing consistency in this instance—to his conviction that he is a backwoods boy and that playwriting with him must continue to be an avocation rather than a vocation. His job, he believes, is to stick close to Chapel Hill, teaching philosophy to both eager and lackadaisical students of his classes at the University of North Carolina, while he confines his dabblings in art to his week-ends, his holidays and a few of his evenings.

As a result the last eight years have brought few plays from his pen. He won the Pulitzer prize with "In Abraham's Bosom" in 1927 and since then only four Green plays have come to production in New York, two of which were, I have an idea, about ready for showing when the news of the prize winning "Abraham" burst suddenly upon him.

The new plays are "The Field God," "The House of Connelly," "Roll Sweet Chariot" and "Johnny Johnson." Of these "Johnny Johnson" stirred the most definite interest, and that largely controversial. This is a fantastic probing of the soul of the average man. Johnny Johnson, pacifist, drawn into the Great War by President Wilson's promise that it was to be a war to end war, suffers a series of disillusionments culminating in his escape from a hospital with a tank of laughing gas which he sprays over the French High Command and almost ends the war. In the asylum to which he is assigned Johnny, the only sane man present, organizes a debating society which functions comically. On his release he is reduced to selling toys and singing pacifistic ballads on the street. Kurt Weil composed the incidental music.

"The House of Connelly" served an organization of Theatre Guild juniors well in the early days of their organization. It is one of Author Green's finest dramas, a study of the disintegration of the old South through one of its proudest families, and the promised ascendancy of the new South through the breaking down of class prejudices.

"Roll, Sweet Chariot" was a further experiment in form, being a "symphonic play of the Negro people," as Mr. Green classified it, revealing the moral and physical disintegration of Potters Field, a Negro settlement. A musical setting was written by Dolphe Martin.

"The Field God" dealt with the tortured soul of a would-be atheist who comes to see the light after his denial of God is followed by a series of personal catastrophes. The note of bitterness, the hymn of defeat that runs through the Green dramas, stabs the attention of the thoughtful in the theatre but keeps the unthinking populace away from the box office. If that is the way it must be, Mr. Green is content to accept the verdict, regret it though he may.

"Stay at home, read books, ignore artificial critical standards and keep a steady job. Those are my precepts for youngsters who want to write," the playwright told Virginia Swain while "In Abraham's Bosom" was still playing in New York. "They're the only rules for success I've ever known, and I've followed them religiously. Even if I made a fortune by my plays—which does not seem likely —I'd keep my little old job in the university in Chapel Hill and go on living the simple life in the 'sticks.' "

New York's introduction to Paul Green, dramatist, came through two channels. He wrote the short play, "The No 'Count Boy," with which the Dallas Little Theatre players won the Belasco trophy in the Little Theatre Tournament in 1925, and he was formally presented as a writing man by Barrett H. Clark in a preface written for a book of his short plays carrying the title of "Lonesome Road."

"People who read plays and playbooks were made conscious of the young Carolinian's existence by the praise of him by Mr. Clark and by the satisfaction with which a few hundred of them read 'Lonesome Road,'" runs the previously printed account.

"And then, after several commercial producers had refused it, the Provincetown Players put 'In Abraham's Bosom' into rehearsal and presented it in their converted stable theatre in Macdougal Street, Greenwich village.

"This was in December, 1926. The 30th, to be exact. And uptown the holiday influx of new drama was keeping the play reviewers a little more than comfortably busy. They sent their assistants into the village to report the Green drama and the assistants returned saying, in general, that 'In Abraham's Bosom' was just another of those Negro plays, done by a Negro cast, professional only in so far as the Negro theatre has attained professional status. It was, they thought, nothing much to worry about.

"Shortly rumors began to circulate along Broadway that 'Abraham's Bosom' was seriously being considered as the Pulitzer winner. This stimulated interest in the play just about the time the Provincetowners were preparing to withdraw it. Raising additional capital from the always hopeful backers of such enterprises they moved the play to that cradle of the Theatre Guild, the Garrick theatre in 35th Street, and the run was extended several weeks. The play was now seen for the first time by many of the reviewers who had missed it before, and several were enthusiastic in praise of it. But still the public remained away, and finally the engagement was brought to a close.

"In May the Pulitzer award was made. Again the Provincetown Players revived 'Abraham' in their Village theatre, and this time for six or eight weeks they did a profitable business. The Green drama registered some-

thing like 200 performances, counting its numerous revivals, before its run was ended.

"Going back to his beginnings for the sake of the record, Professor Green was born on a North Carolina farm
hard by the village of Lillington. The year was 1894. As
a boy he collected stone bruises, adventures in the woods
and probably an occasional lamming for being at the swim-
ming hole when he should have been at other tasks. He
grew up as a farmer's son, working hard through the long
Spring and Summer and getting such schooling as he could
a few months each Winter.

"He had a chance to attend Buie's Creek academy when
he reached his middle teens and graduated in 1914, when
he was 20. Then he taught country school for two years
'saving up' to go to the University of North Carolina.
He was admitted in 1916, and was just settling down to
intensive work, including that of studying drama with Professor Koch, when the United States decided to enter the
Great War.

"The Green war record, as he states it, is quite unevent-
ful. But to anyone familiar with what it takes to earn promotion in any man's army it means a lot. Paul Green started
as a private, became a corporal, a sergeant, and then a
sergeant-major with the 105th Engineers, of the Thirtieth
Division, and later, in Paris, was promoted to a second lieu-
tenancy.

"He had four months' service on the Western front and
then the armistice brought him home. He went back to the
university in 1919 and was graduated in 1921. He took
post-graduate work at North Carolina and at Cornell, and
became a member of the faculty of his alma mater, where,
as noted, he is still teaching philosophy.

Mr. Green's produced plays:

"The No 'Count Boy." Produced at Little Theatre Tournament. Wallack's Theatre, New York, May 6, 1925.

"In Abraham's Bosom." Produced by Provincetown Players. Provincetown Theatre, New York, December 30, 1926.

"The Field God." Produced by Edwin R. Wolfe, Inc. Greenwich Village Theatre, New York, April 21, 1927.

"The House of Connelly." Produced by Group Theatre, Inc. Martin Beck Theatre, New York, October 28, 1931.

"Roll, Sweet Chariot." Produced by Margaret Hewes. Cort Theatre, New York, October 2, 1934.

"Hymn to the Rising Sun," "Unto Such Glory." One-act plays produced by The Theatre Union. Civic Repertory Theatre, New York, January 12, 1936.

"Johnny Johnson." Produced by Group Theatre, Inc. Forty-fourth Street Theatre, New York, November 19, 1936.

GEORGE KELLY
"Craig's Wife" (1926)

I HAVE an idea that by the time we are ready to launch a third edition of this book of playwrights, the gods being that propitious, George Kelly will again be active in what was for so long known as the legitimate theatre, but is now more frequently referred to as the living theatre. Mr. Kelly continues to be potentially a leader among American writers for the stage, with a background second to few and a gift for the sane direction and balanced casting of his own plays that is quite notable. But for the last five or six years he has been coasting. In Hollywood mostly.

In October of 1929 a Kelly play called "Maggie the Magnificent" was produced by his early patron, Rowland Stebbins, who continues to produce plays as Laurence

Rivers, Inc. It was a domestic problem comedy having to do with the ambitious daughter of a vulgar mother who left home and mother in her search for a more inspiring environment. "Maggie" was distressingly truthful, as Kelly plays have a way of being, and the general playgoing public would have none of it. The mother complex is still strong in the theatre. This reaction depressed the playwright considerably and he threatened then to have no more to do with the theatre—not, at least, with the Broadway theatre. Incidentally, two members of the "Maggie" cast were Joan Blondell and James Cagney, later to make their names in pictures.

Mr. Kelly, however, was lured back for another trial two years later. In January of 1931 Mr. Stebbins produced his "Philip Goes Forth," which was also of the domestic problem series. Philip was the son of a business man who hated business and refused to follow in his father's footsteps. He wanted rather to write plays. After a quarrel with his father Philip went to New York on his own, found a job to which he devoted his days while he worked at night on his plays. He was a success as a daytime salesman, but a failure as a nocturnal dramatist, and this led, via an added love interest, to a reconciliation of sorts with the father.

"Philip Goes Forth" also failed to excite the playgoing public sufficiently to pay back its investment, and this time Mr. Kelly made good his threat to let Broadway and its misunderstanding critics shift for themselves. He left New York and was heard of no more for ever and ever so long. When word came from him he was again in Hollywood. His determination, however, was as set as ever. He would have nothing more to do with the theatre—until, a year or so ago, he hit upon a story for a play that intrigued him and he wrote the comedy that afterward became "Reflected Glory." This helped Tallulah Bankhead to a success of proportions and brought the playwright back to Broadway.

"Reflected Glory" is, we feel, something of a compromise. It is more Broadway than Kelly, being builded of the glamour and romance that have long been the theatre's most salable exhibits. An emotional actress of great popularity is convinced at the height of her career that she wants to leave the stage and settle down as a housewife and mother. Still, whenever opportunity offers and the test has to be met she is never quite prepared to meet it. In the end she seems destined to marry her manager and continue in the business.

When, in 1929, I wrote George Kelly, asking him to contribute a few biographical facts to this collection he was an unconscionable time in replying. Then he wrote, reluctantly and with just a tinge of normal resentment at my prying into his affairs, as follows:

"Much as I should like to be of assistance I find myself a trifle temperamental in the matter of inclusion in the book —that is, as far as my personal life is concerned. Isn't there some way in which you can pass me by quietly, and probably just say that I'm a young man who may do something some day? I don't care to what devastation my work is subjected, but I do really dislike any publicity concerning myself. That kind of thing, as far as a writer is concerned, always seems to me like the exhibition of moving picture directors' photographs in front of the cinema theatres. I see no reason for it.

"However, my name is George Kelly—I was born and raised in Philadelphia. I had no early inclination toward the stage—have decidedly less now. I like bridge, golf, riding and travel. The tragedy of my life is the Winter. In fact, that is my one genuine distinction—that I have hated cold weather more than any other human being. And my ability to stay up longer than anyone else has never been questioned.

"As to the state of the drama, the theatre, etc.—you cannot tempt me. I'm probably tired: but I'm enormously uninterested."

As it happens Mr. Kelly has continued to be "enormously uninterested" a good part of the time since, but there was a time when he was an active enthusiast. The essential facts of his career include his introduction to vaudeville, when he was 21, influenced in no small part probably by the success of his older brother, Walter Kelly, a favorite story teller of a former generation who trouped for years as "The Virginia Judge." Young George was a successful actor in vaudeville before he began contributing sketches to the trade. He wrote all his own material, too.

His first long play was "The Torchbearers," an amusing and pertinent satire on the early Little Theatre movement. He followed this with a three-act comedy expanded from a sketch he had written called "Poor Aubrey." In the expanded form it became "The Show-off" and missed the Pulitzer prize by not more than a flickering eyelash. The next season the playwright delivered his first serious drama, "Craig's Wife," and this did win the Pulitzer, which sort of evened things.

The next year's contribution, that being 1926, was "Daisy Mayme," a comedy quite in the Kelly manner but none too flattering to native pride. It failed. So, too, did the Kelly play the following year, one called "Behold the Bridegroom." This, too, was an incisive and unflattering picture of a lady waster. It was about that time that George decided to let them as would write plays for a fickle and cruel public. His produced plays to date are these:

"The Torchbearers." Produced by Stewart and French. Forty-eighth St. Theatre, New York, Aug. 29, 1922.

"The Show-off." Produced by Stewart and French, Inc. The Playhouse, New York, Feb. 5, 1924.

"Craig's Wife." Produced by Rosalie Stewart. Morosco Theatre, New York, Oct. 12, 1925.

"Daisy Mayme." Produced by Rosalie Stewart. Playhouse, New York, Oct. 25, 1926.

"A La Carte" (a series of musical skits). Words by Kelly. Music by Hupfeld, Alter, Gregg, Lanin, Creamer and Johnson. Produced by Rosalie Stewart. Martin Beck Theatre, New York, August 17, 1927.

"Behold the Bridegroom." Produced by Rosalie Stewart. Cort Theatre, New York, December 26, 1927.

"Maggie the Magnificent." Produced by Laurence Rivers, Inc. Cort Theatre, New York, October 21, 1929.

"Philip Goes Forth." Produced by Laurence Rivers, Inc. Biltmore Theatre, New York, 1931.

"Reflected Glory." Produced by Lee Shubert. Morosco Theatre, New York, September 21, 1936.

SIDNEY HOWARD
"They Knew What They Wanted" (1925)

THERE is something very human and exciting about the professional activities of Sidney Howard, dramatist. He takes his play themes where he finds them, develops them as they appeal to him with great care, sees them through the throes of production watchfully, demanding that they be given the best chance possible, and then promptly passes on to another job. This may be concerned with a new play or a problem having to do with the organization of his fellow playwrights of the Dramatists' Guild, of which he is the reigning president. One week he is in Hollywood, where he won an Academy award for his scenario adapted from Sinclair Lewis' "Arrowsmith" in 1932. The next we hear he is back in New York fussing with another potential prize winner among the dramas.

We left Howard with the production of "Salvation" in 1928. This drama, based suggestively upon the career of Aimee Semple McPherson, was written in collaboration with Charles MacArthur and was not a success, being withdrawn after thirty-one performances. After a couple of years devoted principally to pictures Mr. Howard had an original drama, "Alien Corn," produced by Katharine Cornell in 1933, and followed with two outstanding dramas in 1934, the first an adaptation of Sinclair Lewis' "Dodsworth," in the staging of which the author had a part, and the second a laboratory drama called "Yellow Jack," inspired by a chapter in Paul de Kruif's "Microbe Hunters."

"Alien Corn" related the struggle of a small-town college teacher of music whose ambition is set on a career as a concert pianist but who finds herself in love with the head of her college, and he already burdened with an unloved wife. The heroine gives up her love and eventually resumes her career. A soundly reasoned, brilliantly produced drama, its success was no more than moderate.

The dramatized "Dodsworth" was promptly voted the most vigorous and vital exposure of a ruthless type of big business American that had come to the stage. With Walter Huston playing the name part, supported by Fay Bainter as Fran Dodsworth and Nan Sunderland as the sympathetic Edith Cortright, the play ran through one season and most of the season following, with a lengthy road tour following. "Yellow Jack," following the heroic sacrifices of Walter Reed and his associates in Cuba while they were tracking the yellow fever microbe, was also beautifully produced and splendidly acted. Its appeal was to a limited public, however, and it was withdrawn by Producer Mc-Clintic after seventy-nine showings, to the freely expressed resentment of its enthusiastic defenders.

There followed a series of original plays and adaptations, the most notable of them being "The Late Christopher Bean," taken from the French of René Fauchois ("Prenez Garde à la Peinture") and deftly transferred to a New England setting. This was an amusing story of a Cinderella triumph on the part of a hired girl and, with Pauline Lord featured, had great audience appeal. "Olympia," from the Hungarian of Ferenc Molnar, the story of a haughty peasant's revenge upon a proud princess who had sent him away; "Half-Gods," a study in the cure of a quarreling and misunderstanding couple through psychoanalysis; "Marseilles," from the French of Marcel Pagnol, the romance of a lad who would wander the world and is held temporarily by his father and his sweetheart, but released in the end; "Ode to Liberty," from the French of Michel Duran, the story of an escaping Communist who is first sheltered by a beautiful Parisienne and later helped on his way to freedom and love, popularized for a considerable run by Ina Claire, and "Paths of Glory," from the novel of Humphrey Cobb, a depressing tragedy of the war in which a defeated French General, as a matter of discipline, orders the execution of soldiers from each regiment taking part in a charge that was repulsed—these were other activities of Mr. Howard which paid him dividends, either in satisfaction or cash, and frequently in both.

The dramatist's most recent contribution was "The Ghost of Yankee Doodle," a Theatre Guild production of 1937 with Ethel Barrymore and Dudley Digges featured. It is the story of a liberal family's last stand against the on-rushing next war that threatens to engulf the world, and ends in the practical defeat of the forces that would make for sanity and understanding in the treatment of human-ity's problems.

"On the face of the record Mr. Howard, after having successfully attended to the matter of being born in Oak-land, California, in 1891, took with the usual reluctance to being educated. He kept at it, however, or was kept at it by his not overly indulgent parents, until he reached the University of California. He was graduated in 1915.

"The year he graduated certain eminent diagnosticians thought they discovered a spotty condition in his lung tissue. Mr. Howard was not at all convinced that they were right, but agreed to spend a year in Switzerland on the chance that they might be.

"Having been an enthusiast of the theatre through his college years—an enthusiast who wrote or planned pag-eants, class plays, and such—Mr. Howard decided on his return from Europe, to study drama with Prof. George Pierce Baker at Harvard. But just after he was well started a certain historical war was announced and the drama stu-dent left English 47, to drive an ambulance on the Saloniki front. After that he transferred to the American air forces in France.

"Before the fuss was over he had achieved the command of a combat squadron and a feeling about aviation that has, so far as report goes, kept him on the ground ever since.

"Mr. Howard came home from the war still interested

in writing, but not particularly concerned about the drama. The theatre in those days, and, particularly to those who had played parts in the most tragic drama of our times, must naturally have seemed rather a puny, painted thing. He went in for what might be called radical reporting. He did a series of stories for the *New Republic* on the industrial spy system, later using the material in a novel called 'The Labor Spy.' He did a series of stories for Mr. Hearst's *International Magazine* which exposed the traffic in narcotics, and accepted an assignment as a sort of war correspondent in Pennsylvania when a coal miners' strike was on. He was, his employers agree, very good at these jobs.

"Yet when he was ready to make his debut as a playwright, or at least when the opportunity offered, he came forward with a highly poetic drama of Italian background called 'Swords.' Clare Eames, making progress at the time as an actress, brought the play to Brock Pemberton, whose first success as a producer had been won the season before with the comedy 'Enter Madame' starring Gilda Veresi."

"Swords" was beautifully produced, in a gorgeous Robert Edmond Jones setting of a medieval castle, but proved caviare to the general. Thereupon Mr. Howard married Miss Eames and retired temporarily from the local scene. Coming back later he did a few translations, "S.S. Tenacity," "Casanova," and a piece called "Bewitched," which he wrote with Edward Sheldon. Nothing much happened to any of these. The real change in the Howard fortunes took place in 1924, when he returned from Europe with the script of a play called "They Knew What They Wanted" in his suitcase. This, a story of the Napa, California, vineyards telling the exciting adventure of an Italian who advertised for a wife and sent the picture of his handsome overseer to inspire confidence, was generously cast by the Theatre Guild and played to the hilt by Richard Bennett, Pauline Lord and Glenn Anders. It ran the season through and won the Pulitzer award of that year, beating down so strong an opponent as the Stallings-Anderson "What Price Glory?" to the expressed dismay of many persons and several critics.

Mr. Howard followed with "Lucky Sam McCarver," in which a blue book society lady married the physically attractive owner of a night club; "Ned McCobb's Daughter," in which a smart Yankee girl tricked a Boston bootlegger out of ill-gotten profits, and "The Silver Cord," a serious and holding discussion of the devastating influence of a selfish mother-love that approaches the fanatical. These may all be set down as critics' successes, but the paying playgoing public rose only to "The Silver Cord" with any great enthusiasm. The McCobb and McCarver casts featured Miss Eames. "The Silver Cord" may also have been written with this actress in mind, but the part was afterward given to Laura Hope Crews. Miss Eames died in 1930. In 1931 Mr. Howard married Polly Damrosch, daughter of Conductor Walter Damrosch. They have spent much of their time in California since their marriage.

Mr. Howard's plays have included the following:

"Swords." Produced by Brock Pemberton. National Theatre, New York, September 1, 1921.

"S.S. Tenacity." Produced by Augustin Duncan. Belmont Theatre, New York, January 2, 1922.

"Casanova." Produced by A. H. Woods and Gilbert Miller. Empire Theatre, New York, Sept. 26, 1923.

"Sancho Panza." Produced by Russell Janney. Hudson Theatre, New York, November 26, 1923.

"Bewitched" (with Edward Sheldon). Produced by John Cromwell, Inc. National Theatre, New York, Oct. 1, 1924.

"They Knew What They Wanted." Produced by Theatre Guild, Inc. Garrick Theatre, New York, Nov. 24, 1924.

"Michel Auclair" (adaptation). Produced by Provincetown Players. Provincetown Theatre, New York, March 4, 1925.

"Lucky Sam McCarver." Produced by William A. Brady, Jr., Dwight Deere Wiman and John Cromwell. Playhouse, New York, October 21, 1925.

"The Last Night of Don Juan" (adaptation). Produced by Macgowan, Jones and O'Neill. Greenwich Village Theatre, New York, Nov. 9, 1925.

"Morals" (adaptation). Produced by Actors' Theatre. Comedy Theatre, New York, Nov. 30, 1925.

"Ned McCobb's Daughter." Produced by Theatre Guild. John Golden Theatre, New York, Nov. 29, 1926.

"The Silver Cord." Produced by Theatre Guild. John Golden Theatre, New York, December 20, 1926.

"Salvation" (with Charles MacArthur). Produced by Arthur Hopkins at the Empire Theatre, New York, Jan. 31, 1928.

"Olympia." Produced by Gilbert Miller. Empire Theatre, New York, Oct. 16, 1928.

"Half Gods." Produced by Arthur Hopkins. Plymouth Theatre, New York, Dec. 21, 1929.

"Marseilles." Produced by Gilbert Miller. Henry Miller Theatre, New York, Nov. 17, 1930.

"The Late Christopher Bean." Produced by Gilbert Miller. Henry Miller Theatre, New York, Oct. 31, 1932.

"Alien Corn." Produced by Katharine Cornell. Belasco Theatre, New York, Feb. 20, 1933.

"Dodsworth." Produced by Max Gordon. Shubert Theatre, New York, Feb. 24, 1934.

"Yellow Jack." Produced by Guthrie McClintic. Martin Beck Theatre, New York, March 6, 1934.

"Ode to Liberty." Produced by Gilbert Miller. Lyceum Theatre, New York, Dec. 21, 1934.

"Paths of Glory." Produced by Arthur Hopkins. Plymouth Theatre, New York, Sept. 26, 1935.

"The Ghost of Yankee Doodle." Produced by the Theatre Guild. Guild Theatre, New York, Nov. 22, 1937.

OWEN DAVIS
"Icebound" (1923)

No ONE knows just how many plays Owen Davis has written. Not even Owen Davis. He has been at it for forty years, and he is a persistent worker, though not as persistent as he used to be. A play or two a season satisfies him these days. If they do not he edges in a scenario or two between plays.

The newest activity in the Davis play shop is the introduction of Donald Davis, Owen's eldest son, as a dramatist. Donald had some difficulty making up his mind about the playwriting business. He was convinced as a lad that he wanted to go to sea. He trained for the sea, in a manner of speaking, after he was through with grammar schooling in Yonkers and high schooling at Pomfret and Horace Mann. He took a course with Prof. "Benny" Leonard to fit him for a career at Annapolis. He had two years at the Naval Academy, and a course in navigation at Columbia after that. And then he went before the mast for two years as an able seaman.

Donald still was at rather loose ends when he came home. He wanted more book learning, for one thing, so he went to Cornell for a spell and took a couple of night courses at New York University. Then the writing germ, which had been getting in its insidious work all these preparatory years, broke forth with unexpected virulence and young Davis went to Hollywood. He was there four years. He wrote a play about it. "The Promised Land" he called it, but when Brock Pemberton tried it in Philadelphia he changed the title to "Gone Hollywood." It never got as far as it should have because just about that time a couple of other fellows, George S. Kaufman and Moss Hart, also wrote a Hollywood play called "Once in a Lifetime." That took the edge off Hollywood plays for several seasons.

Now there came a job of playwriting on which Owen Davis felt that he could jolly well use a young and eager mind, collaboratively, a job on which he wanted a youthful slant. This was the dramatization of Pearl Buck's sensational seller, "The Good Earth." It took some persuading to convince Donald that he was the boy for the job. The young sailor did not lack confidence, but he had inherited that Yankee independence of spirit which prompted him to stay on his own. He had no ambition to ride piggyback into fame. Or even to ride piggy-back. However, it was finally arranged that the two Davises should do the dramatization of "The Good Earth." The play was literally assured a handsome profit by the terms of its sale. The New York Theatre Guild bought the dramatic rights for a goodly sum and the Metro-Goldwyn-Mayer picture interests took on the picture rights, sight unseen.

The Davises did a good, workmanlike job with "The Good Earth," Donald being credited with most of the writing, Owen with the mapping and consultation. But there was no transferring to the stage the charm of the novel's writing, neither its style nor its warmth. As soon as the theatre's crudely affected realism got between the spectator's imagination and the book, the appeal of the latter was blotted out. "The Good Earth" lasted little longer than the Guild's subscription list in New York and only briefly on tour.

Two years later the Davises took over the job of re-cre-

ating a drama from Edith Wharton's "Ethan Frome." This
had been tried in a version by Lowell Barrington, but had
not worked out as expected. Max Gordon, the producer,
turned to the Davises, and they, being Yankees by birth
and inheritance, accepted the assignment with considerable
enthusiasm. The result was a drama the reviewers ear-
marked as representing the best and most lucid transference
of novel to stage of any of which there was recent record.

Donald Davis has one other play to his credit, a comedy
he wrote with Sam Ornitz called "Haunch, Paunch and
Jowl." It has not yet reached production in the English
theatre, but the season of 1935-36 it was translated into
Yiddish and included in the repertory of the Artef theatre.

Owen Davis' activities since last we visited with him in
1929 have been somewhat curtailed. For a time his interest
reverted to the tricky mystery play. One he did was called
"To-night at 12." In this a suspicious wife had a great time
running down the writer of a note who, she felt sure, was
trying to arrange an assignation with her husband. One
was "The Ninth Guest," in which a dinner party of eight,
being locked in by the host, was informed that before anyone was released all should be killed. Death was to be the
ninth guest. The dinner party was pretty thoroughly deci-
mated, only two young lovers being spared. The host, it
transpired, was a madman filled with hate and revenge.

Next thing anyone knew the elder Davis had gone social
and offered a tragic drama exposing the lengths to which
gangland had gone and was going in the racket game. This
was "Just to Remind You," and told the experience of an
honest fellow whose laundry business was literally bombed
out of existence, the proprietor being shot in the back just
as a grafting politician was reading the Gettysburg address

at a school dedication across the street.

Still in reformative mood, the next Davis opus was "A Saturday Night," which tore down the shutters shielding a typical American home of the throbbing present. A middle-aged wife had planned a wild little celebration of her birthday with her husband. Before she could get started her young son was brought home injured from a basketball game, her daughter was brought home tight from a party to which she had gone without permission, a former suitor had proposed that she divorce her husband and fly with him and the husband himself had admitted an infidelity or two. Still, the wife decided to stick by her family. A Davis melodrama called "Jezebel" was intended for Tallulah Bankhead and given to Miriam Hopkins when Miss Bankhead was not available. The story was of a hot-headed Southern girl who quarreled with the cousin she loved and left him. She came back three years later prepared to forgive cousin, only to find that he had married a Northern girl. Thereafter she sought a cruel revenge and was not conquered until a yellow fever scourge laid her loved one low. Then she sent his Northern wife home and went to the pesthouse to nurse him.

"Too Many Boats" was an assignment job, a dramatization of a novel by Charles L. Clifford, that quickly failed, and "Spring Freshet" was another of the Yankee character studies which was expected to carry on in the tradition of "Icebound." This was the story of a hard old matriarch of Maine who crushed her grandson's romance and forced his marriage with a girl of her choice to guarantee the family line should be carried on. When she was thwarted by a lack of issue from this marriage she adopted an illegitimate child fathered by the grandson and raised it legitimately, again to preserve the line.

The senior Davis deliberately attached himself to the playwriting profession because he early developed a passion for that form of creative work. He had started out with some intention of becoming a civil engineer, studied two years at the University of Tennessee and two years at Harvard. His first move away from college, however, was to invade the offices of Harris, Sullivan and Woods, the firm that was at that time specializing in melodramas written mostly by Theodore Kremer, Charles A. Blaney and Charles W. Taylor (Laurette Taylor's first husband) and announce to Mr. Woods that he could write as good melodramas as any of these established playwrights. Mr. Woods' reply was that he would like to be shown.

"A week later Mr. Davis, who worked slowly in those days, submitted to Mr. Woods the manuscript of a four- or five-act melodrama entitled 'The Confessions of a Wife,'" the earlier account relates. "Another fortnight and he came in with 'The Gambler of the West.' From that beginning he gradually wrote his way into the melodrama field until he, and not Mr. Kremer, was the chief contributor of popular plays. He wrote under many aliases and frequently he had as many as eight dramas in circulation at one time."

The Davis melodrama factory continued running full blast for many years. In 1910 it began to falter. The infant movies were learning to walk, even though they had not yet begun to talk. Trade was poor and the Davis ambition to do higher class drama was matched by Mr. Woods' ambition to move into the $2-theatre zone. Davis wrote a comedy called "The Wishing Ring" for Marguerite Clark, another called "Lola" for Laurette Taylor and a series for

Alice Brady including "The Family Cupboard," "Sinners" and "Forever After." In 1921 he won the respect of the critics with "The Detour," a tragi-comedy of Maine life and character, and followed it in 1923 with "Icebound," similarly patterned, which won him the Pulitzer prize. Shortly after this he did a comedy called "The Nervous Wreck" which returned him a sizable fortune. Thereafter Davis plays followed in numbers too numerous to mention, many successful, many not, but the average largely in the playwright's favor.

Owen Davis was born in Portland, Me., in 1874. In 1902 he married Elizabeth Drury Breyer of Chicago, at that time a leading woman in a Davis drama. Their two sons are Donald, the growing playwright, and Owen Jr., a growing actor who is now having his fling at the movies after an experience that took him through a course of writing and studying with Prof. George Pierce Baker at Yale, as well as the playing of several parts on Broadway. The Davises represent the happiest of stage families, which is a source of complete satisfaction to Owen Sr. His offstage activities have embraced a good deal of golf and considerable work in the interest of the Dramatists' Guild. His produced plays from 1919 to date include:

"At 9.45." Produced by Wm. A. Brady. Playhouse, New York, June 28, 1919.
"Those Who Walk in Darkness." Produced by Messrs. Shubert. 48th Street Theatre, New York, August 14, 1919.
"Opportunity." Produced by Wm. A. Brady. 48th Street Theatre, New York, July 30, 1920.
"Marry the Poor Girl." Produced by Oliver Morosco. Little Theatre, New York, September 25, 1920.
"The Detour." Produced by Messrs. Shubert. Astor Theatre, New York, August 23, 1921.

"Up the Ladder." Produced by Wm. A Brady. Playhouse, New York, March 6, 1922.

"The Bronx Express" (adaptation). Produced by Mr. and Mrs. Coburn. Astor Theatre, New York, April 26, 1922.

"Dreams for Sale." Produced by Wm. A. Brady. Playhouse, New York, September 13, 1922.

"The World We Live In" (adaptation of "The Insect Comedy"). Produced by Wm. A. Brady. Jolson Theatre, New York, October 31, 1922.

"Icebound." Produced by Harris, Lewis and Gordon. Harris Theatre, New York, February 10, 1923.

"Home Fires." Produced by Messrs. Shubert. 39th Street Theatre, New York, August 20, 1923.

"The Nervous Wreck." Produced by Harris, Lewis and Gordon. Cohan Theatre, New York, October 9, 1923.

"The Haunted House." Produced by Harris, Lewis and Gordon, Cohan Theatre, New York, September 2, 1924.

"Lazybones." Produced by Sam Harris. Vanderbilt Theatre, New York, September 22, 1924.

"Easy Come Easy Go." Produced by Harris, Lewis and Gordon. Cohan Theatre, New York, October 26, 1924.

"Beware of Widows." Produced by Crosby Gaige. Elliott Theatre, New York, December 1, 1925.

"The Great Gatsby." Produced by Wm. A. Brady. Ambassador Theatre, New York, February 2, 1926.

"The Donovan Affair." Produced by Al Lewis. Fulton Theatre, New York, August 30, 1926.

"Sandalwood" (with Fulton Oursler). Produced by Robert Milton. Gaiety Theatre, New York, September 22, 1926.

"Gentle Grafters." Produced by Sam Harris. Music Box, New York, October 27, 1926.

"The Triumphant Bachelor." Produced by Donald Burton. Biltmore Theatre, New York, September 15, 1927.

"Carry On." Produced by Carl Reed. Masque Theatre, New York, January 23, 1928.

"To-Night at 12." Produced by Herman Shumlin. Hudson Theatre, New York, November 12, 1928.

"Spring Is Here" (musical comedy with lyrics by Lorenz Hart and music by Richard Rodgers). Produced by Alex A. Aarons and Vinton Freedley. Alvin Theatre, New York, March 11, 1929.

"The Ninth Guest." Produced by A. H. Woods (by arrangement with S. M. Biddell). Eltinge Theatre, New York, August 25, 1930.

"Just to Remind You." Produced by Sam H. Harris. Broadhurst Theatre, New York, September 7, 1931.

"A Saturday Night." Produced by Wm. A. Brady. Playhouse, New York, February 28, 1933.

"The Good Earth" (with Donald Davis). Produced by The Theatre Guild. Guild Theatre, New York, October 17, 1932.

"Jezebel." Produced by Katharine Cornell and Guthrie McClintic. Ethel Barrymore Theatre, New York, December 19, 1933.

"Too Many Boats." Produced by Wm. A. Brady, Jr. Playhouse, New York, September 11, 1934.

"Spring Freshet." Produced by Lee Shubert. Plymouth Theatre, New York, October 4, 1934.

"Ethan Frome" (with Donald Davis). Produced by Max Gordon. National Theatre, New York, January 21, 1936.

"Virginia" (with Laurence Stallings; music by Arthur Schwartz). Produced by Rockefeller Center, Inc. Center Theatre, New York, September 2, 1937.

HATCHER HUGHES
"Hell Bent fer Heaven" (1924)

ZONA GALE
"Miss Lulu Bett" (1920)

JESSE LYNCH WILLIAMS
"Why Marry" (1918)

OF THE three others who were included in the Honor Group of prize-winning dramatists in the first edition of "American Playwrights," none has continued a contributing factor in the theatre. Neither Hatcher Hughes (Polkville, N. C., 1883), nor Zona Gale (Portage, Wisconsin, 1874), has properly capitalized the gifts that brought them the Pulitzer prizes. Prof. Hughes won in 1924 with "Hell

Bent fer Heaven" and Miss Gale in 1920 with "Miss Lulu Bett."

It was the awarding of the 1924 prize to Prof. Hughes, who has taught playwriting at Columbia College since 1912, first as assistant to Prof. Brander Matthews and later as head of the department, that caused the most violent of many minor outbreaks against the Pulitzer award. Two members of the committee that year voted for George Kelly's "The Show-off" and only one for the Hughes play, but the awards committee at Columbia sided with the Hughes choice. Owen Johnson, novelist and chairman of the sub-committee on play selection, thereupon resigned and sometime later both Prof. William Lyon Phelps of Yale and Prof. Clayton Hamilton of Columbia also retired.

"Hell Bent fer Heaven" was Prof. Hughes' third play to reach production since 1919. The others were "Wake Up, Jonathan," written in collaboration with Elmer Rice and played by the late Minnie Maddern Fiske, and a second drama of the South called "Ruint." The last several years this playwright has fathered "It's a Grand Life" (1930), written with Alan Williams, and "The Lord Blesses the Bishop" (1934). The first was produced for Mrs. Fiske by George C. Tyler and A. L. Erlanger. It was as bold a play in story as any you might have expected the proper Mrs. Fiske to have offered in that day. It related to a self-sacrificing heroine of Park Avenue who holds her home together by ignoring the moral lapses of her husband and children. This wife even gave house room to one of her husband's mistresses who was brought to bed with child while visiting her. It was, however, rather a preposterous story and the play was withdrawn after twenty-five performances.

"The Lord Blesses the Bishop" was given a none too competent production at the Adelphi Theatre in November, 1934. The huge auditorium was entirely unsuited to the intimate drama. This one also concerned a bold attempt on the part of the author to offer a solution of a lightly fantastic domestic situation. A husband wanted to become a father. His wife preferred reform work to motherhood. They separate. The wife goes home to her father, a bishop. The husband engages a practical young woman to become the mother of his child. In due time the wife returns to her husband's home and offers to buy the baby from its mother, who refuses to sell. "The Lord Blesses the Bishop" was a quick failure, lasting no more than seven performances.

Prof. Hughes taught English at the University of North Carolina after he was graduated from that institution. He later took post-graduate work at Columbia and thus worked into the drama department. He served as a captain in the 18th Division during the Great War.

Zona Gale, who gained the award in 1920 with her first play, "Miss Lulu Bett," which she dramatized from her own novel of that title, wrote one other play that gained production in 1924. This was "Mr. Pitt" which brought Walter Huston to the legitimate theatre from a long and successful career in vaudeville and served as a stepping stone to the fame he has since gained as one of America's outstanding actors. These two plays accomplished and a couple of her novels, "Papa Le Fleur" and "Faint Perfume" dramatized but never produced on Broadway, her curiosity as a playwright was evidently quite satisfied and she went back to story writing, a profession at which she is an old and successful practitioner. Miss Gale has her A.B. and an

M.L. from the University of Wisconsin, is an honorary
Phi Beta Kappa of Western Reserve, and a member of the
Board of Regents of her alma mater. She had considerable
experience as a newspaper woman before she took to writing stories.

Jesse Lynch Williams, the winner of the first Pulitzer
award in 1918, died September 14, 1929, just after the publication of the first edition of "American Playwrights." He
had not been active as a dramatist since 1922, when a companion play to "Why Marry?" called "Why Not?" was
produced by Equity Actors, Inc., Tom Powers and Margaret Mower playing the leads. "Why Not?" discussed divorce with the same philosophic levity that "Why Marry?"
expended upon marriage. Mr. Williams gained fame as a
young man, both as a historian of Princeton College
("Princeton Stories," 1895, and "History of Princeton,"
with John DeWitt, 1898) and as the author of many short
stories and novels. His best known early drama was a newspaper play called "The Stolen Story," made from one of
his more popular fictions.

POTENTIAL WINNERS

In addition to those dramatists of the first line who have been singled out for prize awards there is a considerable number of potential prize winners, also of the first line, who, from season to season, continue to serve the American theatre with such distinction as to keep it in the forefront of the world's theatre. In this chapter are included leaders in this particular playwrights' group whose dramas have, from year to year, been included in "The Best Plays," the annual year book of the theatre.

RACHEL CROTHERS

THERE are not many finer records in the American theatre than that achieved by Rachel Crothers. She has been an active worker for approximately thirty-seven years. She has written and assisted with the production of some thirty-odd plays, has scored more successes than failures and has never had to apologize for either the character or quality of any play that she has written or with which she has been associated, despite the fact that she has herself acknowledged a deep disappointment in many of them.

Miss Crothers never has permitted her rather definite convictions on social issues to dominate her dramatist's duty of providing sane and acceptable entertainment. A majority of her plays have dealt lightly and humorously with recognizable domestic problems, and while this Crothers' tendency has lost nothing in firmness of statement the last several years, it has taken on a mellowness and humanness in story that has added greatly to the popularity of her plays.

Just after we left this dramatist a little abruptly in the first issue of "American Playwrights," in which it was recorded that her then most easily recalled output had included "A Little Journey" and "39 East" in 1918, "Nice People" in 1921, "Mary the Third" in 1923, "Expressing Willie" in 1924 and "A Lady's Virtue" in 1925, Miss Crothers formed a sort of friendly producing partnership with John Golden. By the terms of their agreement the dramatist was to have the selection of her own casts and attend to the direction of her own plays. Mr. Golden might make suggestions and help when help was needed, at both of which jobs he is a particularly able showman, but the burden of the work was to be definitely assumed by the lady herself.

The first production under this arrangement was that of "Let Us Be Gay," produced in February, 1929. Mr. Golden had gone to Florida. The telegraph wires informed him the day after the opening that he was, in a manner of speaking, stepfather to a hit. "Let Us Be Gay," which had to do with a wife's experimenting with the masculine code of a double standard of morals, after she had divorced her husband, ran for a hundred and thirty-two performances. Francine Larrimore played the feminine lead opposite Warren William, with Charlotte Granville prominently cast in support.

Two seasons later Miss Crothers produced a second social comedy, this one called "As Husbands Go," under conditions similar to those obtaining in the case of "Let Us Be Gay." And "As Husbands Go" ran for one hundred and forty-eight performances. This one was an intimate and observant study of the restless wife who, in her early middle years, again looks favorably on romance and struggles feverishly to retain at least a finger-tip hold upon her illusions. The heroine meets and thinks she loves a young man in Paris and returns to her Middle Western American home convinced that she should divorce her plodding and somewhat stodgy husband that she may be free to marry her new love. She tries desperately to go through with this program, but in the end the sounder, finer, more dependable qualities of the husband return her to normalcy.

Later that same season Miss Crothers succumbed to one

of the few compromises with expediency that she has made and wrote a comedy inspired by the interest in mystery plays. This was called "Caught Wet," concerned the adventure of a bored house party that resorted to the theft of the hostess's pearl necklace to relieve the tedium and was caught in its own trap. The pearls actually did disappear. "Caught Wet" suffered the fate of all compromises and was withdrawn after thirteen performances.

In October, 1932, Miss Crothers returned to the social drama she has served so faithfully and with "When Ladies Meet" scored another outstanding success. The ladies were the wife of a publisher and an attractive novelist who thought she was in love with him. The wife and the would-be wife meet at a country house without either being aware of the other's relationship to the publisher involved, and each seeks to justify her feeling toward him by free and open argument. The situation, which involves a quartet of vitally interested humans, in place of the usual triangle, does not flare up and out in a happy ending of orthodox cut. It merely suggests a possible adjustment and leaves the auditor's imagination free. "When Ladies Meet" was played for a total of 191 performances on Broadway, and later did considerable touring.

America's first lady dramatist was born in Bloomington, Ill. Her parents were both physicians. Which, concluded the daughter, was enough medicine for one family. She took to the drama in school, was made the director of a local dramatic club and topped this experience by taking a course at the then popular Stanhope-Wheatcroft School of Acting in New York. Finishing this course she stayed on as an instructress, employing her spare hours in the writing of one-act plays for the use of the students.

After this she turned actress, touring in support of Mme. Rhea and being a member of an early cast of "The Christian." Although early plays called "The Rector," "Nora" and "The Point of View" are credited to her authorship, as produced at the Savoy Theatre in New York in 1903-04, Miss Crothers feels that she made her real debut as the author of a full length play with "The Three of Us" in 1906, which was, for her, "the beginning of Heaven." After that until 1925 she averaged practically a play a year. Of her early output probably "A Man's World," in 1909 did more than any other to establish her importance and confirm her promise as a playwright with something to say.

In 1918 she organized the Stage Women's War Relief, was its first president and one of its most active workers. In the early years of the depression she was also an organizer of the Stage Relief Fund, designed to help members of the acting profession and associated callings through the hard times. In 1924 she was active in the conduct of the Actors' Theatre, an organization stemming from the Actors' Equity and inspired by a desire on the part of serious-minded players to do something worthy for the legitimate theatre.

Between the time she wrote "When Ladies Meet" and the recent production of "Susan and God" Miss Crothers spent the better part of five years in Hollywood writing and adapting scripts for the motion picture manufacturers, and marveling at the things that happened to them after they were written.

The success of "Susan and God," with the English comedienne, Gertrude Lawrence, playing the name part, is quite in line with the experience Miss Crothers has enjoyed with her other social dramas. In this instance she poses the experience of a flighty member of the social register set who, being burdened with an alcoholic husband, parks her daughter in high schools and Summer camps and runs away to England. There she contacts one of the newer religious movements and is spiritually reclaimed. Returned to her home filled with enthusiasm for her new happiness she seeks to convert her friends, to spread the blessings of an intimate communion with God to all the world, excepting the husband. She is quite eager to save the world, but the husband problem is too embarrassingly intimate to interest her. Circumstances impel her finally to meet the repentent husband half way. She agrees to reopen their Summer home, send for the daughter and give the husband a chance to find the same spiritual help that she has found in her new religion. Their relationship is to be merely friendly and should he backslide even once he agrees that she may claim the divorce he previously has denied her. The experiment is threatened with success through the husband's steadfastness of purpose and their mutual rediscovery of the daughter, and then threatened with failure through the wife's lack of faith in the permanence of the husband's reformation, but the ending is a happy one.

Going back to 1919, when the "American Playwrights of Today" record was begun, the Rachel Crothers productions have included the following:

"39 East." Produced by Messrs. Shubert. Broadhurst Theatre, New York, March 31, 1919.
"Nice People." Produced by Sam H. Harris. Klaw Theatre, New York, March 2, 1921.
"Everyday." Produced by Mary Kilpatrick. Bijou Theatre, New York, November 16, 1921.

"Mary the Third." Produced by Lee Shubert. 39th Street Theatre, New York, February 5, 1923.

"Expressing Willie." Produced by Equity Players, Inc. 48th Street Theatre, New York, April 16, 1924.

"A Lady's Virtue." Produced by Messrs Shubert. Bijou Theatre, New York, November 23, 1925.

"Venus." Produced by Carl Reed. Masque Theatre, New York, December 26, 1927.

"Let Us Be Gay." Produced by John Golden. Little Theatre, New York, February 19, 1929.

"As Husbands Go." Produced by John Golden. John Golden Theatre, New York, March 5, 1931.

"Caught Wet." Produced by John Golden. John Golden Theatre, New York, November 4, 1931.

"When Ladies Meet." Produced by John Golden. Royale Theatre, New York, October 6, 1932.

"Susan and God." Produced by John Golden. Plymouth Theatre, New York, October 7, 1937.

S. N. BEHRMAN

THERE is something about the sound of Samuel Nathaniel that does not please S. N. Behrman. At any rate he greatly prefers to be known as plain "S. N." and consistently clings to his initialed signature, though he lets his intimates call him Sam.

S. N. Behrman, then, thought modestly to storm Broadway as a playwright with ambitions as far back as 1923. At least there is a record of sorts to the effect that in that year he and Kenyon Nicholson had written a play entitled "Bedside Manners," which evidently was frankly a bid for the attention of boudoir farce promoters of the early or A. H. Woods school. It did not, so far as I know, achieve production.

Three years later, however, the Behrman name did

loom large upon the metropolitan hoardings. On April 11, 1927, the Theatre Guild produced his "The Second Man," which was the first of his full length plays to be written without the comfort of a collaborator, and a week later the Messrs. Jones and Green produced a comedy entitled "Love Is Like That," which was written by Mr. Behrman and Mr. Nicholson. "Love Is Like That" lasted no more than twenty-four performances, but "The Second Man" ran on for a total of 178 performances, establishing Mr. Behrman as a most promising white hope of the living theatre, and a dear friend of the Theatre Guild.

"The Second Man" will be recalled as the brightly humorous romance of Clark Storey, an irrepressible and irresponsible novelist. Clark was inclined to marry the wealthy Mrs. Frayne and thus feather his nest, though he was conscious of a definitely stronger urge for Monica Grey, a younger but financially less secure attraction. Monica, conscious of the threatened loss of Clark, boldly announces that she is to become the mother of his child. The novelist's reaction to this enormously exaggerated statement does not satisfy Monica that he loves her as he should and she turns to another man, leaving Clark to rebuild his affair with Mrs. Frayne if possible.

Nothing more came from the Behrman pen after that, due probably to one of those flattering Hollywood offers, until January of 1929. Then Jed Harris produced a second romance that was greatly beloved of the theatre's severest critics but not too generously approved by the seat-buying majority. This was "Serena Blandish," and it was notably strengthened by the presence of Ruth Gordon in the name part. It proved a lightly fantastical tale of a wide-eyed child who, being in debt to a jeweler, agrees to let him decorate her with expensive jewels. These she is to parade in Mayfair and thus attract trade to his shop. The jeweler works in association with a sort of professional chaperon who undertakes to provide Serena also with a rich husband. Serena, however, being without that certain subtle something that works to the advantage of salable ingénues, fails to lure the proper man and elopes finally with quite the least important of her suitors. "Serena Blandish" continued for ninety-three performances, but success never came closer than a fair beckoning distance.

A similar experience was that of the Behrman entrant of the 1929-30 season, a drama called "Meteor" which the Theatre Guild produced. This, too, was a brilliantly written account of an egotist's flight. Raphael Lord married the daughter of a famed psychologist whose work had imbued him with vision and unconquerable determination. By a kind of uncanny clairvoyance Raphael forged to the head of the world's speculators, acquiring great wealth and power. Failure threatens him, his wife leaves him, his friends are driven away by his insufferable egotism. But he is never conquered. And at the play's end is busy fashioning a new career.

Popular success came back to the Behrman camp with his writing of "Brief Moment," a social comedy in which Francine Larrimore was the star and that popular raconteur of the radio, Alexander Woollcott, did a bit of modest town crying from a sofa. The dramatist was through now with fantasy and genius. "Brief Moment" was a straight story of theatrical romance, always the most salable of the theatre's offerings. A young man of wealth and social position, given to periods of deep introspection, decides to marry out of his class in the hope of re-establishing his self-esteem. He takes to wife a singer of blues songs in a night club. Their understanding is perfect. This is to be an adventure in matrimony. And it is. When the first break comes the wife tries to go back to a former love. It does not work. In the end there is a compromise and the adventure goes on.

"Brief Moment" continued through the season. The Behrman position was established. When, a year later, his "Biography" was produced by the Theatre Guild, with Ina Claire in the heroine's role, the reception of star, play and author was more or less ecstatic. "Biography," a notable series of character etchings, revolved about the more or less casual love life of a gifted daughter of Tennessee who became a great portrait painter, specializing in world celebrities. She thought to keep herself free and independent, and did, save for a more or less serious attachment for a radical magazine editor who insisted that she write her biography and shame the world. The play ran through one season and well into the next, counting a successful road tour.

Another period of scenario servitude was worked out in Hollywood before Mr. Behrman came again to Broadway. This time he brought "Rain from Heaven," which embraced his personal reaction to those citizen boycotts that had reached a peak in Nazi Germany. He expanded this thought to include the bitterness and prejudice that had stemmed from the Russian Revolution. In "Rain from Heaven" the Lady Violet Wyngate of England seeks to compose a variety of these racial and social problems by bringing together a music critic barred from Berlin, a Russian scholar and a Russian pianist set adrift by the revolution, a big business American and his younger romantic brother. Two, the idealist brother and the music critic, are in love with Lady Violet, but she cannot risk marriage with the one and the other sacrifices his love to get back into the fight for liberalism. The play was a little muddled in appeal, and was not continued long after its subscription period, despite the personal popularity of Jane Cowl as Lady Violet.

After another two years devoted to the bolstering of the bank account in golden California the playwright was back with "End of Summer" which the Guild also produced. This is another of those adult comedies in which the observant Behrman looks on life and finds it both amusing and stimulating. His attention is now focused on the youth movement and the puzzle it presents to the generation that is forced to take it. The heroine here is the flighty widowed mother of a daughter in love with a boy who feels that he cannot marry her without a sacrifice of his radical convictions, she being rich and he merely a worker without an established future. Mother finds this problem baffling enough, but when it is complicated by the discovery that the learned psychologist whom she has really selected for herself is in love with her daughter the impact of disappointment is almost too much to bear. She has nowhere to turn at last, unless it be toward a handsome young radical who is set on establishing a magazine that shall do justice to the proletariat in the great work of remaking the world.

"End of Summer," starting in February, ran the season out, finally adding up 137 performances, but never quite equaling the popularity of the previous Claire-Guild success, which was "Biography."

When Alfred Lunt and Lynn Fontanne went touring

with "Idiot's Delight" in the Spring of 1937 they took a
Behrman script with them. This was the playwright's
adaptation of "Amphitryon 38," from the original of Jean
Giraudoux, which had been a Paris success in 1929, a Berlin success in 1931 and a Stockholm success in 1934. Showing that the American theatre, while undoubtedly it leads
the world, is not always completely abreast of the times.

The Lunts produced "Amphitryon 38" in San Francisco in late June, took it to Los Angeles in July, scored
record-breaking successes in both cities, and retired to
their Wisconsin farm for the summer. In October they
started forth again, polishing "Amphitryon 38" in Baltimore, Washington and Cleveland and bringing it to New
York November 1, 1937. It ran through till Spring, when
the Lunts revived Chekhov's "The Sea Gull."

"Amphitryon 38" says M. Giraudoux, is, by his reckon-
ing, the thirty-eighth version of the legend that brings
the god Jupiter to earth in quest of amatory adventure.
This time Jupiter comes disguised as a husband, as the
warrior Amphitryon, no less, and, sending Amphitryon off
to the wars, spends some time in dalliance with the beautiful Alkmena, his wife. Disappointed that the impression
he creates is no greater than that of any husband, and his
pride severely bruised when Alkmena is loath to admit
even his supremacy as a god, Jupiter returns to his heaven
a wiser and, it may be, a sadder deity.

The Behrman theatre urges developed early. He was in
his teens in Worcester, Mass., where he was born in 1893,
when he began falling desperately in love with all the leading women appearing with the local stock company, and
collecting as many actor autographs as possible. While still
in school he wrote a one-act sketch and, what is much

more important, sold it and acted a part in it on what was then known as the Poli circuit. At that point, however, the family arm was outstretched to drag him back to Clark university, and here he developed a new interest in study. He went from Clark to Harvard, where he took an A.B., and also went through the English 47 course with Prof. George Pierce Baker. He went on to Columbia and added an M.A. there. Then he went to work, writing book reviews first for the *New Republic* and later the New York *Times*. The old theatre urge bobbed up again about this time, however, and he became, first, a play reader; and, second, a press agent, which led him naturally into playwriting. His first efforts, as noted, were in collaboration with Kenyon Nicholson, himself a professor of drama at Columbia.

The Behrman play record to date is as follows:

"The Second Man." Produced by The Theatre Guild. Guild Theatre, New York, April 11, 1927.

"Love Is Like That." Produced by A. L. Jones and Morris Green. Cort Theatre, New York, April 18, 1927.

"Serena Blandish." Produced by Jed Harris. Morosco Theatre, New York, January 23, 1929.

"Meteor." Produced by The Theatre Guild. Guild Theatre, New York, December 23, 1929.

"Brief Moment." Produced by Guthrie McClintic. Belasco Theatre, New York, November 9, 1931.

"Biography." Produced by The Theatre Guild. Guild Theatre, New York, December 12, 1932.

"Rain from Heaven." Produced by The Theatre Guild. Golden Theatre, New York, December 24, 1934.

"End of Summer." Produced by The Theatre Guild. Guild Theatre, New York, February 17, 1936.

"Amphitryon 38" (adapted from comedy by Jean Giraudoux). Produced by The Theatre Guild. Shubert Theatre, New York, November 1, 1937.

"Wine of Choice." Produced by The Theatre Guild. Guild Theatre, New York, February 21, 1938.

CLIFFORD ODETS

THE most promising playwriting talent that has come into the theatre the last ten years is the possession of a young man named Clifford Odets. It is the most promising talent, I believe, because its possessor's background has been conditioned almost exclusively by the theatre. He was an actor before he turned twenty and continued as an actor for twelve years before he wrote a play. His achievements to date include three full length plays, "Awake and Sing," "Paradise Lost" and "Golden Boy," and two striking one-act plays of protest, "Waiting for Lefty" and "Till the Day I Die."

As the record runs Odets always had the urge to write but lacked confidence. Also it was necessary that he should earn a living. At 19 he was doing this by reading dramatic poems over the radio, romantic pieces by Rudyard Kipling and Robert W. Service. He got a job as a juvenile in a Camden, N. J., stock company. Followed by a job in New York as understudy to Spencer Tracy who was testing a drama called "Conflict." "Conflict" did not stand the test, even though in addition to Tracy the cast boasted the presence of several good actors, including Edward Arnold and Albert Van Dekker. It was Van Dekker who a year later introduced Odets to the Theatre Guild. He went touring in several Guild productions and came back to find a piece called "Roar China" in rehearsal. He got a job in that. And later in "Midnight," also a Guild production, written by Paul and Claire Sifton. But neither play ran past its subscription period.

It was about this time that the young people of the Guild organization were beginning to seethe with ambition. Harold Clurman, a playreader, was one of them. Herbert Biberman, who had staged "Roar China," was another. Cheryl Crawford was a third. They wanted to organize a sort of Junior Guild of their own, and did. With the backing and friendly co-operation of the Guild. They held meetings in Steinway Hall and Odets was among the enthusiasts who joined. That was the beginning of the Group Theatre, Inc. Odets was a charter member. The Group spirit enthused him. He set to writing feverishly. But not plays. He thought he would do a few novels first.

"I always had an ambition to be a writer," the playwright confessed. "Later I wanted to be a great pianist. But it had to be great. Instead I wrote a poor novel about a great pianist who lost his left hand in an accident—and I got to be a playwright."

He continued acting during his experimental writing days, but with less and less zest. He wanted to write. The fact that he had to act in order to live, or thought he did, irritated him. He did quite a bit of fuming those days, becoming one of the best of the younger fumers in his group. It was out of this experience that the idea of "Awake and Sing" began to grow. It was, his friends insist, a protest against such strangulations of family life as he had known as a boy. He shared an apartment with other Groupers. His room was furnished with a cot and a trunk. He slept on the cot and put "Awake and Sing" in the trunk. When the Group went into the country to rehearse that Summer they tried the second act of "Awake and

Sing" and promptly forgot it. Local boy couldn't make good with them, not just then. They were too excited about a play called "Men in White" written by another ambitious young fellow whose name was Sidney Kingsley. "Men in White" was destined not only to set the Group up as a successful producing unit, but also to win a Pulitzer prize and start young Mr. Kingsley on a career.

With the success of "Men in White" the Group Theatre executives forgot all about "Awake and Sing," which Odets had meantime completed, so he sent the script to a friend who took it to a producer with ambition but little capital. This was Frank Merlin, who bought an option on the Odets opus for $500, and dug up a second $500 when that option was about to lapse. A thousand dollars, in cash, for an unproduced play! Now Odets knew that writing was to be his real vocation. He looked at his first check and went to his room to start work on "Paradise Lost."

The following Summer, which would be the Summer of 1934, the Group Theatre again went to the country to prepare for the season to come. Again they could not see their acting pal's "Awake and Sing," but turned rather to a piece called "Gold Eagle Guy," by Melvin Levy, probably because it had a flashy part for J. Edward Bromberg, who had scored as a famous surgeon in "Men in White." In Boston, while they were trying "Gold Eagle Guy" and Odets was playing a part in it he heard of a contest for one-act plays sponsored by a New Theatre League in New York. There were only a few days left during which plays might be entered. Odets locked himself in his hotel room and wrote "Waiting for Lefty" in three days and entered it in the New Theatre contest.

Back in New York "Gold Eagle Guy" failed to enthuse

the subscribers or the general public. During the time it lingered the New Theatre League staged the best of its contest plays one Sunday night at the Civic Repertory Theatre. "Waiting for Lefty" was one of them. The furor it created was tremendous. The Group Theatre players were wildly enthusiastic. Now they quite suddenly became aware of their friend and associate. Now they were prepared not only to bring "Waiting for Lefty" to Broadway, but "Awake and Sing" as well. They thought at the time they could play them as a double bill, but "Lefty" was too long and would not stand cutting. Odets agreed to do another short play to go with it. "Till the Day I Die," a bitter arraignment of the Nazi purge in Germany, was the result. "Awake and Sing" was produced in February and was a success. "Till the Day I Die" and "Waiting for Lefty" followed in March, and also created a minor furor. Clifford Odets had unmistakably arrived. I asked the playwright some time later what were his reactions to this first success. What did he think about it?

"I didn't think about it," he answered. "I felt, and I felt sad, shocked, as if I'd been hit on the head and was lying in a dark room unconscious while critics and others were talking about some impostor with the same name."

This conclusion, I think, may reasonably be ascribed to the normal detachment of genius, the unawareness of those gifts which a slow-witted public has, to its own satisfaction, at least, finally discovered. Stimulated, in Mr. Odets case, by a very honest doubt of the value of a Broadway verdict.

"I have no attachments for the Broadway theatre such as it is," Odets added in this same confessional. "It always seems to me a depressing spectacle; dismal, inhuman, as far removed from genuine human problems as we are from Mars. An interest in trifles is the first sign of decadence, has always been so, in the history of an art. And our theatre is for the main interested in trifles. Talented theatre people go to Hollywood, and why shouldn't they? What does Broadway offer them? Does it offer other people mutually interested in certain themes, in common world points of view? Does it offer a place where there is not 'the money anguish,' a slight shelter so that they may work together, helping each other in craft and understanding, in technical development, in growth and sure expansion of their original talents? Actors might stay together on Broadway if they could get these things. As they stay together in the Group Theatre, which is one of the reasons I personally happen to be of the opinion that the American theatre must more and more turn to carefully-trained, mutually-reactive 'collectives,' where the whole theatre is what the Russian director, Vachtongov, once called 'an ideologically cemented collective,' in terms of direction, in terms of life content, in terms of sheer acting and directorial technique.

"If one wants to know the ghastly tragedy of the American theatre one must ask himself about the fates of Jeanne Eagels, Ethel Barrymore, Pauline Lord, Marjorie Rambeau, Laurette Taylor, etc., all extraordinary talents. The American theatre failed them, and they in turn failed their talents, and all because the sad, bitter truth is that there was no American theatre!"

Following the lukewarm reception of "Paradise Lost" in December, 1935, Odets decided to give up the Broadway theatre, at least temporarily. He had received many flattering financial offers from the picture folk in Hollywood, and in his present state of mind these now appealed to him with particular force. To Hollywood he went, and shortly after his arrival word came back to Broadway that the most promising of the new talents had been sold for-ever. It looked as though the reports might be true as months passed with no word of creative writing for the stage from the Odets camp. But finally, in late 1936 and early 1937, the tenor of the reports changed.

Odets had not given up the theatre. Odets was finishing a promised play for the Group Theatre that was to be called "Golden Gloves." In time the play came through. The title had been changed to "The Manly Art" and then to "Golden Boy." In November, 1937, this salty saga of an Italian prizefighter who was torn between a conflicting urge to become a great violinist and feed his soul and a consuming ambition to become a prizefighter and make his fortune, was produced and enthusiastically hailed as proof that the Odets genius still held and the Odets interest in the living theatre had been reborn.

Clifford Odets was born in 1906 in Philadelphia and brought up in the Bronx, New York; his early schooling was gained in the common and high schools of New York; his education was continued in the theatre, as noted, and is still expanding. He does most of his work at night, lives, when in New York, in the Washington Square district.

"I plan to spend as much of my time as possible travel-ing around the country where great themes are lying like gold nuggets on top of the ground," the playwright has written. "It is a dangerous time to be living in, but a happy time for writers and artists once they actually contact the life around them. Civilization is groaning in its sleep, wak-ing. I am very much interested in civilization. Believe an artist should be. That means being against war, against Fascism. It means open eyes, too. So, my chief occupation is—open eyes."

The Odets plays produced to date include:

"Awake and Sing." Produced by The Group Theatre, Inc. Belasco Theatre, New York, February 19, 1935.

"Waiting for Lefty." Produced by The Group Theatre, Inc. Longacre Theatre, New York, March 26, 1935.

"Till the Day I Die." Produced by The Group Theatre, Inc. Longacre Theatre, New York, March 26, 1935.

"Paradise Lost." Produced by The Group Theatre, Inc. Longacre Theatre, New York, December 9, 1935.

"Golden Boy." Produced by The Group Theatre, Inc. Belasco Theatre, New York, November 4, 1937.

PHILIP BARRY

WHEN we left Philip Barry in the first edition of "American Playwrights" eight years ago, he was holding what we considered an extremely promising position. He had, starting with a Harvard prize play, "You and I," in 1923, added some half dozen other dramas to his record and stood, we thought, an excellent chance of one day being numbered with the winners of Pulitzer prizes. Not that that would have made any particular hit with Mr. Barry, he being an independent sort and modest as to his achievements and his potentialities. But it would have pleased us to have been prophetically right about this playwright's immediate future.

As it happens, Mr. Barry did some of his best work in the early thirties, despite the depression, and the gradual recession of the theatre in general. He followed a somewhat fanciful mystery drama, "Cock Robin," which he had written in 1928 with Elmer Rice in a spirit of mockery, with a drama entitled "Holiday." This proved a searching and satisfying comedy dealing analytically with another of those problems of living which have been bothering the more thoughtful children of the rich since the beginning of the capitalistic era. The hero of "Holiday," engaged to the daughter of a great industrialist, had the courage (nerve, the girl's father called it) to insist that he did not think much about making money. Give him just a little security and he would be content to take a long holiday while he was young enough to enjoy it. The confession practically broke off the engagement, but it brought our hero in contact with his fiancée's sister, and he discovered that she thought a good deal the way he did. Which was fine. "Holiday" proved a popular hit, playing for 229 performances. Hope Williams came out of society and The Amateur Comedy Club to appear in it with Ben Smith and Donald Ogden Stewart, who thought some of being an actor at the time.

A year after that young Mr. Barry went serious on us, writing the first of the no-intermission dramas, a two-hour psychological study of the eternal mysteries in one act called "Hotel Universe." In this Barry brought together a sextette of unhappy and wondering souls. Fantastically he gave each of them a reminiscent peek at the particular act or decision of his or her youth that was responsible for such disturbances, material and spiritual, as each had suffered. The Theatre Guild gave the play a handsome production, with Katherine Alexander, Franchot Tone, Glenn Anders, Ruth Gordon and Earle Larimore in the cast. The subscribers were mystified and not too well pleased with

"Hotel Universe." It was withdrawn shortly after the subscription period was passed.

Two more popular successes came from the Barry writing retreat in Cannes the next two seasons, "Tomorrow and Tomorrow" in 1931 and "The Animal Kingdom" in 1932. "Tomorrow and Tomorrow" was frankly a rewriting of the Biblical legend of Elisha and the Shunammite woman. You may recall that the prophet stopped at the woman's house and was impressed by her kindness to him and her evident loneliness and heaviness of spirit. Learning that she would greatly love to have a child Elisha saw to it that she was so blessed. Years later, when the child was about to die, the woman summoned Elisha and the prophet brought the lad back to life. So, in the Barry play, a psychoanalyst, being billeted while on a lecture tour at the home of a childless couple, discovers a similar state of unhappiness on the part of the young wife. A great passion accompanies the discovery and, months after the lecturer has resumed his tour, a son is born to the wife and thereafter brought up as the son of her husband and the idol of his eye. The unknowing husband, however, is forever trying to bend the boy to his way of living and to a sharing in his athletic enthusiasms. This brings about the boy's nervous breakdown. His life is despaired of and the psychoanalyst is summoned. He is able to bring the lad out of his mental confusion and restore the happiness of the home. But when he would take the wife and her son away with him, the wife decides she must remain loyal to the man she married. A company headed by Herbert Marshall, Zita Johann and Osgood Perkins won acclaim in "Tomorrow and Tomorrow."

"The Animal Kingdom" was also an exposure of the

tangle mismated marriages can weave. In this instance a young man of property and ideals puts aside an artist mistress with whom he has been happy for some years and marries into what is properly his own social set. The wife proves theoretically all that a wife should be, but actually a greater disappointment than the young man can assimilate. There is no understanding sympathy between the two. In time the mistress and the wife have, so far as the husband is concerned, changed roles. When a break comes he goes happily back to the understanding artist. Leslie Howard being the unhappy husband in this instance, the popularity of "The Animal Kingdom" grew apace until 183 performances were counted, this being twenty odd less than were given of "Tomorrow and Tomorrow."

But now the Barry star, for some reason unaccountable at the time, began to set. Three failures followed in 1934, 1935 and 1936. The first of these was "The Joyous Season," the story of a tactful and understanding sister of charity written for Maude Adams' return to the stage. After weeks of indecision that timid star of former years decided not to play it. Lillian Gish took up the role Miss Adams laid down, but Arthur Hopkins, the producer, withdrew the play after sixteen performances.

"Bright Star," following a season later, told of a young man who married a girl he did not love because she and her money fitted in with certain idealistic schemes he had for the rejuvenation of his home town. Three years of domesticity and mental disturbance determine the hero to remove himself from the picture. The wife, sensing the cause of his desertion, dies of a heart stroke. Lee Tracy and Julie Haydon made this something of a motion picture cast, but even then there was no public for it. Seven performances and it was gone.

"Spring Dance," which came early in the season of 1936-37, was, so far as Mr. Barry was concerned, a rewrite job. Two college girls, Eleanor Gordon and Eloise Barrangon, had written a college romance telling of a college girl's hope of marriage and a tragedy that threatened it. Work being necessary to bring this story into focus and the play to production, Mr. Barry agreed to do the job as adapter. Even his experienced hand could not save it, however, and it lasted but three weeks.

This third failure so discouraged the playwright that he decided to take a long rest. He was still resting when this record was being compiled, but his return to an active interest in the theatre was being broadly hinted.

We quote from the earlier edition:

"Mr. Barry is another of the younger men who, compared with the forerunners of their profession, seem slightly abnormal in their native reticences.

"He is willing to admit, the record being what it is, that his name is Philip Barry and that he was born in Rochester, N. Y., 32 years ago. He will even go so far as to confide that he escaped from Rochester in 1913 and returned only occasionally thereafter to see his family, and never to stay for long at a time."

He received his early education from priests and nuns, and his later education at Yale and Harvard. He was graduated from Yale in 1919 and promptly ran over to Harvard to study drama in Professor Baker's English 47 class.

When Mr. Barry won the Harvard prize with "You and I" (1923), he started seriously upon a playwrighting career. His chief objective, quite reasonably, was success with honor, in the commercial theatre. He had had some experience with a clerkship in the State Department in Washington; had filled a berth as a member of the staff of the United States Embassy in London. He had also given some time to writing copy in an advertising agency. But none of these jobs really appealed to him.

Following "You and I" he did a piece called "The Youngest" (1924), having to do with the life of Benjamin Franklin, which was a moderate success. He wrote "In a Garden" (1925), which Laurette Taylor played for Arthur Hopkins in a beautiful setting designed by the oncoming Robert Edmond Jones. But neither Miss Taylor nor the scenery could sell it to the women, the theme being that every married woman is at heart mistress of the man who first awakened romance in her soul.

Eager now for a further wing-stretch the young playwright wrote a fantastic satirical comedy called "White Wings" (1926), having to do with the evolution of an honest street cleaner. Winthrop Ames produced it and this, too, was frowned upon by the common or ticket-purchasing playgoers. He next tried a Biblical drama based on the life of John the Baptist. A sensitive and finely written work, "John" (1927), was not too wisely cast and also proved a failure.

By this time the playwright was pretty bitter about the whole business, but managed to finish another play done in his best comedy manner. This was "Paris Bound" (1927), a discussion of adultery and the unfair importance attached to a husband's inadvertent slip in those marriages that are presumed to represent a spiritual sacrament. "Paris Bound" put the playwright back in the popular-hit group. Its success was followed by another fairly lengthy vacation which, as previously noted, brought forth nothing more important than the Rice-Barry collaboration with "Cock Robin."

Mr. Barry's produced plays to date include:

"A Punch for Judy." Produced by Professor Baker's 47 Workshop. Morosco Theatre, New York, April 18, 1921.

"You and I." Produced by Richard Herndon. Belmont Theatre, New York, February 19, 1923.

"The Youngest." Produced by Robert Milton. Gaiety Theatre, New York, December 22, 1924.

"In a Garden." Produced by Arthur Hopkins. Plymouth Theatre, New York, November 16, 1925.

"White Wings." Produced by Winthrop Ames. Booth Theatre, New York, October 15, 1926.

"John." Produced by Actors' Theatre Inc. Klaw Theatre, New York, November 4, 1927.

"Paris Bound." Produced by Arthur Hopkins. Music Hall, New York, December 27, 1927.

"Cock Robin" (with Elmer Rice). Produced by Guthrie McClintic. Forty-eighth St. Theatre, New York, January 12, 1928.

"Holiday." Produced by Arthur Hopkins. Plymouth Theatre, New York, November 26, 1928.

"Hotel Universe." Produced by The Theatre Guild. Martin Beck Theatre, New York, April 14, 1930.

"Tomorrow and Tomorrow." Produced by Gilbert Miller. Henry Miller Theatre, New York, January 13, 1931.

"The Animal Kingdom." Produced by Gilbert Miller and Leslie Howard. Broadhurst Theatre, New York, January 12, 1932.

"The Joyous Season." Produced by Arthur Hopkins. Belasco Theatre, New York, January 29, 1934.

"Bright Star." Produced by Arthur Hopkins. Empire Theatre, New York, October 15, 1935.

"Spring Dance" (adapted from play by Eleanor Golden and Eloise Barrangon). Produced by Jed Harris. Empire Theatre, New York, August 25, 1936.

MARK REED

ONE of the most satisfying of recent elevations to first line prominence in the theatre was that of Mark Reed, whose "Yes, My Darling Daughter," was one of the brighter items of the 1936-37 season. This comedy, the story of a progressive mother whose Greenwich Village past catches up with her when her twenty-year-old daughter insists upon her own right to a love life of complete freedom, ran through the season in which it was produced, with Lucile Watson and Peggy Conklin featured, and well into the season following. Which served to set Mr. Reed up in a manner of which he had dreamed when he first gave up architecture to write for the theatre. He got frightfully tired, he has said, of designing bathrooms, which was his first assignment in his first job out of school—ten floors of bathrooms for a hospital.

Reed was born in Chelmsford, Mass. Attended Dartmouth to study football, Massachusetts Institute of Technology to study architecture and Harvard to take Professor Baker's "English 47" and allied courses on the drama. Wrote a couple of plays under Mr. Baker's tutelage but before they were produced and while he was acting as editor of the suffragists' magazine "Women's Journal" he enlisted in the army and was assigned to the camouflage division of the A.E.F. The day he returned from France he was summoned to the first rehearsal of "She Would and She Did" in which Grace George was starred. This, his first play, was produced at the Vanderbilt Theatre, New York, in 1919.

The next ten years Mr. Reed spent writing innumerable short stories and came back to Broadway in January of 1929 with "Skyrocket" which Gilbert Miller produced at the Lyceum. Neither of his first two plays was successful. The next, "Petticoat Fever," however, produced by Richard Aldrich and Alfred de Liagre at the Ritz, with Dennis King the star, received good notices and ran for 137 performances.

Mr. Reed acknowledges a private little prayer of his own. "I devoutly pray that the living theatre may triumph over the talking pictures," he has written, "and after 98 per cent of the pictures I see I suspect my prayer has already been answered." He has no home life, insists this bachelor, and his off duty time is spent playing tennis, driving a car, collecting stamps and going to the theatre.

Mr. Reed's produced plays since 1920 have been:

"She Would and She Did." Produced at the Vanderbilt Theatre, New York, Sept., 1919.

"Skyrocket." Produced by Gilbert Miller. Lyceum Theatre, New York, January, 1929.

"Petticoat Fever." Produced by Richard Aldrich and Alfred de Liagre. Ritz Theatre, New York, March, 1935.

"Yes, My Darling Daughter." Produced by Alfred de Liagre. Playhouse, New York, February, 1937.

GEORGE ABBOTT

EIGHT years ago we placed George Francis Abbott at the head of the great collaborators and predicted that, in the words of the greater biographers, he would go far. Or at least farther. And he has. His last work as co-author in the 1929 "American Playwrights" was "Coquette," a sad but exciting little drama about a sweet Southern girl who died for love. He wrote "Coquette" with Ann Bridgers. During the years immediately following, Mr. Abbott continued his career as a collaborator with considerably more artistic success than financial profit. Happily he is one who worries little about profits.

In 1928 he helped E. E. Paramore and Hyatt Daab write a comedy called "Ringside," which Gene Buck produced. It was the story of a boxer (Robert Taber) who fought his way to a championship through a lot of skullduggery and a variety of conspiracies framed to undo him. It was withdrawn after thirty-seven performances. Next he helped S. K. Lauren with "Those We Love," the story of a misunderstanding two who separated temporarily for the good of their work, threatened to make it a permanent arrangement when the husband was caught cheating, and were finally brought together by the needs of their son. This lasted for seventy-seven performances.

In 1932 there was a brief revival of the George Abbott-Philip Dunning partnership in the writing of "Lilly Turner," which was the story of a model who just could not make up her mind about men until her husband, a poor thing but her own, was tossed through a skylight and needed her greatly if he ever was to recover. Twenty-four showings and this one, too, was gone.

The season following, "Heat Lightning," which Abbott extracted from an original script by Leon Abrams, telling of an Oklahoma girl who was compelled to shoot a gangster husband before she could be rid of him in Arizona, likewise suffered a short run, going out after forty-four showings.

In 1934 our busy hero helped Lawrence Hazard and

Richard Flournoy with the rewriting of a rather involved opus called "Ladies' Money." In this two unemployed actors and a clerk were doing the housework in a rooming house while their wives supported them. Complications involving a gunman, a bevy of pursuing coppers and a thief who left a wad of money behind him when he ran from the law were plot features, but not sufficiently intriguing to keep the play going. "Ladies' Money" was also short-lived.

Now the resourceful Abbott turned again to that type of swiftly paced comedy which is his particular forte. Working with an idea and a script submitted by John Cecil Holm, he produced a comedy farce called "Three Men on a Horse," selecting his own cast and staging the play. It was the story of a mild-mannered greeting card writer whose hobby was the picking of winners from the racing forms. The morning he quarrels with his wife and is late for work, due to his defiantly taking a drink or two, he is kidnapped by a trio of professional racetrack touts who have discovered magic in his selections. Under duress he picks winners for them until they have rolled up a fortune, but breaks the spell the first time he personally puts down a bet. Then he is permitted to return to his anxious wife.

"Three Men on a Horse" proved the comedy sensation of its season (1934-35). It was the forerunner of a quartet of laugh producers similarly staged and directed by Mr. Abbott the money making equal of which has not been known since the early days of the John Golden-Winchell Smith partnership which started with "Turn to the Right" and continued with "Lightnin'," "Three Wise Fools," "The First Year, etc."

The Abbott winners included, in addition to "Three Men on a Horse," the Spewacks' "Boy Meets Girl," spoofing Hollywood, "Brother Rat," saga of the Virginia Military Institute written by two graduates, John Monks, Jr. and Fred J. Finklehoffe, and "Room Service," a wildly farcical tale of shoestring play promotion on Broadway by John Murray and Alan Boretz. Mr. Abbott took no part in the rewriting of these jolly plays, though naturally, as director he unquestionably had a free hand in pointing up the lines and building up the more riotous scenes. All four plays were big box-office successes, and duplicated on tour their success in the big city.

However, the mighty can fall as well as rise. In the Fall of 1936 a hunk of Abbott profits were sunk in a modernized version of "Uncle Tom's Cabin" called "Sweet River," and recently this master of flippant comedy turned back to a murder mystery melodrama called "Angel Island." This was not a very successful turn either. "Angel Island," written by a lady who signed herself Bernie Angus (Bernie being short for Bernadine) followed the old form brought closest to popular perfection with the Avery Hopwood-Mary Roberts Rinehart "The Bat" the season of 1920-21. Abbott managed to point up its comedy and give polish to its mysterious crimes, which included a couple of ice-pick murders mysteriously consummated during a single evening spent by a house party on an island, but despite all he could do "Angel Island" remained a pretty average shriek and shiver number and that was all.

In addition to his later works George Abbott has worked with James Gleason, Winchell Smith, John V. A. Weaver, Maxwell Anderson, Frank Craven, Paul Dickey, Philip Dunning, Ann Bridgers and Dana Burnett in the fashioning of plays, a list of which is hereafter appended.

"In some instances I suspect he did most of the work, and in others the material was probably pretty well shaped before he took it over," I wrote in the first edition of this work. "But you will find, I am also convinced, a very definite something that is George Abbott in each of these plays, because that is the sort of person he is, and that is the kind of talent which is his particular gift.

"Geographically Abbott belongs to both the East and the West. The family lived in the little town of Salamanca, N. Y., in the near neighborhood of 40 years ago. Salamanca is generally given as his birthplace. As a matter of truth he was born in the neighboring village of Forestville while his mother was visiting there and George refused to delay his arrival until she could get home.

"He was no more than 7 when his father became a government land agent in Wyoming and took George along with him to Cheyenne. When he was big enough they sent him to the military academy at Kearney, Neb., and when the family moved east again he went to high school in Hamburg, N. Y., and from there to the University of Rochester.

"The playwriting urge began to trouble George during his sophomore year in college, but he could not induce the dramatic clubs to produce his plays. Not until his senior year. After that they tried several. He was the happy author of the senior farce his graduation year, which was 1911.

"The next year he, too, studied with Prof. Baker in Harvard, and did well enough as a student of English 47 to have one of his plays produced by the Harvard Dramatic Club. Another, called 'The Man in the Manhole,' won a prize and was played in one of the Keith theatres in Boston."

With this encouragement Abbott packed up his plays and invaded New York. Producers were not interested. Rather chilly, in fact. So he turned actor and for the next eight years served time as a good trouper.

"During an engagement in a touring company playing 'Dulcy,'" continues the record, "Abbott met James Gleason who also had playwriting ambitions. Together they wrote 'The Fall Guy,' and when this comedy was produced in March, 1925, it helped to put one Abbott foot, which is of generous size and solid enough to support the six feet of bulk that towers above it, on one of the lower rungs of the Broadway ladder. He followed it promptly with the other foot and he has never taken either off the ladder except to climb a rung higher.

"His acting years were also productive in another way. By 1923 he had acquired stature as a leading man in plays demanding the healthier he-men types. He enjoyed personal successes in 'Zander the Great,' with Alice Brady, in Maxwell Anderson's 'White Desert' and Hatcher Hughes' prize-winning 'Hell-bent fer Heaven.' They tried to make a sort of star of him in 'Lazybones,' but it did not take. He played prominently in 'Processional,' and his last try was in 'The Terror,' which he and Winchell Smith made over from its Maxwell Anderson-George Abbott beginnings."

As it turned out playing the lead in "The Terror," which was a failure, was not the last appearance of Mr. Abbott as an actor. In 1934 he got hold of a play by an English school teacher, Ronald Gow, which sought to do for John Brown of Osawatomie what John Drinkwater had done for Abraham Lincoln. "John Brown" as a play took hold of the Abbott imagination and fired George not only with a desire to produce it but also with a conviction that, seeing there was no one else available, he could play the part. He could, too, but not very convincingly. He was impressive in whiskers but, curiously, his voice didn't fit. It emerged as something of a misplaced falsetto, intensifying the suggestion of old John's fanaticism but playing hob with his appeal as an heroic martyr. "John Brown" was Abbott's last appearance to date as an actor. He read the reviews and withdrew the drama after the second performance.

"Abbott is a modest enthusiast and believes sincerely in the modern theatre," to go on with the story. "He belongs to the group that figuratively took to throwing its caps in the air when the 'debunking' processes that have stripped the drama of much of its cheaper artifice the last few seasons set in.

"A clean minded, clean-living type himself, he will fight long and hard for the honesty and freedom of a scene that to him demands a touch of profanity to give it character. Either cut the scene or play it right is his rule. Either eliminate the character or give it every chance for honest development and expression. His enthusiasm may lead him astray at times, but in the end his sound common sense and native good taste will save him."

The Abbott collaborations to date have been:

"The Fall Guy" (with James Gleason). Produced by Messrs. Shubert in association with George B. McClellan. Eltinge Theatre, New York, March 10, 1925.

"A Holy Terror" (with Winchell Smith). Produced by John Golden. George M. Cohan Theatre, New York, September 28, 1925.

"Love 'Em and Leave 'Em" (with John V. A. Weaver). Produced by Jed Harris. Sam H. Harris Theatre, New York, February 3, 1926.

"Broadway" (with Philip Dunning). Produced by Jed Harris. Broadhurst Theatre, New York, September 16, 1926.

"Four Walls" (with Dana Burnett). Produced by John Golden. John Golden Theatre, New York, September 19, 1927.

"Coquette" (with Ann Bridgers). Produced by Jed Harris. Maxine Elliott Theatre, New York, November 8, 1927.

"Ringside" (with Edward E. Paramore, Jr., and Hyatt Daab). Produced by Gene Buck. Broadhurst Theatre, New York, August 29, 1928.

"Those We Love" (with S. K. Lauren). Produced by Philip Dunning. John Golden Theatre, New York, February 19, 1930.

"Lilly Turner" (with Philip Dunning). Produced by Abbott and Dunning. Morosco Theatre, New York, September 19, 1932.

"Heat Lightning" (with Leon Abrams). Produced by Abbott and Dunning. Booth Theatre, New York, September 15, 1933.

"Ladies' Money" (previously written by Lawrence Hazard and Richard Flournoy). Produced by Courtney Burr. Ethel Barrymore Theatre, New York, November 1, 1934.

"Three Men on a Horse" (with John Cecil Holm). Produced by Alex Yokel. The Playhouse, New York, January 30, 1935.

"On Your Toes" (a revue written with Richard Rodgers and Lorenz Hart). Produced by Dwight Deere Wiman. Imperial Theatre, New York, April 11, 1936.

"Sweet River" (adapted from "Uncle Tom's Cabin"). Produced by George Abbott. 51st Street Theatre, New York, October 28, 1936.

A. E. THOMAS

A. E. Thomas had been coasting leisurely during the late twenties. His record had been something like a play a year previous to that time. Henry Miller had depended greatly upon him. It was in Mr. Thomas' "Embers" that Mr. Miller was playing just before he died in 1926. After that the playwright collaborated with George Middleton on "The Big Pond" in 1928. This was an amusing criticism of the attitude of many Americans toward many foreigners. A big rubber man from the Middle West takes his family abroad and hires a handsome courier to show them about. His daughter thinks she is in love with the courier. Papa will be damned if he lets her marry any man who isn't a go-getter in the true American tradition. To expose the courier Papa offers him a job in the rubber business. Back in Vernon, Ohio, the courier becomes even a greater Rotarian than his patron. But daughter doesn't like him that way. So she goes back to the town boy she first loved.

George Cohan produced a Thomas comedy called "Vermont" the season following. This was a serious study of the evils wrought by prohibition in weakening the character fiber of some of Vermont's oldest and most stalwart citizens. A Vermont Carter, after generations of honorable Carters, accepts a bribe from the rum runners to permit them to use his barn as a hideout. He would use the money to provide medical treatment for a son who has been blinded by poisoned liquor. His daughter finally induces him to return the bribes, but before he can do this he is killed in a fight between rum runners and hijackers and his youngest son is jailed as an accessory. Covering the trial that followed Playwright Thomas wrote himself into the script as a district attorney and gave himself a nice exit when, as the attorney, he let the Carter boy out on bail. "Vermont" found the playgoing crowd fed up on prohibition and all the arguments that went with it, particularly the depressingly tragic arguments. "Vermont" was withdrawn after two weeks' playing.

As a courtesy to the Players' Club Mr. Thomas made a new acting version of "Uncle Tom's Cabin" in the Spring of 1934, and the Players led by Otis Skinner as Ol' Uncle Tom, made back a little of the losses they had suffered during the prohibition era when they had to give up their bar. The year following he came back into his own with a considerable rush with the writing of "No More Ladies." This was a deft and lightly satirical comedy having to do with the satisfied sophisticates of the period. Two young people who knew each other well enough to be apprehensive as to the possible success of their marriage, were still eager to take the chance. Being married they suffered the familiar disappointment. The young husband acquired a new interest and the young wife determined to get even. A new adjustment of home values was promised as a result. Lucile Watson, playing an outspoken and keenly observing lady of a passing generation, did much to help the success of "No More Ladies," which ran for a hundred and sixty-two performances.

Mr. Thomas took another long rest after this happy adventure. Recently he appeared as the adapter of a Georgette Heyer murder comedy called "Merely Murder." In this a cast of irresponsibles baffled Scotland Yard by rather frankly making themselves individually suspect following the murder of a widely unpopular man. The players enjoyed the comedy more than the audience.

"As far back as 1919," to quote from the earlier edition, "Mr. Thomas was still a reporter working with the Dana heirs and assigns on the New York *Sun*. He had been there since 1895. He was known then to the city editors of the opposition as the *Sun's* star man. It may be possible that in those days he could have been forced to admit the honor if pressed, though I doubt it. But even to this star reporter the newspaper business had lost its glamour. He wanted most awfully to get out of it.

"He had written one novel, 'Cynthia's Rebellion,' and a play, 'Her Husband's Wife.' The novel, published in 1903, did fairly well. The play finally came to the notice of Henry Miller, was bought, was played by Mr. Miller and Laura Hope Crews, achieved a considerable success and made it possible for Mr. Thomas to quit being a reporter."

His early plays included "What the Doctor Ordered," "The Rainbow" and "Come Out of the Kitchen," adapted from the Alice Duer Miller story. He is a playwright of serious mind tempered with a nice sense of humor. He was born in Chester, Mass., in 1872, and took an A.B. and an A.M. at Brown University. He was christened Albert Ellsworth, and his pet peeve for years was being mistaken for the late Augustus Thomas. In the old days to say to Mr. Thomas: "I certainly think 'Arizona' is the best play you ever wrote," was to invite a poke right on the nose.

The Thomas plays since 1920 have included:

"Just Suppose." Produced at the Henry Miller Theatre, New York, November 1, 1920.

"The Champion" (with Thomas Louden). Produced by Sam H. Harris, at the Longacre Theatre, New York, January 3, 1921.

"Only Thirty-eight" (from short story by W. P. Eaton). Produced by Sam H. Harris. Cort Theatre, New York, September 13, 1921.

"The French Doll" (adapted from French of Armont and Gerbidon). Produced by Ray Goetz. Lyceum Theatre, New York, February 20, 1922.

"Our Nell" (with Brian Hooker). Produced by the Hayseed Productions Inc., at the Bayes Theatre, New York, December 4, 1922.

"The Jolly Roger." Produced at the National Theatre, New York, August 30, 1923.

"Fool's Bells." Produced by Donald Gallagher and James W. Elliott, at the Criterion Theatre, New York, December 22, 1925.

"Embers" (an adaptation). Produced at the Henry Miller Theatre, New York, February 1, 1926.

"Lost" (with George Agnew Chamberlain). Produced by Ramsey Wallace, at the Mansfield Theatre, New York, March 28, 1927.

"The Big Pond" (with George Middleton). Produced by Edwin H. Knopf and William Farnsworth. Bijou Theatre, New York, August 21, 1927.

"Vermont." Produced by George M. Cohan. Erlanger's Theatre, New York, January 8, 1929.

"Her Friend the King" (with Harrison Rhodes). Produced by Lawrence Weber, Longacre Theatre, New York, October 7, 1929.

"Uncle Tom's Cabin" (revision of G. L. Aiken's melodrama). Produced by Players' Club. Alvin Theatre, New York, May 29, 1933.

"No More Ladies." Produced by Lee Shubert. Booth Theatre, New York, January 23, 1934.

"Merely Murder" (adapted from book by Georgette Heyer). Produced by Laurence Rivers, Inc. The Playhouse, New York, December 3, 1937.

GEORGE M. COHAN

GEORGE MICHAEL COHAN's recent theatre activities have been concerned with acting rather than playwrighting or play production. Which is an interesting departure for this generously admired and most versatile of native stage favorites. In fifty years of trouping Mr. Cohan has spoken lines written by other playwrights just three times: Once during the Great War, when he took part in a whirlwind tour of Hartley Manners' "Over There" with an all-star cast that raised $750,000 for the Red Cross; again when he played Nat Miller in Eugene O'Neill's "Ah, Wilderness!" for the Theatre Guild, and now when he is topping all his previous successes appearing as President Franklin D. Roosevelt in "I'd Rather Be Right." The fact that this actor has been able to play the President with such amazing amiability and such disarming charm that he has received the frank commendation of that worthy's political friends and foes alike is, I think, as perfect a tribute to his individual gifts as any that could be written.

Back in 1929, when we were last considering the case of Mr. Cohan as playwright and producer, he had just presented a musicalized version of his own "Broadway Jones," renamed "Billie," with Polly Walker in the name part; Ring Lardner's stage version of his own "You Know Me, Al," called "Elmer the Great," with Walter Huston as the boneheaded but well-meaning hero, and "By Request," a light comedy written by J. C. and Elliott Nugent. None of these did especially well, though "Billie" did get 112 performances. "Elmer" held on for forty and "By Request" got two less than that.

The season following Mr. Cohan started early, producing an original play called "Gambling" in August. In this, as the father of a girl who had been murdered, the actor played his gambler's hunches in tracking down the murderer after the police had failed. "Gambling" ran through until early Spring and then was taken on tour, it being the Cohan intention at the time to play through to the coast and there have another try at pictures. He had a contract in his pocket that promised him half the world, or its equivalent. But something happened between New York and Chicago. Cohan had not played that territory in twenty years, and he was both amazed and touched by the reception a delighted following gave him. There may also have been some further discussions about the proposed screen engagement. In any event, by the time he reached Chicago George was as stage struck as any juvenile making his first tour. Then and there he tore up the motion picture contract and announced that he was back on the stage to stay. He returned to New York, playing revivals of "The Song and Dance Man" and "The Tavern" on the way. Arrived on Broadway he played "The Tavern" for four weeks and "The Song and Dance Man" for another two.

A little something called "Friendship" was the Cohan contribution to the early season of 1931-32. In this George told of an honest fellow's experience with a young woman, a night club hostess by profession, whom he had supported for three years. At the end of that time the girl decided that her patron looked upon her as nothing dearer than the subject of an experiment, and decided to capitalize the education she had been able to acquire by becoming a writer, marrying a writer and eventually paying back all that she owed the man who had been good to her. After a scene with the father of the writer she hoped to marry she was glad to return to her man and marry him. Even the Cohan popularity could not keep "Friendship" playing more than three weeks.

After that the playwright rested and invited inspiration. At the end of a year he decided to write another play about an engaging eccentric who preferred the society of pigeons to the society of humans. "Pigeons and People," as he called it, with an explanatory sub-caption declaring the play to be "a comic state of mind in continuous action."

"Pigeons and People" played for nearly two hours without an intermission. It told the adventure of a strange person called Parker (played by Cohan), who had been picked up by a socially minded young man named Heath in the park where for years he (Parker) had made a daily habit of feeding and talking to flocks of pigeons. Parker is taken home by his new friend and urged, in fact he is practically forced, to remain there until, as Heath puts it, he can "get a fresh start, with his feet stuck in the ground." Heath is fascinated with the idea of rejuvenating Parker, even if Parker appears reluctant about being rejuvenated.

The adventure proceeds. Soon Parker has created a doubt in Heath's mind. The doubt grows. Now Heath is ready to dismiss Parker and forget the whole thing. But Parker isn't ready to be dismissed. It may be he's a crook. It may be Heath's a crook. Who knows anything about anybody? But he does not intend to be picked up and set down just to amuse an idle busybody. Before the evening is finished the police have taken a hand. And a variety of mystified friends have dropped in. Finally, when they do get rid of Parker, there is little satisfaction in the dismissal. They still don't know anything about him—unless they believe the story he told in the park.

"Pigeons and People" was almost as mystifying to the Cohan public as it was to the actors in the play. It was favorably reviewed but George withdrew it after the seventieth performance, and went again into the silences.

During the Summer came the offer from the Theatre Guild. Would Mr. Cohan consider playing a part for the Guild in a new O'Neill comedy called "Ah, Wilderness!"? Mr. Cohan would at least agree to read the script. Having done that Mr. Cohan agreed he would love to play the part, other arrangements being satisfactory. The Guild saw to it that they were. Mr. Cohan was the first actor ever to be what might be called star-featured by the Guild and one of the preferred few who were paid a percentage of the gross receipts in addition to a guaranteed salary.

This was also an exceptional adventure in other ways.

Mr. Cohan suddenly found himself discovered as a great actor. Play reviewers who had known him and thought of him only as a gifted and versatile contributor to the theatre, and a song and dance man at base, began writing columns in praise of the Cohan art, the actor's finish and poise, of his incisiveness in characterization and his deep understanding. Editorials appeared in many papers extolling the Cohan virtues. And these were true discoveries and greatly deserved. But—when, two seasons later, Mr. Cohan, having left the Guild and "Ah Wildnerness!" and having gone back on his own, so to speak, and gave quite as finished a performance in a comedy of his own writing called "Dear Old Darling," and again three years later, when he fashioned for himself another part quite similar in character to the one played in "Ah Wilderness!" in a comedy he rewrote from an original by Parker Fennelly called "Fulton of Oak Falls," there were no editorials and comparatively few kind words from the critics. Going to show that emotional reactions play a great part in drawing superlatives from the writing profession.

A good deal was written at the time "Fulton of Oak Falls" was produced about the re-establishment of the old firm of Cohan and Harris. And these two did, in fact, present the play jointly. But there was no reviving of the old firm. Mr. Harris continues as an independent producer, and if Mr. Cohan should get hold of a play, or write a play, that he wants to produce, in all reasonable probability he will again act independently of Mr. Harris. There has never been any real break in their friendship, despite the actors' strike and all the arguments it started. And no break at all in their admiration for each other. It is entirely possible that they still may join forces in the production of many plays. But the old firm of Cohan and Harris is through, and has been through for nineteen years.

Mr. Cohan was in Europe when it occurred to Mr. Harris, or perhaps to George Kaufman or Moss Hart, the authors, that he was the ideal choice for the role of the President in "I'd Rather Be Right." They sent him a cable asking if he would consider the part. He asked to see the script. They sent him the script. He read that and cabled his acceptance. The opening was in Boston. A vast crowd, feverishly interested in this reported "attack" on the Government and the New Deal, stormed the opening. The national press associations sent representatives to report the liberties taken in this assault upon the Administration. It was, underneath the surface, a kind of supreme test of the rights of free speech. And the resulting ballyhoo was terrific. No play within my memory has ever been so amazingly advertised. By the time "I'd Rather Be Right" reached New York at least half the town knew sections of the dialogue and all the jokes by heart.

But the most amazing of all the reactions were those of the audiences. Having gathered either in the hope of applauding a satirical slap at the President and all his works, or with a determination to protest in the name of the country's honor against the perpetration of an outrage, both parties to the investigation remained to laugh and to sympathize, first with the President and his troubles and, second, with the poor old tax-ridden economic royalists who were the Administration's victims. It still is a question whether the Cohan performance added sympathizers to the President's party or donation-payers to the Liberty League. This experience was, as I have said, the supreme achievement of the Cohan career.

George Cohan will always be numbered with the great of the American theatre, whatever his rating among its greater actors may be. He never has thought much about himself as an actor, nor talked much about it. He is content to play the part that lies within his range and let others do the talking. In the first edition of this book I wrote this of him:

"There are very few chapters in this book into which the story of George Michael Cohan would not fit. I might write of him as one of the Significant Influences of the American theatre. Or as is so frequently done, as an American Institution. He could be placed at the head of the words and music lads, or among the most successful writers of American comedy. He is both a many-sided and a one-sided man. He commands great versatility of mind and talents, and yet so definite is the Cohan individuality that all he does is unmistakably dominated and colored by all that he is.

"George's parents were show folk, Jere John Cohan (Keohane was the family name the generation previous) and Helen Costigan Cohan, his wife. Their son, born to the theatre, was considerate enough to arrive in the summer. The date was July 4, 1878, which many people have sought to regard as significant. Especially press agents.

"He toured with the family when touring was necessary, pecked at such school books as were put in his way and studied the violin. There was a time, so I have heard, when there was no instrument in the orchestra on which George could not play a tune of some character, and play most of them very well. Which made him a sort of prodigy.

"He was 9 years old when he first made a public appearance. The event occurred in Haverstraw, N. Y., and the play was 'Daniel Boone.' After that as a boy he played the hero in one of the 'Peck's Bad Boy' comedies and had a lot more fun than any other member of the cast. That was in 1890.

"Mostly, however, he toured with the other Cohans, his father, mother and sister Josephine. Father and mother played dramatic and comedy sketches, George played the violin and Josephine danced. The variety season over they would join a stock company for the summer months. Sometimes they continued in stock all winter."

He was writing songs when he was 15. Songs like "Why Did Nelly Leave Her Home?" and "Venus, My Shining Star." He was 20 when he wrote "I Guess I'll Have to Telegraph My Baby," which endeared him to Ethel Levy, who sang it. They were married shortly after and in time Georgette Cohan was born to them.

So far as the Cohan career in the legitimate theatre is concerned it started with the expanding of a vaudeville skit called "The Governor's Son" into a full length play the season of 1899-1900. Followed by another, "Running for Office," which was similarly treated. Soon after there occurred the famous meeting of Cohan and Sam H. Harris at a Staten Island clam bake. Mr. Harris, then directing the destinies of Terry McGovern, prize fighter, was looking for a theatre star. Mr. Cohan, with his eye set upon success in the first-class, or "$2 theatres," was looking for a manager. Their mutual confessions resulted in a handshake and an informal verbal agreement that endured for eighteen years and made them both rich men. They began with "Little Johnny Jones" and went through a list including "Forty-five Minutes from Broadway," "George Washington, Jr.," "The Yankee Prince," etc., to the first straight comedies written or adapted by G. M. C., these including "Popularity," "Get-Rich-Quick-Wallingford," "Seven Keys to Baldpate," and on to "The Miracle Man," "Hit-the-Trail Halliday" and "A Prince There Was."

The Cohan-Harris compact endured until 1919 when Mr. Cohan elected to side with the managers against the Actors' Equity Association and Mr. Harris took his chances with the actors. Mr. Cohan helped to organize an opposition "union" called Actors' Fidelity Association and contributed a check for $100,000. In spite of which the Equity actors won. Embittered and for a time of a mind to retire, George came back into the theatre as an author and producer in 1922 with a melodramatic farce called "Madeleine and the Movies." In the cast he presented his daughter, Georgette. She played opposite James Rennie. Later Cohan himself took the Rennie part, but when "Madeleine" was sent to Chicago it was with Donald Brian in the lead, the title being changed to "Garrison and the Girls."

Since his return to the theatre Mr. Cohan has written and directed many plays. A list of them is appended:

"Madeleine and the Movies." Produced by the author, at the Gaiety Theatre, New York, March 6, 1922.

"Little Nelly Kelly." Produced by the author, at the Liberty Theatre, New York, November 13, 1922.

"The Rise of Rosie O'Reilly." Produced by the author, at the Liberty Theatre, New York, December 25, 1923.

"The Song and Dance Man." Produced by the author, at the Hudson Theatre, New York, December 31, 1923.

"American Born." Produced by the author, at the Hudson Theatre, New York, October 5, 1925.

"The Home Towners." Produced by the author, at the Hudson Theatre, New York, August 23, 1926.

"Baby Cyclone." Produced by the author, at the Henry Miller Theatre, New York, September 12, 1927.

"Merry Malones." Produced by the author, at the Erlanger's Theatre, New York, September 26, 1927.

"Whispering Friends." Produced by the author, at the Hudson Theatre, New York, February 20, 1928.

"Billie." Produced by the author, at the Erlanger's Theatre, New York, October 1, 1928.

"Gambling." Produced by the author at the Fulton Theatre, New York, August 26, 1929.

"Friendship." Produced by the author at the Fulton Theatre, New York, August 31, 1931.

"Pigeons and People." Produced by the author at the Sam H. Harris Theatre, January 16, 1933.

"Dear Old Darling." Produced by the author at the Alvin Theatre, New York, March 2, 1936.

"Fulton of Oak Falls" (from story by Parker Fennelly). Produced by George M. Cohan and Sam H. Harris. Morosco Theatre, New York, February 10, 1937.

PHILIP DUNNING

PHILIP DUNNING was not content to take the profits the melodrama "Broadway" had brought him and retire. He went on writing plays after he had his wife and daughter comfortably settled in Westchester. "The Night Hostess," which John Golden produced in 1928 brought him additional prestige, and a modest profit. We left him with that ten years ago. The season following Mr. Dunning took up melodramatic arms against the racketeering that prohibition had developed and the crooks in office who were fattening on it. The play was "Sweet Land of Liberty" (1929), and it waxed sarcastic in exposing the deal that Jack and Charlie got the time they tried honestly to report a murder in one of their restaurants. In the play

Charlie is framed and Jack is shot in the back.

Two years later Mr. Dunning teamed again with George Abbott, the two becoming producers as well as collaborators, and a first play was "Lilly Turner." This was a fairly hectic account of the love affairs of a girl who was doing Venus poses with a traveling health exhibit. Being married to a property man who drank, Lilly shared her favors with a strong man in an asylum temporarily. Lilly, still lonesome, turned to his successor. But the strong man got out of the asylum and came back to knock the new favorite out and throw Lilly's protesting husband through a skylight. This served to sober the husband and convince Lilly that, after all, he really needed her most of all her men. "Lilly Turner" lasted but three weeks.

In 1934 Mr. Dunning undertook to fix up a play called "Kill That Story," written originally by Harry Madden. This one concerned the determination of a newspaper reporter to clear his name of a charge that he had wronged a stenographer with whom he worked. The girl had killed herself and left a note thanking the reporter for his kindness. The reporter succeeded finally in putting the blame on his boss, where it belonged. "Kill That Story" managed to hold on for a hundred and seventeen performances.

That same season Mr. Dunning undertook another bit of patchwork with a play written by Joseph Schrank. This one was called "Page Miss Glory" and told the somewhat extravagant story of two promoters, one a former photographer, who, being broke in a New York hotel, entered a synthetic photograph of a beautiful girl in a picture contest. The photograph had been craftily developed to include the most striking features of all the Hollywood beauties, having Garbo's eyes, Dietrich's legs, etc. The picture won the contest and a prize of $2,500. But when they were urged to produce the girl for a screen test and a variety of advertising contracts the boys were stumped. They finally selected a pretty chambermaid for the job and their troubles expanded comically.

Since then Mr. Dunning has confined his theatre activities for the most part to the production rather than the writing of plays. He was born in Meriden, Conn., and ran away with a carnival show when he was quite a lad. He refused to follow parental advice to return to school the following winter, and got himself a job in vaudeville, dancing mostly and singing if urged. He wrote several vaudeville skits, helped with a couple of soldier shows during the war and finally came to Broadway. He was stage managing the Marilyn Miller company at the New Amsterdam Theatre in "Sunny" the night his "Broadway" drama was produced two blocks away. He took time out to see how it was going and practically never went back to stage managing.

The Dunning plays, produced since 1919, include:

"Broadway" (with George Abbott). Produced by Jed Harris. Broadhurst Theatre, New York, September 16, 1926.

"Get Me in the Movies" (with Charlton Andrews). Produced by Laura Wilck. Earl Carroll Theatre, New York, May 21, 1928.

"Night Hostess." Produced by John Golden. Martin Beck Theatre, New York, September 12, 1928.

"Sweet Land of Liberty." Produced by Erlanger & Tyler. Knickerbocker Theatre, New York, September 23, 1929.

"Lilly Turner" (with George Abbott). Produced by the authors. Morosco Theatre, New York, September 19, 1932.

"Kill That Story" (with Harry Madden). Produced by Abbott-Dunning, Inc. Booth Theatre, New York, August 29, 1934.

"Page Miss Glory" (with Joseph Schrank). Produced by Laurence Schwab and Philip Dunning. Mansfield Theatre, New York, November 27, 1934.

"Remember the Day" (with Philo Higley). Produced by Philip Dunning. National Theatre, New York, September 25, 1935.

JOHN HOWARD LAWSON

JOHN HOWARD LAWSON (New York, 1886), although he has been writing plays since the year of his graduation from Williams in 1914, has enjoyed his most active period as dramatist the last few seasons. In 1932 he came close to a popular success with his slightly depressing "Success Story." In 1934 he had two plays produced, "Gentlewoman" and "The Pure in Heart," and in 1937 we had his "Marching Song" and a revival of his "Processional."

Mr. Lawson, who has given the theatre and its output long and deep thought (as may be confirmed by a reference to his splendidly complete work, "Theory and Technique of Playwriting," published by Putnam in 1936), has not so far been able so to clarify his texts as to make them appealing to those average audiences that are the sustaining force of the commercial theatre. His early plays, "Roger Bloomer" (1923), and "Processional" (1925), the first of the native expressionistic dramas, brought him a good deal of attention, stamped him as a writer of originality and promise and drew to him a considerable public that eagerly awaited his future development. His next three plays served only to confuse this public. They were "Nirvana," a search or at least a discussion of a universal religion; "Loud Speaker," a radical cartoon farce hitting at the American political set-up and "The International," picturing a future world revolution in which the forces of Capitalism devastated thousands of workers and were still triumphant.

"Success Story" revealed a further search for contentment on the part of a brilliant young Jew who came to dominate the Gentile concern with which he was associated and who was made miserable by his knowledge of the misery his climb to power had caused. Having gained the world at the cost of his soul he died of a gunshot wound for which the Jewish girl he had cheated was accidentally responsible.

"Gentlewoman," the tale of an unhappy wife married to a man of millions who tries to embrace love and poverty and discovers the compromise will not work, and "The Pure in Heart," in which a small town girl comes to New York prepared to make any sacrifice demanded for the sake of a career but finds her true love in an escaping convict wanted for murder with whom she is shot down by the law—these two plays, produced almost simultaneously the season of 1933-34, approached as close to conventional drama as Mr. Lawson has ever permitted himself to come. Following a similarly liberalized playwrighting pattern Mr. Lawson wrote the history of a sit-down strike in 1936 called "Marching Song" which also flirted with success. This again was a story of industrial strife from the workers' viewpoint, the strikers being menaced in body and soul by the ruthless and bitter forces of greed represented by the employers.

There has never been any doubt in this young man's mind as to what his career should be. He had two plays finished the year of his graduation and both were produced. One was called "Standards." Cohan and Harris bought it and Bert Lytell played its try-out performances upstate, where it was abandoned. The other was a little number entitled "Servant-Master-Lover" which was sold to Oliver Morosco in California and presented by that manager in 1917. "It was terrible," Mr. Lawson has frequently confessed.

Out of college the playwright worked with Reuter's, Inc., in which his father was an executive, for a year and when the war broke he drove an ambulance on both the Italian and French fronts, coming back from that experience pretty bitter about the whole business. After the armistice he stayed on in Rome and Paris for another year working for the Red Cross.

He went over to pictures in 1928 and has done a good deal of writing for Metro-Goldwyn-Mayer and RKO. He has been president of the Screen Writers' Guild and helped with the preparation of the writers' code for the NRA.

Mr. Lawson's plays produced in New York since 1919 are:

"Roger Bloomer." Produced by The Equity Players, Inc. 48th Street Theatre, New York, March 1, 1923.

"Processional." Produced by The Theatre Guild. Garrick Theatre, New York, January 12, 1925.

"Nirvana." Produced by Noble-Ryan-Livy, Inc. Greenwich Village Theatre, New York, March 3, 1926.

"Loud Speaker." Produced by New Playwrights Theatre. 52nd Street Theatre, New York, March 7, 1927.

"The International." Produced by New Playwrights. New Playwrights Theatre, New York, January 12, 1928.

"Success Story." Produced by Group Theatre, Inc. Maxine Elliott Theatre, New York, September 26, 1932.

"The Pure in Heart." Produced by Richard Aldrich and Alfred de Liagre. Longacre Theatre, New York, March 20, 1934.

"Gentlewoman." Produced by Group Theatre, Inc. in association with D. A. Doran, Jr. Cort Theatre, New York, March 22, 1934.

"Marching Song." Produced by Theatre Union. Nora Bayes Theatre, New York, February 17, 1937.

SAMSON RAPHAELSON

SAMSON RAPHAELSON (New York, 1897) is an Easterner advantaged by a Western bringing up. He started in the New York public schools, but he was shortly moved on to the schools of Chicago and finally finished at the University of Illinois. He is also to be reckoned as one of the young hopefuls among the dramatists who was spoken of for some years as being promising who has made good the prophecy. He wrote three box-office successes his first ten years out, and never had reason to blush for any of them. These three were "The Jazz Singer" (1925), "Young Love" (1928), and "Accent on Youth" (1935). The first ran for three years, the second ran through a season in New York and became something of a playgoing habit on the continent, and the third continued for two hundred twenty-nine performances in New York and several months on tour.

"The Jazz Singer," starring George Jessel, was the sentimental adventure of a Jewish boy, born of a long line of Jewish cantors, who tried going Broadway but was won back to the calling of his fathers. "Young Love," with Dorothy Gish, was the less sentimental recital of an investigating pair who were not content to accept marriage as a customary convention, but must first experiment to be sure of their love. Their experiments eventually brought them back to each other content to accept convention as it stood.

"Accent on Youth," the most substantial though not the most popular hit of the three, tells of an aging playwright who has written a serious play about an old man's last love, but laughs himself out of the idea he can sell it. His young and attractive stenographer, however, has as much faith in the play as she has in the playwright. Inspired by her enthusiasm the playwright finishes and produces the play. It proves a great hit. In the enthusiasm of their mutual interest the stenographer and the playwright drift into a love affair, handicapped by the playwright's continuing fear that the stenographer will sooner or later hear the call of youth and leave him. Their love approaches a tragic denouement before he finally is convinced. Constance Cummings and Nicholas Hannen played it.

Mr. Raphaelson spends half the year in Hollywood, where he has had considerable success working with Ernst Lubitsch on such screen productions as "Trouble in Paradise," "One Hour with You," "The Merry Widow," etc. His recent play offerings have missed, notably a piece called "White Man." He is not, however, through with the living theatre.

"The theatre, because it functions through the original human actor and not his image, will always remain unindustrialized, like the back-street cigar store," he has written. "Therefore it will always speak to comparatively special audiences which, I choose to believe, means superior audiences." Mr. Raphaelson is married and the proud father of two children, 8 and 6.

His plays produced in New York since 1919 are:

"The Jazz Singer." Produced by Lewis and Gordon in association with Sam Harris. Fulton Theatre, New York, April 18, 1927.
"Young Love." Produced by Kenneth Macgowan and Sidney Ross. Masque Theatre, New York, October 30, 1928.
"The Wooden Slipper." Produced by Dwight Deere Wiman. Ritz Theatre, New York, January 3, 1934.

"Accent on Youth." Produced by Crosby Gaige, Inc. Plymouth Theatre, New York, December 25, 1936.

MARTIN FLAVIN

A NUMBER of interesting plays and at least three successful ones may be chalked up to Martin Flavin's credit and there is every reason to hope that more are on the way. His first to be produced in New York, "Children of the Moon," which had over a hundred performances at the Comedy in 1923, proved a minor sensation. A weird tragedy, it was splendidly acted by Henrietta Crosman, Beatrice Terry and Whitford Kane. "The Criminal Code," produced by William Harris, Jr. at the National Theatre in the Fall of 1929 is listed as one of the ten best plays of 1929-30. It was fast approaching 200 performances when it closed. A couple of months after the opening of "The Criminal Code" two other plays from Mr. Flavin's typewriter were being presented on Broadway: "Cross Roads" a college comedy which failed of popular support and "Broken Dishes" (which had been tried out as "Shucks") with close to 200 performances at the Ritz. His latest play "Around the Corner" produced by Lodewick Vroom at the 48th Street Theatre in December of 1936 wasn't quite important enough to overcome the Broadway handicap although it was a good play, well staged and competently cast. Martin Flavin was born in San Francisco in 1883. He attended the University of Chicago and remained in that city as a business man before he took to writing plays. Of late he has spent much time in Hollywood writing for the screen and for production in non-commercial theatres. These latter productions include "Spindrift" and "Dancing Days," of 1930, "Amaco" of 1933 and "Caleb Stone's Death Watch" played in a Little Theatre Tournament in Jersey City. The Flavin plays since 1919 include:

"Children of the Moon." Produced by Jacob A. Weiser associated with A. L. Jones and Morris Green. Comedy Theatre, New York, August 17, 1923.

"Lady of the Rose." Produced by Jacob A. Weiser. 49th Street Theatre, New York, May 19, 1925.

"Service for Two." Produced by A. L. Erlanger. Gaiety Theatre, New York, August 30, 1926.

"The Criminal Code." Produced by William Harris, Jr. National Theatre, New York, October 2, 1929.

"Broken Dishes." Produced by Marion Gering. Ritz Theatre, New York, November 5, 1929.

"Cross Roads." Produced by Lewis E. Gensler. Morosco Theatre, New York, November 11, 1929.

"Achilles Had a Heel." Produced by Walter Hampden. 44th Street Theatre, New York, October 13, 1935.

"Tapestry in Gray." Produced by B. P. Schulberg. Shubert Theatre, New York, December 27, 1935.

"Around the Corner." Produced by Lodewick Vroom. 48th Street Theatre, New York, December 28, 1936.

KENYON NICHOLSON

Kenyon Nicholson, playwright and teacher of playwrights, is probably one of the most prolific of native writers for the stage. His produced output, however, at least so far as Broadway is concerned, is fairly limited. From which it is reasonably to be concluded that a good many of the Nicholson scripts do not reach production, or, having met that test in the tryout territory, are withdrawn for correction.

We left Mr. Nicholson in 1928, just after the production of "Eva the Fifth," in the writing of which John Golden, the producer, also took a hand. That was in August. In the following April a new Nicholson comedy, called "Before You're 25," was produced by Lawrence Boyd. This proved a sympathetic study of a young radical who refused to go into the furniture business to suit his Chicago father. He runs away to New York, becomes the editor of a radical monthly and takes on a companionate wife. The Government drives the pair out of New York. On the train the "wife" gives birth to a baby and they stop off at Chicago for her convalescence. While the young radical is in jail the wife lives with her in-laws, notes the advantage of conservative living and induces the father of her child not only to marry her, but also to adopt the furniture business for the sake of their security. "Before You're 25" lasted two weeks.

The season following, Arthur Hopkins produced a Nicholson comedy called "Torch Song" which also flirted with success. In this a singer of torch songs is deserted by her lover and joins the Salvation Army in search of consolation. She becomes an ardent worker in the army until she again meets the lover. Praying for the salvation of his soul, while trying to keep him away from other women, her old love is awakened. She would blame God for her second fall and quit the Army, but is reclaimed by an army pal who is stronger in the faith. "Torch Song" had a run of eighty-seven performances. That same season an adaptation of Helen Zenna Smith's "Stepdaughters of War" brought Mr. Nicholson a second production. This was the romance of an ambulance driver who, disillusioned and disgusted as to the glories of war, and suddenly recalled from a long-overdue leave, seeks consolation by surrendering to an awakened love for a newly-met captain. Later, having resigned her commission and become engaged to marry a home boy, the heroine is called back to the front and comes upon the captain of her romance badly wounded. In this dilemma she decides that she belongs more to the dead than to the living and begs her shattered love to marry her. This play proved another unhappy failure.

Mr. Nicholson was probably a little bitter by this time, but his reward was close at hand. In 1933 he collaborated with Charles Robinson in the writing of a farce called "Sailor Beware" which achieved an overnight success. It ran on and on until five hundred performances had been achieved and the Nicholson strong boxes were well lined. "Sailor Beware" will be recalled as a bawdy comedy of the Canal Zone in which a handsome sailor famed for his easy conquest of women is pitted against a Canal Zone hostess, equally famed for her long success in keeping suitors in their place. Wagers were laid on the outcome of the contest, which waxes warm and warmer, and is finally concluded in a sort of draw. The sailor's commanding officer calls all bets off, which makes the hostess very sorry for her opponent.

The "Sailor Beware" success served to keep the Nicholson muse content for the better part of three years. Then the same collaborators tried to repeat with another farce written along similarly broad lines. This was called "Swing Your Lady" and had to do with a dumb wrestler whose manager matched him against a lady blacksmith in a backwoods town in Missouri. The wrestler falls in love with the blacksmith, who is only wrestling to save her home, and refuses to risk doing her an injury. A bearded substitute is found for the lady blacksmith and the match is held with grotesquely comic results. "Swing Your Lady" ran for 105 performances, but never approached the success of "Sailor Beware."

Mr. Nicholson's first successful theatre bid was "The Barker" produced in 1927, with Walter Huston in the chief role. He collaborated with S. N. Behrman on "Love Is Like That." He was born in Crawfordsville, Indiana, in 1894, and after graduating from high school in New York he began acquiring a higher education at Wabash College in Indiana, taking courses later at Cambridge in England and Columbia in New York. He has been associated with the English and dramatic department of Columbia for many years.

The Nicholson plays so far produced include:

"The Barker." Produced by Charles L. Wagner in association with Edgar Selwyn. Biltmore Theatre, New York, January 18, 1927.

"Love Is Like That" (with S. N. Behrman). Produced by A. L. Jones and Morris Green. Cort Theatre, New York, April 18, 1927.

"Confession." Produced by Manhattan Little Theatre Club, Inc., for Little Theatre Tournament. Frolic Theatre, New York, May 2, 1927.

"Eva the Fifth" (with John Golden). Produced by John Golden and Edgar Selwyn. Little Theatre, New York, August 28, 1928.

"Before You're 25." Produced by Lawrence Boyd. Maxine Elliott Theatre, New York, April 16, 1929.

"Torch Song." Produced by Arthur Hopkins. Plymouth Theatre, New York, August 27, 1930.

"Stepdaughters of War" (from book by Helen Zenna Smith). Produced by Charles Frohman, Inc. Empire Theatre, New York, October 6, 1930.

"The Vanderbilt Revue" (sketches). Produced by Lew Fields and Lyle D. Andrews. Vanderbilt Theatre, New York, November 5, 1930.

"Sailor Beware" (with Charles Robinson). Produced by Courtney Burr. Lyceum Theatre, New York, September 28, 19

"Swing Your Lady" (with Charles Robinson). Produced by Milton Shubert. Booth Theatre, New York, October 18, 1936.

DAN TOTHEROH

DAN TOTHEROH was known in the West some years before we made his acquaintance in the East. As a native son of California, born in Oakland in 1895, he had gone through high school in Marin County and had a few years at the University of California. Out of college he took to acting seriously, playing kid parts with stock companies and in vaudeville, and quit when he decided he would always be a baby-faced juvenile. He hated baby-faced juveniles. Couldn't make good his getaway, however. Had to write a one-acter he called "Her Kid Brother," and the success of this was so marked that it kept him playing in vaudeville for several years.

Then he wrote "Wild Birds." That would be in 1922. It was a pretty plain-spoken tragedy for those days, the story of an orphan girl and a reform school boy who seek release from their miseries as drudges in a cruel farmer's home by acknowledging their love and trying to escape. The cruel one catches them, beats the boy to death and the girl kills herself by leaping in the well.

"Wild Birds" was awarded a University of California prize by a committee of three—Eugene O'Neill, Susan Glaspell and George Jean Nathan. It was also given private performance in San Francisco, but met with censor trouble. Two years later it was obscurely produced in New York in the Cherry Lane Theatre, in Greenwich Village and attracted such attention that it was continued for forty-four performances.

Since then Mr. Totheroh has had several plays produced, and has missed a popular success by narrow margins. In New York Guthrie McClintic staged "Distant Drums," a story of pioneer days and the Oregon trail, in 1932; Bushar and Tuerk tried "Moor Born," a story of the Brontë sisters, in 1934, which continued for sixty-three performances. The same producers staged "Mother Lode," the authorship of which was shared by Mr. Totheroh and George O'Neil, in 1934. This was a quick failure, though Helen Gahagan and Melvyn Douglas were its stars.

Naturally Mr. Totheroh, who has been devoting the last several years to Hollywood tasks, is not greatly encouraged by the present state of the living theatre. But neither is he discouraged. The American theatre is still more alive than any other in the world, he agrees, but he is afraid it will take a good many transfusions to keep it so.

The Totheroh plays produced in New York so far have been:

"Wild Birds." Produced by Cherry Lane Players, Inc. Cherry Lane Theatre, New York, April 9, 1925.

"Distant Drums." Produced by Guthrie McClintic. Belasco Theatre, New York, January 18, 1932.

"Moor Born." Produced by Bushar and Tuerk. Playhouse, New York, April 3, 1934.

"Mother Lode" (with George O'Neil). Produced by Bushar and Tuerk. Cort Theatre, New York, December 22, 1934.

"Searching for the Sun." Produced by Albert Ingalls, Jr. 58th Street Theatre, New York, February 19, 1936.

JOHN WEXLEY

JOHN WEXLEY, being a nephew of Maurice Schwartz, actor and producer, developed an early ambition to be associated with the theatre. He admits that he wanted to be an actor, director and playwright. The Washington Square Players presented a trio of his early minor achievements: "Machine Guns," "What Is Your Desire?" and "Rules." Obsessed with a desire to write about life he had actually seen and known, he occupied himself with various jobs. At different times he tried being bellboy, waiter, salesman, floorwalker. He has installed Diesel engines, drilled oil wells and stoked ships. For a while he was social director at Summer adult camps. Becoming interested in the psychology of criminals, and having access to notes made by a condemned man in a Texas penitentiary, he wrote "The Last Mile," which was his first full-length play. Produced in February, 1930, it had a run of 300 performances. Following this, Wexley spent some time in Europe and Hollywood and then wrote "Steel" (1931), "They Shall Not Die" (1934), a propaganda play dealing with the Scottsboro Negroes who fought for their lives in a prejudiced court, which was produced by the Theatre Guild. At Ottsville, Pa., Mr. Wexley is "sandwiching in four or five hours of writing, haphazardly, between farm chores and general repairs on an old stone Dutch farmhouse," where he lives the year round. He was born in New York City in 1907 and attended the New York University.

Mr. Wexley's produced plays are:

"The Last Mile." Produced by Herman Shumlin. Sam H. Harris Theatre, New York, February 13, 1930.

"Steel." Produced by Richard Geist, Inc. Times Square Theatre, New York, November 17, 1931.

"They Shall Not Die." Produced by The Theatre Guild. Royale Theatre, New York, February 21, 1934.

NEW BLOOD

This was to have been a chapter devoted to debutants—the newcomers among the playwrights who, with one play or more, have shown such promise that the American theatre of the immediate future may reasonably be said to rest at least partly with them. There are, however, a number among them who can no longer be thought of as debutants. They may still be fairly inexperienced, and they may have written but one successful play, but they are already seasoned practitioners in the Broadway experiment, and, in several instances, stand high in the list of its most gifted contributors.

E. P. CONKLE

THE approach of Ellsworth Prouty Conkle, both toward recognition and a position of standing in the theatre, has been steady and persistent. As plain E. P. Conkle his work first attracted attention in 1932 when the manuscript of his first play to be offered for sale, a little something entitled "Forty-nine Dogs in the Meat House," began making the Broadway rounds. Not strange that it should first be accepted as a laugh and later taken with sufficient seriousness to find a purchaser. It was, however, never produced. Four years later a second Conkle play, "200 Were Chosen," was bought and produced by Sidney Harmon and received with a fair amount of enthusiasm by the reviewers. It ran for thirty-five performances. Later this drama was taken up by the WPA Federal theatre and produced over its circuit. It offered a human and holding story of the adventure of those pioneer families that were moved out of the dust bowl into the Mantanuska valley in Alaska in the early days of New Deal experiments.

The third Conkle play was "Prologue to Glory" and this proved one of the major successes of the WPA Federal theatre season in 1937-38. "Prologue to Glory" offers a picture of the the 22-year-old Lincoln during his earliest political adventures in New Salem, Ill., and is written around the rail-splitter's first romance, his love for pretty Ann Rutledge, who died just before he started for Springfield and began the climb that made him his country's most beloved hero.

At the University of Iowa Professor Conkle is the assistant professor of the Department of Speech and director of the University theatre. He was born in Peru, Nebraska, in 1899, and comes of pioneer stock. This, his biographers insist, explains why all his plays bear upon the theme of the unconquerable American pioneer spirit.

Dramatist Conkle received both his Bachelor's and his Master's degree from the University of Nebraska. Interested in the drama, he studied with Prof. George Pierce Baker at Yale. He went to Europe on a Guggenheim fellowship and he has taught at both the University of North Dakota and the University of Delaware. He earned his doctorate in "creative dramatic literature" with his play, "200 Were Chosen," which, according to Prof. Edward Mabie of the University of Iowa, is the first award of its kind. Samuel French has published two volumes of short plays of the Conkle authorship, "Loolie and Other Plays" and "Crick Bottom Plays."

"With me playwriting has been a kind of avocation," Professor Conkle explains. "I've never been able to make a living at it. I've made my life insurance, my daily bread and my wife's shoes teaching school."

CLARE BOOTHE

CLARE BOOTHE, who wrote "The Women" and thus added to the joys and the discussions of the theatre seasons of 1936-37 and 1937-38, spells her maiden name with a final e, and her married names include a Brokaw and a Luce. She was, when she first took to literature in a serious way, Mrs. George Tuttle Brokaw, and, after divorcing Mr.

Brokaw in 1929, she married Henry Robinson Luce, editor of both *Time* and *Fortune*, in 1935. None of which has to do with Miss Boothe's career as a playwright, but is apparently of absorbing interest to the growing Boothe public, being the first facts mentioned in any reference to her theatre activities.

"The Women" is not Miss Boothe's first produced play. She wrote a domestic problem drama in 1935 called "Abide with Me" which disclosed definite playwrighting talent but was not of sufficient holding interest in story to please playgoers, nor of a dramatic quality that pleases critics. She had before this written three other plays by way of practice. One was a farce called "Entirely Irregular," one was a comedy entitled "The Sacred Cow," written in collaboration with Paul Gallico, the sports authority, and the third a political satire called "O, Pyramids," which made sport of the NRA and was quite sadly whipped in a bout with the Blue Eagle, an unbeatable bird in 1932-33.

Miss Boothe was for some years managing editor of *Vanity Fair*. Some years ago she startled her social intimates and thrilled the proletariat with a satirical fling at the leaders of the social game which she called "Stuffed Shirts." Her bent has always been satirical and her attacks incisive. "The Women" so effectively pillories selected exhibits taken from the feminine world that it has been described both as an insult to womanhood and as the most brilliant social satire of its time. The fact that it ran the better part of two seasons would seem to prove conclusively that its types are not only recognizable but generously appreciated.

Miss Boothe is a native New Yorker, acknowledges her thirty-five years without hesitancy and is counted among the most popular social registerites who care something less than a hoot for society as such. They are, these society independents, a little boastful of that distinction.

CLIFFORD GOLDSMITH

ONE of the happier incidents of the Spring theatregoing season of 1938 was the emergence in the Broadway theatre of a comedy called "What a Life." It was, so far as the records immediately available provided information, a first play by a young man signing himself Clifford Goldsmith, and it was a success. Deeper research revealed the fact that, technically at least, "What a Life" was really Mr. Goldsmith's second play. Some years back he had helped Elliott Nugent fashion one called "Charlie," which they sold to, or at least loaned to, Stuart Walker, at that time directing an enterprising stock company venture in Cincinnati and frequently producing pieces like "Six Who Passed While the Lentils Boiled." Mr. Walker also produced "Charlie," but nothing came of that play and Mr. Goldsmith went back to earning a living in more or less legitimate fashion. He has for some years been a lecturer on food values and the healthy rearing of children, working in co-operation with Boards of Education and talking for the most part in High School auditoriums. It was from his experiences as a High School lecturer, and from such stories as he was told, that he pieced together the incidents which form the plot basis of "What a Life." He sent the play to George Abbott, fully expecting to have it back within a week or two. To his surprise it did not come back, and to his further surprise he one day received a letter from Mr. Abbott asking him if he would mind stopping in one day to sign a contract. "What a Life" is a story of the High Schools which serves to humanize the adventures of an undergraduate who is neither very responsive on the mental uptake or very quick in formulating explanations covering his delinquencies. The number of playgoers who find him recognizably reminiscent is prodigious. Mr. Goldsmith was born in East Aurora, N. Y., and was for many years a neighbor of Elbert Hubbard, East Aurora's most famous sage. His own farm is located at Paoli, Pa.

PAUL OSBORN

PAUL OSBORN was accepted as one of the outstanding hopefuls of the native theatre with the production of his "Vinegar Tree" in 1930, but he did not achieve the fullness of that promise, nor any considerable part thereof, until seven years later. In February, 1938, Mr. Osborn's comedy, "On Borrowed Time," which he adapted from a novel by Lawrence Edward Watkin, bounded into an immediate popularity that carried it triumphantly through the season. Dudley Digges, who had for twenty years been one of the stalwarts of the Theatre Guild, achieved stardom in the new play. "On Borrowed Time" is the quaintly fantastic tale of an 84-year-old grandfather who is boldly determined to fight, even in the face of Death's call, for the protection and care of his 5-year-old orphaned grandson, Pud Northrupp. Gramps literally chases Death up a bewitched apple tree and keeps him there until the neighbors, counting the old gentleman demented, arrange for his incarceration in an asylum. When there seems no other way out, Gramps agrees to go with Death (a Mr. Brink in the cast of characters), and Mr. Brink, to save Pud from what promises to be an unhappy adventure in life, decides to take him, too.

Mr. Osborn's "Vinegar Tree," the amusing story of a restless wife who strives desperately to recapture the memory of a purple afternoon she had, as a young woman, spent with an artist, proved one of Mary Boland's happiest stage roles, running through the season of 1930-31. But there also had been a definite promise indicated in the first Osborn play to reach Broadway production. This was a comedy called "Hotbed," having to do with morality and a co-ed college, produced by Brock Pemberton in 1928. "A Ledge," a drama, was an Osborn contribution to the following season, but that failed of success, as did a piece called "Oliver Oliver," tried in 1934.

Mr. Osborn was born in Evansville, Ind., in 1901; attended the University of Michigan, taking his A.B in 1923 and adding an M.A. in 1924. In 1927 he studied playwrighting with George Pierce Baker at Harvard. He taught English at the University of Michigan in 1925-26 and for the last ten years has been living in Brattleboro, Vt.

GEORGE HAIGHT

GEORGE HAIGHT came out of Yale University ten years ago well fortified with ideas. He had gone to Yale from Washington College, and had four years of academic work, including many sessions with Professor Baker and English 47. All his ambitions were centered in the theatre, but it did not matter greatly to him whether he wrote plays or produced them, doctored plays or directed them. He just was a little theatre mad. His first ventures were linked with those of Henry C. Potter, a Yale buddy and also a theatre enthusiast. Together they organized the Hampton Players and proceeded to establish a sort of Summer Theatre Laboratory down Long Island. It was their plan to try out plays that had been rejected by the professional Broadway producers on the theory that all rejections could not possibly be as bad as Broadway said they were. Out of their first eleven original plays, covering three Summers of experimentation, they sold seven, which was a pretty startling average. Not all of these came through to a Broadway success later, but most of them reached the stock company circuit or Hollywood. One, "Up Pops the Devil," was a long-run success and another, "Good-bye Again," which Mr. Haight wrote with "Allan Scott," ran for 216 performances with the late Osgood Perkins as a featured player.

As a producer the Haight judgment was upheld with such productions as "Double Door" (1933), "Wednesday's Child" (1934), "Post Road" (1934), which afterward became "Leaning on Letty" with Charlotte Greenwood on the road, and "Kind Lady" (1935), in which Grace George starred successfully. In both "Double Door" and "Kind Lady" Mr. Haight was a collaborator, but let the credit go and watched the box office.

Also in 1935 Mr. Haight worked with Richard Maibaum and Michael Wallach on a play entitled "Sweet Mystery of Life," which Herman Shumlin produced extravagantly, but which did not prove popular. Then both Mr. Potter and Mr. Haight, together with practically all their associates, were gathered in by the picture makers. "The drama is healthy; the living theatre will always live, but, somehow, we are all in Hollywood today," wrote Mr. Haight in 1936. Conditions have not changed perceptibly since then, though the retreat from Hollywood is growing in both popularity and importance to the theatre. "I ultimately hope to slow down and write one play a year, produce it on the stage, then write the screen play and produce it on the screen," Mr. Haight has confessed. "Whether I will feel like this when I think I have mastered both mediums, I wonder!" This playwright is a native of Newark, N. J., and has arrived at the brave age of 33.

ROBERT ARDREY

Just how wisely and well Robert Ardrey writes for the theatre his critics have been at some pains to analyze to the advantage of their critiques. But of just how wisely and well he writes of the theatre there can be little or no question. Mr. Ardrey, incidentally, is one of the newer dramatists of greater promise who came to the theatre with his first play in 1936. That was a satirical comedy of life among the Polish-American "pipple" of Chicago entitled "Star-Spangled." It was handsomely produced by Arthur Hopkins, variously received by the New York reviewers and withdrawn after twenty-three performances.

"The state of the theatre is no different from that of American economic life today," Mr. Ardrey declares in a notation recently made. "The producers (actors, authors, managers) are healthy and active; the consumers (the potential audiences) are eager and wise. But the processes of distribution (in the theatre, critical evaluation) are uniformly confused. They are torn between the insincerities of today's democratic sympathies, and the formal, patterned, traditional insincerities of another era. The theatre's crisis is no different from that of American life."

Mr. Ardrey, who at 29 can afford to take his time, did not return to the theatre, following the failure of "Star-Spangled," until February of 1938. Then he appeared with two new plays which were produced within a fortnight of each other—Guthrie McClintic staging a comedy with serious overtones called "How to Get Tough About It," and the Group Theatre, Inc., following with a comedy of similar quality called "Casey Jones" ten days later.

Again disappointment was the Ardrey lot. His professional critics again admitted his promise and the superlative fashioning and writing of individual scenes. But they also insisted that he had still much to learn about preserving both the artistic and narrative coherency of his stories. Like so many long-faced professors they gave the young student B-plus ratings and dismissed him. Without, as is the traditional custom, inquiring as to the influence or interference of his producers and directors.

"How to Get Tough About It" offered the romance of a pair of aspiring souls caught in sordid surroundings. A waitress in a water front café falls for a tough labor leader, is disillusioned and turns to a young boatbuilder who spends many quiet hours wondering what it is that forces a kind of decency-urge upon him. In the end the two groping idealists are left to work out their salvation.

"Casey Jones" related the somewhat doleful experience of the physical deterioration of a loyal railroad engineer whose eyes went bad in his fiftieth year. They retired

Casey to a flag-stop station but he could not take it. He was starting West to build a new life at the curtain's fall.

Both these Ardrey dramas developed a realism that was a little too fine to work entirely to their advantage, a realism that passed the point of conviction and permitted an audience to again become theatre-conscious. "How to Get Tough About It" became a shade too tough to insure average audience acceptance. "Casey Jones" rolled a practical locomotive excitingly across the stage and set its audiences tittering as well as trembling. But both plays established the Ardrey gifts for the writing of sharp and pungent dialogue, and the development of solid and recognizable characters.

The playwright was born and reared in Chicago. His ancestors were Scotch and Scotch-Irish. He was graduated from the University of Chicago in 1930, and made the Phi Beta Kappa, he says, "by the skin of the faculty's teeth." He works hard when he works and plays hard when he plays.

KATHARINE DAYTON

It was just her marvelous luck that propelled Katharine Dayton up among the first line playwrights, according to Miss Dayton. She had not the remotest idea, probably, when she suggested to her literary agent that she thought there was a play in the social trivia of Washington life, if George Kaufman would agree to help write the play, that anything would come of it. But the agent took the idea to Mr. Kaufman and the play, "First Lady," proved to be the outstanding comedy success of the year. Miss Dayton is still a little flabbergasted by her first experience in the theatre. She would, if she could, still give her collaborator the greater credit. But Kaufman, being a truthful as well as a gallant fellow, was the first to insist that it was largely Miss Dayton's inspiration and Miss Dayton's knowledge of the subject that made the play possible. Of course Jane Cowl helped. Jane played a President's daughter married to a Secretary of State who ruled Washington society and finally projected her husband into a presidential candidacy. But it was chiefly a playwright's victory. The play was produced around Thanksgiving in 1935 and ran until the end of the 1935-36 season with 246 performances to its credit. The next season it was widely toured. In February of 1938 Sam H. Harris and Max Gordon produced Miss Dayton's second play, "Save Me the Waltz." Unfortunately it met with no such success. At the end of the sixth performance it silently stole away. Leaving the author still a promising debutante.

Miss Dayton grew up in the writing atmosphere, being the daughter of a newspaper man. Yet she did not take to writing seriously until a few years ago. About six or eight, I should say. Frank Crowninshield bought an article of hers for *Vanity Fair*. The late George Horace Lorimer bought another for the *Saturday Evening Post*. She wrote a series of political satires, "Mrs. Democratic and Mrs. Republican," for the *Post*. These were pretty rough on the Roosevelt reconstruction theories, though the effect on the Roosevelt pluralities was not more than a shade greater than that of the Lorimer editorials. It was while she was in Washington working in Dave Lawrence's Consolidated Press Service and writing the political articles and short playlets for the *Post*, that the "First Lady" idea struck her, with the Kaufman collaboration following. Miss Dayton was born in Philadelphia, which may account for the Republican influence, but moved shortly to Glen Ridge, N. J. Her ancestry is Scotch and English. She was never conscious of any violent theatrical leanings, though she always loved the theatre and is sure of its future. "The theatre will live as long as a trace of imagination is left in Man, and until he outgrows his favorite childhood game of 'let's pretend,'" she wrote recently. "This date, I predict roughly, is about 50,000,000 years from next Tuesday." If the question of age must be brought up, Miss Dayton admits that she never yet has had a vote challenged.

LILLIAN HELLMAN

LILLIAN HELLMAN's first published play, "The Children's Hour," dominated the season of 1934-35, in which it was produced. The Pulitzer prize that season was given to Zoe Akins' "The Old Maid," and a wide popular success was earned by Robert Emmet Sherwood's "The Petrified Forest" (with Leslie Howard). Neither of these plays, however, made as deep an impression or achieved as long a run as the vividly tragic drama which Miss Hellman extracted from the records of a suit for scandal fought through the Scottish courts in the early nineteenth century and later recorded in a published volume by William Roughhead entitled "Closed Doors, or the Great Drumsheugh Case," (Duffield and Green, 1931).

"The Children's Hour" was played for 691 performances in New York. It has been taken on tour since then and has created considerable excitement wherever played. One or two cities, notably Boston, have barred it from a local showing because of its theme, which touches definitely but with discretion upon the unnatural attraction between persons of the same sex. It is the retailing of such a story that explodes the scandal in the play, a scandal traced to the lying of a fiendish child and the malicious gossip of her elders.

Miss Hellman is a New Orleans girl by birth and is in her early thirties. She was educated in New York at Columbia and New York Universities. Her approach to the theatre was through a job as play reader for Herman Shumlin, who produced "The Children's Hour." She has been a book reviewer, a reader of scenarios, a contributor of short stories and articles to the better magazines and a press agent for a summer stock company in Rochester. Since her success with "The Children's Hour" she has been devoting much time to Hollywood, where she directed the preparation of her play for the screen. In December of 1936 her second play, "Days to Come," telling of a settled old-stock American community in the throes of a strike, was produced and ran but a short week.

VICTOR WOLFSON

VICTOR WOLFSON, a native New Yorker, though he has lived much in the West and was adopted with some enthusiasm by his fellow classmen and professors at the University of Wisconsin a few years back, gave the New York playgoers a pleasant shock in April, 1937. A play of his called "Excursion" was produced with little heralding. He had been known to Broadway only as an experimenting playwright of what had been accepted as radical tendencies.

With Victor Trivas he had made an adaptation of Dostoevski's "Crime and Punishment" in 1935 and in 1936 his contribution had been a drama taken from Silone's "Fontemara," renamed "Bitter Stream." Both these plays had been produced by the Theatre Union, a group dedicated to work in the propaganda field. Then came "Excursion" and the surprise of the late season. This proved to be a simple, heart-warming little comedy about an old sea-captain who, having run a Coney Island excursion boat for thirty years, decides suddenly on her last trip to head for the open sea and a tropical island, there to start a new life with so many of his passengers and crew as might want to go with him. "Excursion" was greeted with the cheers of a majority of the professional reviewers, but the time of year and its lightly exaggerated fancifulness limited its popular appeal. It since has proved a great stock company favorite.

ARTHUR ARENT

OUT of the chaos that was the WPA Federal Theatre in the days of its beginnings several outstanding figures wriggled their way to the top and to the attention, first of their appointed superiors and then to that of the public to which their talents were revealed. Prominent among these was a young man named Arthur Arent. Mr. Arent came to notice first through the establishment of that exciting new dramatic form of entertainment called The Living Newspaper. Serving as a sort of editorial supervisor, Mr. Arent and his co-workers evolved a drama entitled "Ethiopia." It never reached production, save at a sort of preliminary showing "against a brick wall, by actors in their street clothes," (January, 1936), but it stirred a small tempest in the WPA teapot. Washington heard of it. Washington heard that its tale of wars and conquests specifically mentioned certain dictatorial personages then serving as cocks of the walk in Europe, and Washington decreed that "Ethiopia" was something that could not diplomatically be sponsored by the United States Government.

This meant curtains for "Ethiopia" and disappointment for Mr. Arent and his associates. As a result of this order Elmer Rice, who had been at the head of the New York State Federal theatre project, resigned with words. Mr. Arent went on. That same year he edited and co-authored "Triple A Plowed Under" and "Injunction Granted." The year following he did "Power," and in 1938 ". . . one-third of a nation . . ." These were all successful. Particularly the last two, when the lads had refined the character and smoothed out the technique of the Living Newspaper form—a form, incidentally, from which Mr. Arent is convinced such last-season novelties as "The Cradle Will Rock" and "Our Town" have sprung, as well as dozens of Living Newspaper productions staged by amateur groups and college dramatic societies all over the country.

Mr. Arent was born in Jersey City, N. J., 33 years ago. His ancestry is Russian-American. He was educated at Lafayette College, New York University and Dwight Preparatory School. He has always been interested in playwriting and is convinced that "the 'living theatre' is just beginning to live. . . . It's in the healthiest state in its history." Last year he wrote a sketch for the Labor Stage revue, "Pins and Needles," and has been awarded a Guggenheim Fellowship to help him continue his playwriting experiments.

MARC BLITZSTEIN

While Marc Blitzstein has confined himself to the study and composition of musical scores, and has had little touch with the drama, his "The Cradle Will Rock" excited more comment as drama than it did as opera. This was largely due to the unusual conditions under which it came to hearing. Made ready for production by Orson Welles and John Houseman of the WPA Federal Theatre forces in 1937, it was barred from a public showing at the last minute on order from Washington. It was finally given in a borrowed theatre with the cast in street clothes, Mr. Blitzstein at the piano serving as orchestra, director and minor characters. The songs were sung, the ensemble numbers suggested, but the effect was almost exclusively dramatic. Mr. Blitzstein was born in Philadelphia in 1905. He studied in the public schools and at the Curtis Conservatory of Music, supplementing his musical education with courses in Paris and Berlin. He has written for musical publications and contributed to the sketches featured in the Labor Stage revue, "Pins and Needles."

LAWRENCE RILEY

The first play that Lawrence Riley brought to Broadway bounced about in managers' offices for three years. It finally came to the notice of one of Brock Pemberton's attention callers and was read by that producer and his associate, Antoinette Perry. They decided something could be done with it, and something was. The play was "Personal Appearance." It ran the season out after it was produced in October, 1934.

Young Mr. Riley (he is 34) was, I assume, surprised as well as measurably elated by this experience. He had had some little touch with the theatre the summer he helped direct a series of little theatre productions in Warren, Pa. But that was as close as he had come to realizing a half-hearted ambition to do something about it. He had devoted his earning years, after a war experience with a medical unit attached to an aviation corps, to the furniture business of his father in New York and the writing of stories for the pulp magazines. He liked writing better than he liked furniture. And, father or no father, he stuck to it. His "Personal Appearance" relates the adventure of a motion picture star who is on a fan-greeting tour of Eastern theatres the time she takes a fancy to a husky young servitor at the filling station in Pennsylvania. She has an idea she would like to take the boy back to Hollywood with her, but is effectively dissuaded following some highly comic adventures working to her disillusionment. At the time he wrote the play Mr. Riley had never met a movie actress in the flesh. He has seen plenty of them since, having been grabbed by Paramount shortly after the success of his comedy. Mr. Riley was born in Bradford, Pennsylvania, and attended High School there. He would have gone to Princeton if it hadn't been for the war.

ARTHUR KOBER

ARTHUR KOBER, a veteran scenario writer, is a debutant as a playwright on Broadway, having written 25 or 30 movies and only one produced play. "Having Wonderful Time," presented by Marc Connelly in February of 1937 was an immediate hit and ran for 372 performances. It is a simple human comedy concerning the adventures of a group of vacationers at a Jewish summer camp in the Berkshires. Katherine Locke, playing the lead, made as great a hit with the public as the play did. Mr. Kober was born in Brody, Poland, in 1901, and came to New York when he was three years old. He went through the public schools, attended the High School of Commerce, took a course in stenography and worked at several jobs from office boy to stenographer. His urge to be a playwright stemmed from his connection with a stock company, where, at thirteen, he took part as a singer in a boys' choir. School theatricals and contributions to the school paper added to the fascination of playwriting. His first play was "A Certain Young Lady" which was bought but never produced. It appears in *The New Yorker* in the "Bella Gross" series of short stories.

JOHN MURRAY, ALLEN BORETZ

JOHN MURRAY, JR., and Allen Boretz knew they wanted to write for the theatre from the time they went to school, John at De Witt Clinton in New York and Allen at Boys' High in Brooklyn. But, to satisfy parental ambition John gave a year to City College, another to Columbia and a couple to Brooklyn Law before he got started writing for the movies. Allen attended City College and took a course in journalism at New York University before his writing career began. An accidental meeting brought their minds together in the writing of a play each one had had in contemplation for some time and, with the help of George Abbott, "Room Service" appeared in May of 1937, has passed its 400th performance and is still running strong.

JOHN MONKS, JR.,
FRED F. FINKLEHOFFE

JOHN MONKS, JR., and Fred F. Finklehoffe, who wrote "Brother Rat," were born in 1910 and were graduated from the Virginia Military Institute in 1932. John Monks, whose birthplace was Springfield, Mass., lives now in White Plains, N. Y., and has his mind set on playwriting. After his graduation he became an actor, following in the footsteps of his English father. Fred Finklehoffe (born in New York City) left V.M.I. for Yale to study law. During their school days at the military institute they were put in the college jug for a prank and while there wrote their first play "When the Roll Is Called." This was submitted as their graduation thesis in English in which they were both majoring. In 1935 they got together again and rewrote the thesis, naming it "Stand at Ease," hoping for a Broadway production. George Abbott saw it, paid out the customary option money, and renamed the play "Brother Rat." It ran for 577 performances before closing in April of 1938, and later was toured successfully.

IRWIN SHAW

IRWIN SHAW decided to compete for a prize offered by a New Theatre League in search of social drama. Whether or not he had seen or read Hans Chlumberg's "Miracle at Verdun," he fashioned his long one-act drama, "Bury the Dead," on that model. He wrote of soldiers killed in the war who refused to be buried. Brought a burial detail face to face with six cadavers they had been ordered to put underground; showed them the dead men rising in their shrouds, and made them listen to protests against their extinction by cruel war. "Bury the Dead" never reached the contest for which it was written, but it was given a production by the League to which it was submitted and attracted the attention of several drama critics who saw it. Six weeks later it was given a professional production and created another round of excitement. Young Mr. Shaw (he is 24 and lives in Brooklyn, though he was born in Manhattan) was hailed as a genius by his more excited critics, and as a playwright of definite promise by even the least excited among them. He had been writing radio scripts for a detective story continuity when the radio scouts found him and sent him to Hollywood. In picture land he has been doing football stories, having played football when he was a student at Brooklyn College. His early ambition, insofar as it was associated with the theatre, he relates, was "to be polite, polished and luxuriantly idle, and to write that kind of play, none of which things has been vouchsafed me." With the excitement of the production of "Bury the Dead" still fresh in his mind he confessed that he had several other plays "violently on the way." One of these turned up at the Longacre Theatre under the management of Norman Bel Geddes in December of 1937. It was called "Siege" and lasted less than a full week. Which leaves Mr. Shaw still a debutant albeit "violently on his way." He is unmarried and glad he did not let his father persuade him to become a salesman of hat trimmings.

LEOPOLD ATLAS

THE usual disappointments preceded the emergence of Leopold Atlas as a playwright. At Yale he had devoted much time to the drama, taking the Drama 47 course and having one play produced there, a piece simply titled "L," in 1928. He also wrote another the same year, "The House We Live In," but it was never produced, so far as my record goes, and was not published until 1934, a delay doubtless due to the depression. He did get a production for "Wednesday's Child" in 1934, but that fine little comedy had been hanging around since 1930. He was pretty discouraged by that time. This play, however, proved an encouraging experience. "Wednesday's Child" was not a great popular success, but many people liked it a lot and said so. It brought Frankie Thomas, who was twelve years old that year, to Broadway notice and it ran for fifty-six performances.

Mr. Atlas' second play, "But for the Grace of God," was produced by the Theatre Guild in January, 1937. It proved a disappointment as convincing entertainment, for all it dealt seriously with the problem of the harassed poor and the crimes they, and particularly the young among them, are forced into through the suffering and the rebellion that poverty creates. Ralphy and Josey Adamec, sons of Frank Adamec, who has been out of work for two years, are supporting the family. Ralphy has a factory job. When his lungs give out Josey takes his place. Ralphy must go to a hospital. Josey and another boy steal a copper's revolver, hold up the proprietor of the factory and shoot him dead when he has but eight dollars to give them. Ralphy dies in the hospital, Josey goes to jail for his crime, the family suffering goes on. "But for the Grace of God" lasted no longer than it took to cover the Guild's subscription list, though it was admirably produced. Atlas was born in Brooklyn in 1907. He is the author of two other unproduced works, "So Long" and "From John Doe to John Dough."

ROSE FRANKEN

THE satisfaction of getting good and mad was partly responsible for Rose Franken's one-play success. It may be that she was so calmed and sweetened by that experience her Muse has since refused to respond to her bidding. Anyway there has not been another Franken play to match her "Another Language," produced in 1932. And "Another Language" was so definite a success that it ran originally for 344 performances and came back for a return engagement that added another 89 performances, making 433 in all. Which is quite a record for a first play. But, about the mad scene: Mrs. Franken, who is the wife of Dr. Sigmund Franken, an oral surgeon of wide renown, had been writing short stories successfully for years when she first tried her hand at playwriting. That resulted in a little something called "Fortnight," which drifted about until it was finally promised a production in a suburban theatre. The promise was not kept, and this experience so irritated Mrs. Franken that she decided to take her anger out on another play. So she gave her cook a vacation, took up the duties of housekeeping and the care of her three children and started work on a comedy she called "Hallam Wives." I pause to explain that Mrs. Franken writes best, she says, when she works hardest. Hence, when in the throes of composition she always insists on doing her own work. At least that's the story. "Hallam Wives" also floated aimlessly until a chap named Arthur Beckhard, who had been a concert manager and had taken up the drama to fill in a Summer, decided to try a production of it in Greenwich, Conn. It was not a very good production, but good enough to indicate that the comedy had value. Beckhard thereupon brought it to New York and managed a late Spring production for it under the new title of "Another Language," with a new and carefully selected cast of actors that included Glenn Anders, Dorothy Stickney, Margaret Wycherley and John Beal. That was the beginning of the success noted above. Also the last record I have of Mrs. Franken. The playwright was born in Dallas, Texas, but she came East at the tender age of 4. A novel of hers, entitled "Pattern," was published in 1925.

FRANK WEAD, U.S.N.

FRANK WEAD, Lieutenant Commander in the United States Navy, retired, whose "Ceiling Zero" is probably the best aviation play so far produced, has written the stories of half a hundred heroes of the sea and skies the last ten years. One day some equally gifted biographer will write the story of Frank Wead, and that will be the most fascinating of all. This playwright, born in Peoria, Ill., 43 years ago, and graduated from the United States Naval Academy at Annapolis in one of the war classes, was assigned to mine-laying duty in the North Sea during the Great War. A pretty task and filled with excitement. When he came home from the war none of the dull routine of three years at sea and three years on shore appealed to him. He made application for a berth with the Navy's flying forces and was transferred to San Diego. His advance was rapid. In a few years he was the holder of five world's records for flying and had gained fame as the captain of the United States Navy team that competed in 1923 for the Schneider cup, defeating France, England and Italy at Cowes. Then, a few years later, he fell down three little steps in his San Diego home and fractured a vertebra. Months of misery in hospitals and specialists' offices; months with nothing to do but wait and worry. Out of which emerged Frank Wead, author. At least he could write about the things he had done and those other things he had hoped to do. He wrote short stories and sold them. He wrote motion picture scenarios and sold them. Finally he wrote a play and sold that. He started to fly from Los Angeles to Chicago with the script to meet Brock Pemberton and Antoinette Perry, who were to fly from New York to Chicago to meet him. As it happened a lot of fog got in the way and all three arrived in Chicago by train, but Wead had the play and Pemberton liked it. The production was made in April, 1935, and it set a first-night audience cheering with the excitement of it. "Ceiling Zero" was probably a shade too realistic for popular sale. Strong men in every audience went white and ladies either swooned or threatened to swoon when a roaring airplane carrying the romantic interest crashed off-stage just the other side of the right upper entrance. Also an April start was not conducive to a long run for a thriller. However, "Ceiling Zero" ran for a hundred and four performances. After which the Warner Brothers, who were interested in both picture and stage rights, withdrew it. Commander Wead is still writing, mostly for the movies. He confesses that, to him, playwriting is easily the most interesting and exciting form of literary expression. But he feels that he probably will wind up as a novelist.

JOHN CECIL HOLM

The man who wrote "Three Men on a Horse" should be back in the theatre with another play pretty soon now. He is an actor, his wife is a playbroker and the first Holm comedy ran for a total of 835 performances on Broadway. Or it may be his profits from his first hit will satisfy the Holm ambition. The story has been told of this author that he was worrying a good deal about a mortgage that was coming due on his Westport, Conn., home the day he stopped in at a drugstore to buy a soda. On the seat next him was a man who was eager to bet on the races but in doubt as to the entries. He took a chance with Holm, and Holm, knowing nothing about the horses either, confidently picked one with a name that interested him. The horse won. And there the idea for the comedy was born.

It did not take long for the playwright to get it on paper, and a much shorter time for the wife to have it typed and started circulating. You could not say that the rejections came pouring in. There were not enough to pour. But there were several. George Abbott liked it, with reservations. Alex Yokel liked it, but was without funds. Finally it came about that Mr. Abbott agreed to work on and produce the farce, while Mr. Yokel interested several backers, among them the Warner Brothers of the movies. The farce at that time was known as "Hobby Horses." Under the present title it did a bit of touring and by the time it got to Broadway was so speeded up and tricked out with all the known aids to farce of which Mr. Abbott is master it proved an overnight hit. Since then it has been played in London and Australia and a French version was a hugh success in Paris. Mr. Holm was born in Philadelphia in 1906. He was a member of the Mask and Wig Club at the University of Pennsylvania, played in the annual shows and got a job in a Philadelphia stock company after he graduated. Since then he has done fairly well on Broadway, understudied Lee Tracy in "Broadway" and played the part of the hoofer-hero on tour.

EMMET LAVERY

ANOTHER young playwright who came quickly to notice during the season of 1934-35 was Emmet Lavery. Mr. Lavery had practiced law and done a bit of newspaper editing in his native town of Poughkeepsie, New York, and had acted a part or two for Hallie Flanagan when she was head of the drama department at Vassar. That would be in the Vassar Experimental Theatre, the work of which played a part in recommending Mrs. Flanagan to the Government for the post she has recently filled with great credit, that of Director in Chief of the Federal Theatre engaged in WPA reclamation work.

Mr. Lavery's introduction to Broadway was with a serious drama called "The First Legion," an impassioned defense, or at least an honestly prejudiced analysis and explanation, of those emotions which might wrack the minds of young men who have given their lives to a holy order. The good fathers of the House of St. Gregory, a Jesuit order, together with certain of their troubled novices, furnish the *dramatis personae*. The theme has to do specifically with the doubt created in the mind of one young priest who comes to believe that a certain miracle of God associated with the healing of a brother priest can be explained by science. At the moment of his greatest doubt he is brought back to the faith by witnessing the performance of a real miracle—the healing of a young boy stricken with infantile paralysis.

"The First Legion," no better than a quasi-success in New York, was afterward toured with great success by its actor-producer, Bert Lytell, and has become one of the outstandingly popular plays of the Continental theatre. Early in his career Mr. Lavery wrote a comedy on a newspaper theme called "Crusade," and is also the author of a second churchly drama, "Monsignor's Hour." He has been writing scenarios of late, but his faith in the future of the living theatre has not been lessened by that experience. He is 36 years old.

ROMNEY BRENT

Romney Brent's real name is Romulo Larralde y Hagueman. He was born in Saltillo, Mexico, in 1902 and became a citizen of the United States in 1928. He received his education in nine different cities: Saltillo, Mexico City, Monterrey, San Antonio, Paris, Brussels, London, Boston and New York, where he finished at the New York University. After acting for ten years—1921-1932—in New York and London, he took to writing. "The Mad Hopes" produced originally in Los Angeles, starring Billie Burke, in the Spring of 1932, was his first play. The next year in London his "Nymph Errant," a play with music by Cole Porter, had a considerable run. He adapted "Tomorrow's a Holiday" from the German of Leo Perutz and Hans Adler. It was produced by John Golden in association with Joseph Schildkraut.

HARDIE ALBRIGHT

Hardie Albright came into the Broadway picture as a playwright in March of 1938 with "All the Living," dramatized from Dr. Victor Small's "I Knew 3000 Lunatics." Mr. Albright, member of a theatrical family, had made a reputation in stock, on Broadway and in Hollywood as an actor, but this dramatization is his first play. Born Pittsburgh, 1903; was graduated from Carnegie Tech; attended Art Institute of Chicago; wanted to be an artist but decided to take up acting.

HARRY SEGALL

HARRY SEGALL wrote the original script of "Lost Horizons" which John Hayden revised for Broadway production. His only play which had reached Broadway prior to that production was "The Behavior of Mrs. Crane." Recently he has completed another one which he says "concerns itself with actual and spiritual characters." It is tentatively called "No Pity in the Clouds." The author, who was born in Vilna, Russia, in 1896, now lives in Hollywood. He came to America when he was a youngster and attended school in Chicago, graduating from Medill High School. In his youth he "burned to act—always on hand amateur nights— and always got 'the hook.'" He is still enthusiastic about the theatre. "With eager, talented little theatre groups dotting the country; with the road showing its old time vigor; with the insatiable demand for flesh and blood entertainment and the hunger for thoughtful plays, the future of the living theatre is nothing to be concerned about," writes Mr. Segall.

JOHN PATRICK

JOHN PATRICK of Carmel, California, was another of the young men who had his first training in scenario writing. This merely whetted his eagerness to write a play script. He thought he had found a story worthy of the living theatre when he wrote a piece called "Hell Freezes Over." He brought it East with him. He had never been east of

Chicago before that. One of his friends in New York invited him to a cocktail party in a penthouse. There he met George Kondolf, present head of the WPA Federal theatre in New York, who frequently dabbles in the production of plays. Kondolf, impressed with the story of "Hell Freezes Over," bought it next day and assembled the capital for its production. The play, splendidly cast and well played, proved too depressing for Broadway audiences. And no wonder. It was the story of twenty-five men who pilot a dirigible over the Arctic wastes in a search for the South Pole. The dirigible crashes, eighteen are killed, and seven survivors sit down in the cabin of the wrecked ship to wait for relief. One by one, sometimes two and two, they are variously snuffed out. The last man alive is chained to the wreckage when he hears the whine of the relief ship overhead. He cannot release himself to signal for help, and dies, as he had hoped to die, on his feet. Patrick is only twenty-eight. With that much plot sense and plenty of time left in which to develop it he should write a lot of plays.

JOHN HAYNES HOLMES

JOHN HAYNES HOLMES may never write another long play. He put a great deal of heart and many long hours into a peace propaganda drama called "If This Be Treason," working with Reginald Lawrence ("Men Must Fight") as a collaborator, and the play failed of success. This was not very encouraging. Yet the Holmes love of the theatre is strong, and he has a one-act piece, "The Unknown Soldier Speaks," with a large number of Little Theatre productions to the author's credit. The Rev. Holmes, however, is a clergyman by profession. His pastorate, the Community Church of New York, takes practically all the time he does not give to public affairs, to lecture tours and similar enterprises. There would not seem to be much time for drama creation.

MARY MACDOUGAL AXELSON

Mary Macdougal Axelson's one play, "Life Begins," was produced by Joseph Santley in 1932. It was a grim little tragedy in which a girl convicted of murder in a vice squad investigation gave birth to a baby in prison, fighting for her right to risk her life for her child when the prison physicians insisted her chance of survival was slim. She died and the infant was left to her loyal husband. It was too depressing a play for an already depressed playgoing public to support, although, after being slightly modified, it did very well as a motion picture. There was so much of promise in Mrs. Axelson's work, it is good to hear she is working a little feverishly on two other plays, "Life Comes to This" and "The Last Day." Mrs. Axelson, married to Ivar Axelson, economist, and mother of Mary Ivonne, aged 7, was born in the village of Selmer, Tenn. Three universities assisted in her education, Borth Texas College, University of Oklahoma and Columbia University.

LAURENCE GROSS

LAURENCE GROSS, whose first play to reach Broadway production, "Whistling in the Dark," was a success, is also a two-play author, but the other one, called "The Conquering Male" did not get beyond a week in Newark and a second week in Atlantic City. Edward Childs Carpenter was collaborator and wet nurse to "Whistling in the Dark," of which Ernest Truex was the star, but the original manuscript was Mr. Gross's and came from Milwaukee, where the author is engaged as a furniture buyer for a department store and also bosses a couple of other departments. His theatre interest, this playwright believes, was born in him but practically eliminated by his parents, who thought it pretty silly. Just for that Mr. Gross refused to do as they wanted him to and go to college. One of his friends in Evansville, Ind., where he was born, was King Cobb, a brother of Irvin's. King at that time was manager of the Evansville Opera House. This friendship served to stimulate the Gross playwriting ambition and now Mr. Gross goes right along writing plays between furniture deals. He has one called "Face Value," which, he says, is ready for rewriting, and he is about to begin another which he has talked over with Walter Huston. He is 48, lives in Wauwatosa, Wis., with a wife, a baby and an Irish terrier dog.

VINCENT YORK, FREDERICK J. POHL

VINCENT YORK, an actor, and Frederick J. Pohl, the husband of a novelist, Josephine Pollitt, extracted an amiable

but unimportant play which they called "Brittle Heaven" from Miss Pollitt's biography, "Emily Dickinson." This is the story in which the author seeks to prove that the love interest in Miss Dickinson's life, said to be responsible for her love poems, was stirred by Captain Edward Bissell Hunt, husband of her old friend, Helen Hunt Jackson, who afterward wrote "Ramona." The play was not without merit, and was well cast, Dorothy Gish playing the poetess of the title with a good deal of charm and Albert Van Dekker doing right by the Captain. But there was no more interest shown in the Dickinson biography by the playgoing public in this instance than had been shown in a former play, "Allison's House," written by Susan Glaspell on the same subject, and for which Miss Glaspell was awarded the Pulitzer prize for 1930-31. Mr. York has worked in the theatre, as actor and stage director, for some years. Mr. Pohl has been teacher of English and dramatics at the Boys' High School of New York City.

MARGARET LEECH, BEATRICE KAUFMAN

MARGARET LEECH PULITZER and Beatrice Bakrow Kaufman may as well be bracketed in this account of their debuts as playwrights. Together they wrote a drama entitled "Divided by Three." It proved a fairly searching and intimate discussion of the problem faced by a wife and mother sentimentally bound to the service of three men— her husband of twenty years, her son just entering man's estate and a lover, who has, she feels, made life endurable for her. Her adultery is discovered by her son, who curses and leaves her. She contemplates divorce and a second marriage, only to be trapped by the crash of her husband's fortunes and his appeal to her wifely loyalty. The drama was classed as being superficial and obviously theatrical by its severer critics, and as a dignified and intelligent social treatise by those who liked it. The playwrights have not since attempted another play. Mrs. Pulitzer (the wife of Ralph Pulitzer of newspaper fame) has her B.A. from Vassar and is the author of several books, including "The Back of the Book," "Tin Wedding," "The Feathered Nest" and a collaboration with Heywood Broun on "Anthony Comstock." She was born in Newburgh, New York. Mrs. Kaufman (who married George Kaufman, playwright, in 1917) was born in Rochester, New York, had a year at Wellesley and another at the University of Rochester. She has done considerable magazine writing and of recent years has served in various editorial capacities including, since 1935, her present position as editor of *Harper's Bazaar*. She has hopes of finding time to write again for the theatre.

JOSEPH M. VIERTEL

JOSEPH M. VIERTEL was only twenty years old when he wrote his first and (up to now) his only play, "So Proudly We Hail," a vital drama and important play even if it did not last long on Broadway. It was a play about the rigid discipline of a military school which conceivably might influence reforms. He was born in New York City in 1916 of Russian-Rumanian ancestry. Preparation for college was at Staunton Military Academy and his college education was obtained at Harvard and Yale Drama School. The vocational trend in the family seems to have been toward teaching and editing, both his parents having been teachers, one uncle a New York City public school principal and another editor of *City Record* and New York City *Green Book*. His father (Jack Shapiro), however, became a theatre builder, constructed over 100 theatres in the United States, dabbled in motion picture production and became half owner of the French Casino. This probably led to his desire to write plays and the year's drama course at Yale.

HOWARD LINDSAY, RUSSEL CROUSE

THE Howard Lindsay star became fidgety in 1933 and began shooting in the ascendant. That was the year he dramatized a novel by Edward Hope called "She Loves Me Not" and made it into the happiest comedy of the season. Produced by Dwight Deere Wiman and Tom Weatherley in November, "She Loves Me Not" (which had Burgess Meredith playing Buzz Jones in the cast) ran through the season and into the next, until it had 360 performances to its credit. With Russel Crouse, Lindsay then revised the book of "Anything Goes," which had 420 performances with Ethel Merman, William Gaxton, Victor Moore and Bettina Hall in the cast. The next year (1935) he wrote "A Slight Case of Murder" with Damon Runyon, produced it and sold it to the movies for a pretty penny.

Again with Russel Crouse in 1936 he helped write the book for "Red, Hot and Blue" and in 1937 that of "Hooray for What," which resulted in many hoorays for Ed Wynn. Playwright Lindsay was born in Waterford, New York, in 1899 and educated at Boston Latin School and Harvard. He started his stage career as an actor in "Polly of the Circus" in 1909. After service with the U. S. Infantry during the war he resumed acting and in 1927 started collaborating with Bertram Russell. Together they wrote three plays: "Tommy" (1928), "Your Uncle Dudley" (1929) and "Oh Promise Me" (1930).

Russel Crouse is a former newspaper reporter and columnist. His first work in the theatre was as librettist for "The Gang's All Here," in 1931. In 1933 with Corey Ford he co-authored a musical comedy called "Hold Your Horses," based on a play by the authors and Charles Beahan.

JAMES WARWICK

JAMES WARWICK, hailing from Chester, England, where he was born in 1897, had been writing short stories and plays, mostly in Hollywood, for the better part of twenty years when he hit upon the plot foundations for one called "Smokescreen." This one had to do with a professor of psychology who engages in a battle of wits with a Dillinger type of gangster and was produced by Gilmore Brown at the Pasadena Playhouse in California. The play reached Broadway in 1935 as "Blind Alley" and ran for 119 performances, being counted one of the best and most exciting of latter day melodramas. Mr. Warwick has recently been living in Greenwich Village, New York. His life has been adventurous. Born of a 60-year-old English physician father and a 19-year-old Irish mother, he was taken to Australia as an infant. His mother died when he was 6, he ran away from home when he was 14, went to war with the First Australian contingent when he was 17. Out of the army he took to the sea and landed finally in California, which is hard by Hollywood.

PHILO HIGLEY

PHILO HIGLEY, whose "Remember the Day" brought him to the theatre with Philip Dunning as a collaborator, was for some time an advertising agency man in the job-holding lists, but an eager dramatist by night. Also Sundays and holidays. He managed to turn out a second piece called "Traveller's Track," which the stock company at Lakewood, Me., gave a production the summer of 1936. He has been working in the theatre recently and also on two other plays. Mr. Higley is a native of Cedar Rapids, Iowa, and was brought up in Colorado, California and Illinois, where he followed up his public school education with the Chicago Latin School and later Princeton University. He is 36, has been married a couple of years and points pridefully to the conviction that any institution that can weather a depression as successfully as the theatre has weathered the last seven years can look forward to a grand future.

JOHN HAYDEN

JOHN HAYDEN, who rewrote "Lost Horizons" from an original script by Harry Segall, is advantaged in being a man of the theatre. His playwriting has been largely a matter of doctoring ailing scripts and collaborating with bemused authors. He worked on "The Sap from Syracuse," produced as "So Was Napoleon," and "The Night of Jan. 16." He and Marie Baumer have recently finished one called "Darby and Joan." Hayden is 49, a native of Hartford, Conn., and is convinced that young playwrights with definite gifts will arise as fast as the veterans fade away.

GEORGE BREWER, JR.

GEORGE BREWER, JR., was enjoying, or at least he was occupying, a job teaching English when he first dabbled in playwriting. This was in 1934, when he collaborated with Bertram Bloch on a piece called "Dark Victory." This happened to be one of the best of the plays that Tallulah Bankhead had been able to uncover for her return to her native theatre after ten years in England, and earned a run of fifty-one performances. It was the story of a young woman who had six months to live and decided, first, to live them riotously, and, on second thought, to marry the young surgeon who had reluctantly condemned her and live happily with him until the summons came. His second play, a solo effort, was a stanch little labor play called "Tide Rising." It brought Grant Mitchell back from the movies to play honest Jim Cogswell, a druggist who was elected sheriff and tried to settle a milltown strike organized by his daughter-in-law. It ran four weeks and was voted a promise of stronger plays to come from the Brewer workroom. Mr. Brewer is a native New Yorker, born 1899; graduated from Yale in 1922.

GERTRUDE TONKONOGY

WHEN Gertrude Tonkonogy (Brooklyn, 1908) was 25, and a very comely young woman, she was reading play manuscripts for John Krimsky. It suddenly occurred to her that she could write a play herself, having learned a lot of technique reading the plays of others. So one evening she gave her young man caller a book to read and wrote a first act. The story goes that two weeks after she started the play it was sold, and that she walked out of the producer's office with $500 advance royalties and trembling knees. The play, which was received with considerable praise, had a fair run. It was called "Three-Cornered Moon" and Richard Aldrich and Alfred de Liagre, Jr., produced it in the Spring of 1933. Shortly after the play was launched, the young playwright married an equally young heart specialist, Dr. Charles K. Friedberg. And apparently gave up the drama.

AYN RAND

AYN RAND, who was born in Russia in 1908 and educated at the University of Leningrad, came to America for the sole purpose of writing and promptly found herself a job as scenario writer in Hollywood. Now she is an American citizen, is married to Frank O'Connor, an American actor, and lives on Park Ave. in New York. An unusual experience in her life is that she sold her first movie scenario, "Red Pawn," her first novel, "We, the Living," and her first play, "The Night of Jan. 16." It was produced first at the Hollywood Playhouse under the name of "Woman on Trial" and a year later, on the night of September 16, 1935, A. H. Woods launched it on a run that continued for 235 performances at the Ambassador Theatre in New York. "We, the Living," published in April of 1936, has also been made into a play.

AND OTHERS

MATT TAYLOR, a magazine writer, and his brother Sam, a Hollywood director, wrote an unusual melodrama called "Stop-Over" (1938). With Arthur Byron, Sidney Blackmer and Muriel Kirkland in the cast it just missed achieving popularity and a run.

Jerome Chodorov and Joseph Fields wrote a satire on Hollywood which Philip Dunning (associated with Lee Shubert and George Jessel) produced at the Ritz in March of 1938. Mr. Dunning cast "Schoolhouse on the Lot" competently and decorated it attractively and it enjoyed a fair success.

Nicholas Cosentino, who is an Italian-American and an actor, came to Broadway early in the season of 1935-36 with a homely folk comedy of the city's streets and dialects. This was "Moon over Mulberry Street." It opened the season and was maneuvered through 303 performances.

Francis Edward Faragoh wrote a play about child laborers in tobacco fields which won a prize in a contest conducted by the International Ladies' Garment Workers' Union, an organization which has lately become theatre-conscious. The Faragoh tragedy, called "Sunup to Sundown," was competently staged and played, with Florence McGee, erstwhile imp of "The Children's Hour" in the cast, but lingered only briefly.

Francis Gallagher, who once served Philip Barry as secretary, wrote a drama about a construction job called "Iron Men" (1936), which Norman Bel Geddes produced and for which he used his genius in designing the setting. The theatre public did not respond to the play, but the scenery aroused great admiration.

Elmer Greensfelder, who wrote "Broomsticks, Amen," won a Drama League-Longsmans, Green prize with it in 1931. Thomas Kilpatrick produced the play in New York in 1934. The play revealed an intimate knowledge of the simple folk of rural Pennsylvania, as well as their primitiveness in the business of witch doctoring at its worst.

Horace Jackson, scenario writer from Hollywood, came to New York in January of 1938 with a play about Richard Steele, the eighteenth century essayist, called "Y^r. Obedient Husband." It was played by the Marches, Fredric and Florence (Eldridge). It met with a mixture of indifference and interest on the part of the critics, and the disappointed producers, Mr. March and John Cromwell, quickly withdrew it.

Leonora Kaghan and Anita Phillips called their first play "A Touch of Brimstone." John Golden produced it at the opening of the 1935-36 season. In it Roland Young, Mary Philips and Cora Witherspoon told the story of an egomaniac who was an actor and playboy as well. Ninety-eight performances.

THEIR BENT IS POETIC

It is Maxwell Anderson's contention that the great American drama of the future will be a poetic drama, even as the great drama of the past from which our drama has stemmed was a poetic drama. Certain it is that poets, and those with the urge of poetry in their souls, are season by season contributing more and more generously to the output of American dramatists. We have collected here a few of those who may be headed toward prize-winning classifications.

GEORGE O'NEIL

GEORGE O'NEIL advances slowly but still promisingly as an American dramatist. He emerged from what might be broadly described as a poetic past (three volumes of his verse have been published by Liveright) to sell "American Dream" to the Theatre Guild. It was produced by the Guild in February, 1933, and just missed being the sort of talked-of hit that stays past the Guild's subscription period. It told of three separated generations of Pingrees, those of 1650, who were Puritans and religion bound; those of 1849, who were greedy industrialists in trouble with their mill hands, and those of 1933 who had pretty much gone to pot. Well written and strongly dramatic, "American Dream" was a bit too revealing to please its American public, and their cousins of foreign extraction were not interested.

Mr. O'Neil rested for a spell and then helped Dan Totheroh (or perhaps Totheroh helped him) with the writing of "Mother Lode." This also dug deeply and dramatically into American history, having to do with the building of San Francisco with a fortune stemming from the Comstock lode. Carey Reid was the hero, popular in his success, deserted in his failure by all save one courageous and self-sacrificing woman, Hannah Hawkins. Melvyn Douglas and Helen Gahagan came home from Hollywood to play the parts, but even they and a large and competent supporting cast, backed by a quantity of excellent scenery, could not save the play. It was withdrawn after nine performances.

Dramatist O'Neil (with one l) was born in St. Louis of an Irish father and an English mother. There were Wilsons and Rowleys in his maternal line, Rowley really being his middle name, and the leading Wilson being one of those who signed the Declaration of Independence. He was sent from Washington University, in St. Louis, to an Eastern preparatory school. He didn't like the school and ran away. The family hoped he would take kindly to their lumber business, but he had too definite a flair for writing. He came to New York after a brief experience in the navy near the close of the war and took such editorial jobs as offered, filling in with short-story writing. He expects to go on with his playwriting.

In fact no longer ago than just the other day he was reported to have completed one called "The Red Pavilion," which was set for production but did not materialize.

STANLEY YOUNG

STANLEY YOUNG, who is literary adviser to The Macmillan Company and writes book reviews for the New York *Times*, is another poet who recently made a first step into the playwright's field. His first Broadway play, "Robin Landing," was produced by Sidney Harmon and T. Edward Hambleton in November of 1937. The play is written in verse, and although the critics were of various minds concerning its worth as a play, they pretty generally agreed that there was unusual beauty in its colorful verse and strength in its simple story. To quote one: "It is rather a pity that a play as fine in texture and as impressive in words as 'Robin Landing' should have to be thrown into the competitive Broadway market and left to succeed or fail by Broadway standards of entertainment." Eleven nights after this was written the play closed. Mr. Young, born in Greencastle, Ind., in 1906, studied at the University of Chicago and the University of Grenoble, France. Then he returned to America and got himself a master's degree at Columbia. For several years he was an instructor at Williams College.

ROBERT TURNEY

ROBERT TURNEY's first and, up to now, his only major contribution to the theatre in the way of drama is his "Daughters of Atreus," one of the more distinguished failures of the 1936-37 season. Of the newcomers among dramatists, however, none gives greater promise of one day being numbered with the leaders of the profession than he. "Daughters of Atreus" was a rewriting and re-shaping of the Atreus legends as told by the Greeks, and retold as the tale of the women involved. It is written in a poetic prose of marked beauty and consistent form. The manuscript was first held by the Theatre Guild, though never produced because of casting difficulties encountered at the time. Dame Sybil Thorndike read it and praised it highly, hoping one day to play any one of its three leading roles in London. The actual production fell to Delos Chappelle, with a cast headed by a German actress, Eleonora Mendelssohn, Maria Ouspenskays and Joanna Roos.

Mr. Turney was born in Nashville, Tenn., in 1900. His paternal grandfather was a governor of the state. He studied at both Columbia University and the University of Toronto, specializing in dramatics. He had a year with Jacques Copeau in Paris; worked at the festival in Salzburg; acted as stage manager for Lawrence Langner at Westport one Summer and later was stage manager for the Theatre Guild's production of Behrman's "End of Summer." His experiences have also included touring with a WPA Federal troupe and a season as dramatic coach at Madison Settlement House on New York's East Side. This he greatly enjoyed, saying, when he left—"The children of the lower East Side are the only ones I ever met really interested in art and culture."

ARCHIBALD MacLEISH

ARCHIBALD MacLEISH is not alone outstanding in the list of modern American poets (he won the Pulitzer thousand dollars for his "Conquistador" in 1935 because the judges rated it the greatest poem by an American written during that year), but he also is the most progressively independent writer among them. So far Mr. MacLeish has no more than dabbled in playwriting. His poetic drama called "Panic" was given showings (several private and one public) under the sponsorship of an organization known as Phoenix Theatres, Inc., in 1935, but nothing more came of that. He wrote "The Fall of the City" exclusively for radio production, and this was heralded as the forerunner of a new art and a new literary expression when it was given over the air by the Columbia Broadcasting System in the Spring of 1937. He also made the adaptation of "Macbeth" which was used over the same network in the Shakespearean cycle of 1937. But even as a dabbler the work and the promise of Mr. MacLeish are too important to be overlooked in any book concerned with the possibilities of our play-producing future. Poet MacLeish was born in Glencoe, Ill., in 1892; was graduated from Yale and Harvard Law School, winning honors in both institutions; was a captain of field artillery during the war and has had published a half dozen novels and volumes of verse.

ARTHUR GUITERMAN

ARTHUR GUITERMAN, also a poet of parts, has made but one try at writing for the stage, and that in collaboration with Lawrence Langner, the Augustin Daly of Westport, N. Y., whose record of playwriting achievements appears on another page. Together they did a rhymed version of Molière's "L'Ecole des Maris," which, reasonably enough, they called "School for Husbands." Mr. Guiterman attended to the rhymes, which brought him many compliments, and Mr. Langner took care of the book and plot adaptations. The play was tried in Mr. Langner's Country Playhouse in Westport the Summer of 1933 and in October of that year was produced by the Theatre Guild in New York. It ran right merrily for three months, and was then sent touring. In addition to this Mr. Guiterman did a good deal of work rewriting the books and lyrics of "The Chimes of Normandy," which happens to have been the first opera he ever heard. This also was produced in the Country Playhouse as "The Chimes of Corneville," but never got out of Westport. It was handicapped, the adapter agrees, by a weak second act. Mr. Guiterman has been working on another operetta for which Oscar Straus has written the music. It is called "Marriette" and is about ready for production. Mr. Guiterman was born in Vienna, Austria, while his parents were temporarily abroad and passed a hale and hearty sixty-sixth birthday anniversary last November. He was graduated with honors from the College of the City of New York in 1891. He lives in Arlington, Vt., five months out of the year, spends three months in some comfortably warm climate and is in New York the other four. He has great faith in the future of the theatre, however much it may suffer financially from newer forms of amusement.

LYNN RIGGS

LYNN RIGGS (Claremore, Oklahoma, 1899) came quietly through a back door to Broadway with the first production of one of his plays, and for the longest time practically no one knew he was in town. The play was called "Big Lake." It was a tragedy about a boy and girl and the love they found and lost, and it was produced at the Laboratory Theatre, conducted at that time by one of the first of the Moscow Art Theatre teachers to become established in America, Richard Boleslavsky.

"Big Lake" received no more than casual mention in the press and Mr. Riggs went back home to write more plays and more poetry, and dream even larger dreams of a possible future as a dramatist. After that he had a production of "Sumpin' Like Wings" at the Detroit Playhouse, and sold three separate options on the play in New York, just as the depression was raising hob with investment affairs.

He also sold "A Lantern to See By" for New York production, but nothing ever came of that, either. He had some little success with Jasper Deeter and his Hedgerow Playhouse near Philadelphia, and then, in 1930, he had his first real New York chance with a romantic comedy of the prairies called "Roadside." Arthur Hopkins gave it a colorful production, but being concerned with a shrill and lightly impossible hero, one called Texas, and he a raring, tearing irresponsible, roaming the roadside and taking romance where he found it, Broadway audience response was not sympathetic. Eleven performances and "Roadside" was gone.

A few months later Mr. Riggs "Green Grow the Lilacs" was produced by the Theatre Guild, and while again the play's reception was what might reasonably be called mixed, many fine compliments were paid the dramatic inventiveness and the poetic writing of the Western author. "Green Grow the Lilacs" continued for sixty-four performances.

Again Mr. Riggs turned to the Hedgerow Theatre for comfort when the commercial producers failed him. At the Hedgerow both "The Son of Perdition" and "The Cherokee Night" were produced, the latter being also given at the University of Iowa and by a WPA Federal group in New York. He did not reach New York again, however, until January, 1936, when "Russet Mantle," a reasonably serious social document with a nice overlay of character comedy, was produced. The reception of this play was pronouncedly favorable and a run of a hundred and seventeen performances resulted. "Russet Mantle" was the story of John Galt, a youthful idealist and poet tramping the West, who stops at the ranch house of the Horace Kincaids. Being given a job, Galt falls in love with a visiting Kincaid niece, and she with him. Being something of a social rebel the girl throws in her lot with Galt. When there are consequences that have to be acknowledged she is reluctant to give up her easy living as the daughter of a Louisville banker. In the end she sticks to her lover and her baby and embraces a conventional marriage.

Out of grammar school Mr. Riggs attended the University of Oklahoma. He has a home in Sante Fe, N. M., and divides his time between writing plays at home from choice and scenarios in Hollywood from economic necessity. He is, so far as the future of the theatre is concerned, what might be described as a poetic optimist. "I feel that the American theatre, now more than ever, must look at and examine minutely the current spiritual ferment. And I feel, too, now more than ever, that a playwright, to be any good, must be also a poet—and use whatever he has of a poet's equipment to see more clearly and to reveal more eloquently than ever before."

LANGSTON HUGHES

LANGSTON HUGHES, the colored poet, has but one Broadway production to his credit, that of a drama called "Mulatto," but he has written other plays and two have been included in the repertory of the Gilpin Players, a Negro producing unit that has been functioning with success in Cleveland, Ohio, the last seventeen years. These are "Little Ham" and "When the Jack Hollers," written in collaboration with Arna Bontemps. "Mulatto," though its reception was none too cordial, was played for many months in New York, and was afterward toured with success. Other Hughes dramas include a long play, "Troubled Island," a story of the Haitian slave trade, and four one-acters, "Scottsboro Limited," "Soul Gone Home," "The Gold Piece" and "Angelo Herndon Jones," which won a New Theatre Magazine prize. Mr. Hughes, 36, was born in Joplin, Mo. His blood carries Negro, Indian and Nordic strains. He is hopeful there will be an expansion of Negro producing units in the theatre.

JOHN DOS PASSOS

JOHN DOS PASSOS, another poet and novelist to become interested in playwriting, wrote "The Moon Is a Gong" and "Airways, Inc." He is a native of Chicago and was born in 1896. He was graduated from Harvard in 1918. He has had no play produced recently, perhaps because he thinks that "unless the theatre continually explores new themes and methods it has no chance to compete with mechanical entertainment," adding: "I don't see much sign of life in it right now."

VIRGIL GEDDES

VIRGIL GEDDES also has a leaning toward the poetic form. He was born on a farm in Dixon County, Nebraska (1897), where his parents of English and Scotch extraction had moved from their home in New England. When he came of age he left the farm and went to Chicago, where he worked as a proofreader on a newspaper. Then he went to Paris where he lived for several years, writing poetry (published abroad) and some prose. When he returned to America he settled in Boston and it was there that "The Frog" was produced in 1927 by the Boston Stage Society. Two years later "The Earth Between," produced at the Provincetown Theatre in New York, although it did not have any run to speak of, met with kindly, even enthusiastic criticism, and Mr. Geddes was proclaimed by admiring critics as a playwright "of great promise in the American theatre." Mr. Geddes has written some 15 plays with the loneliness and isolation of the American farmer as the background and out of these, grouped three into a trilogy under the title "Native Ground." After some changes and the omission of the concluding play of the three it was produced by the Federal Theatre in March of 1937. "Pocahontas and the Elders" was produced in 1933 at Chapel Hill, N. C., but never reached Broadway. Other published but unproduced plays are "Behind the Night," "The Ploughshare's Gleam" and "As the Crow Flies."

THOMAS STEARNS ELIOT

THOMAS ELIOT, a poet much better known in England and France than in America, has transformed one of his dramatic poems into a play which has been successful enough to cause skeptical producers to gasp. It seems that the transformation of this poem began with a suggestion made by an English clergyman to the poet to write a dramatic work for performance in the Chapter House adjoining the cloisters of Canterbury to raise funds for restoration. Mr.

Eliot had previously helped a similar cause with "The Rock" written with the aid of E. Martin Browne and given at Sadler's Wells in London. But this play went much further. It played at the Mercury Theatre in London, went on a long tour through the provinces and was presented by college groups first, then the Federal Theatre and lastly by Gilbert Miller and Ashley Dukes at the Ritz Theatre in New York City. Mr. Eliot has lived so long in England that the American public forgets or never knew that he was born in St. Louis, Mo., and educated at Harvard, receiving his A.B. in 1909. Subsequently he studied at the Sorbonne and at Oxford, contributed to English journals and became the editor of *Egoist*.

WILLIAM BRIAN HOOKER

Brian Hooker (New York, 1880), in the early days of his career as a writer of dramatic poetry, was associated with the opera. His "Mona" (with music by Horatio Parker) was awarded a prize of ten thousand dollars by the Metropolitan Opera Company. In 1923, however, he made an English version in verse of Rostand's "Cyrano de Bergerac" for Walter Hampden which proved that he had a real sense of the dramatic stage. The play had a long run at the National Theatre and was widely played by Mr. Hampden on tour. Four years later (1927), with W. H. Post as collaborator, Mr. Hooker adapted Edwin Milton Royle's "The Squaw Man," making it a musical play in four episodes under the name of "White Eagle." Vincent Youmans, who wrote the music for Hooker's adaptation of Jane Cowl's "Smilin' Through" as a romantic musical play called "Through the Years," produced it in January of 1932. The next year Mr. Hooker adapted Victor Hugo's "Ruy Blas." It was produced in Pittsfield, Mass.

FAMILY STUFF

There are various types of collaborators among
the playwrights, and it is quite startling to find,
particularly among the fledgelings, the great
number who have needed a shoulder to lean
against or smiles of encouragement to inspire a
continuance of effort. But the most interesting of
all are the family collaborators. When papa loves
mama enough to write plays with her, that is important. We also have two teams of brothers and
(if we were to lift the Owen and Donald Davis
duo from the prize winners) we would have
three father and son teams, the Davises, the
Nugents and the Goodmans.

THE LANGNERS

Lawrence Langner should, I think, have been included in the 1929 issue of "American Playwrights." He was barred then, I discover by a reference to the record, because he had not had two full-length plays produced between 1919 and 1929, which was the period and the condition arbitrarily set for that issue. Yet Mr. Langner had been a worker in and a writer for the theatre since he was twenty years old. He came to America from London in 1911. He had passed his examinations and become a Fellow of the British Chartered Institute of Patent Agents. He was in this country primarily to establish himself as an international patent attorney, which, incidentally, he proceeded to do. But his heart was in the theatre. As a lad of seventeen, before the Langner family insistence had sent him to the law, he had worked for a time in the London offices of the late Ben Greet.

"It was part of my job to give Miss Ellen Terry her morning mail, and to watch her rehearsals of 'The Merchant of Venice,'" the dramatist has written. "I, therefore, started my career in the theatre by seeing the work of an actress which has never been bettered since." Well— at least it has never been bettered in the role of Portia.

His first few months in America, plus a residence in Greenwich Village, brought the young attorney in touch with other eager and ambitious amateurs with an eye to theatrical careers. Philip Moeller, Theresa Helburn, Helen Westley and Edward Goodman were among them. The

Washington Square Players evolved from their conferences. "Licensed," a one-act play, was on the first Washington Square program, and Mr. Langner was its author. "Another Way Out" produced shortly after this was one of the Players' most popular items. For several years he devoted himself to the one-act form. His first full-length play was "The Family Exit," a comedy farce done in 1917. The World War temporarily did for the Washington Square Players, but in April, 1919, a reorganization was effected that established the New York Theatre Guild, and Langner was a prime mover in that now historical event.

It was not, however, until the season of 1933-34 that this dramatist moved into the theatre's king row. That season he was co-author of three plays, one a hit called "The Pursuit of Happiness," which he wrote with Mrs. Langner (Armina Marshall); one a modest success, "The School for Husbands," which he adapted with Arthur Guiterman from Molière's "L'Ecole des Maris," and one that did not do so well, "Champagne Sec," a rewriting of "Die Fledermaus."

Since then Mr. Langner has made an adaptation of Wycherley's "The Country Wife" which Ruth Gordon played at Westport, that being the forerunner of her later engagement in a revival of the same play at the Old Vic in London, preceding an engagement on Broadway that amused the sophisticates but left the larger public cold. Two other adaptations of his were "Dr. Knock" and "Love for Love," which Eva Le Gallienne played in Westport and left right there.

As a dramatist, particularly as a collaborating dramatist, the Langner future is fraught with promise. As a founder and director he has long since arrived. He was, as noted, a founder and director of the Washington Square Players. He was founder and director of The Theatre Guild and is now co-director of administration with Theresa Helburn. He was founder and owner of the Country Playhouse at Westport. And he was founder and director of the firm of international patent solicitors known as Langner, Parry, Card & Langner.

Being a stanch defender of the repertory system, and believing ardently that, to bring the art of the theatre back to its best estate it will be necessary for us to build "extremely large theatres, equipped for sound, so that large masses of people can enjoy the theatre at low admission prices, and in this way can compete with the talking motion pictures," I nominate Lawrence Langner as a founder and director of that particular enterprise.

His wife, Armina Marshall, born in Oklahoma in 1898, attended California University, Southern Section, and while there did considerable work in the Greek Theatre, thereby stimulating an early ambition to be an actress. She has had prominent parts in many Broadway successes and has been exceedingly active at the Westport Country Playhouse both as an actress and as a collaborator with her husband in the writing and production of plays. With him she wrote "On to Fortune," "The Compromisers" and "The Pursuit of Happiness." It is not always easy to find the Langners in a card index because they sometimes appear as Alan Child and Isabelle Louden. They are calling their newest play "Suzanna and the Elders." It is a character comedy about up-state New York in 1878.

THE SPEWACKS

SAMUEL SPEWACK was born in Russia and Bella in Hungary in the same year, 1900. Bella came to this country at the age of 3. She started to write by editing the Washington Irving High School magazine, doing newspaper reporting, working on the New York *Call* (with Edwin Justus Mayer, Louis Weitzenkorn, Anita Bloch and David Karsner), press-agenting for various Art and Theatrical groups, editing the literary section for the New York *Evening Mail*, conducting housing investigation for the New York *World*, and free-lancing far and wide. The other member of "Those Writing Spewacks," (who have no routine—just hope for the best) was also a news writer first before he took to the theatre. He was on the *World* reportorial staff just after the Great War and served as correspondent at Moscow and at Berlin from 1922 to 1926. Like Bella, he worked in the free-lance field, writing short stories, and like her, was completely seduced by the theatre.

Bella Spewack had sung in the Victoria Music Hall at the age of 4, had played comedy character parts in school plays, had directed stage productions at Madison House at 14 and was an off-stage voice for George Cram Cook at the Provincetown Playhouse. She first served the Broadway theatre as press agent for "The Miracle" and "Chauve Souris," the musical studio of the Moscow Art Theatre.

Such was the history of this interesting couple before they began to write plays in collaboration. "The Solitaire Man" in 1926 was the first. It was followed by "Poppa" and "The War Song" in 1928, "Clear All Wires" in 1932 and "Spring Song" in 1934. They have spent considerable time in Hollywood writing scenarios and out of that association blossomed their most successful play, "Boy Meets Girl," which took Broadway by storm. It was produced and staged by George Abbott at the Cort Theatre, opening in November of 1935 and closing at the end of the 1936-37 season with 669 performances to its credit.

THE HEYWARDS

DuBose Heyward was born in Charleston, S. C., in 1885. After a fairly successful career in the insurance business he started writing for the better American and English magazines. He organized the Poetry Society of Charleston and wrote many books, among them being "Carolina Chansons" which had for collaborator Hervey ("Anthony Adverse") Allen, "Mamba" and "Porgy." He married a playwright, Dorothy Hartzell Kuhns, and together they dramatized "Porgy." It was produced by the Theatre Guild in 1927, became an outstanding success of the season and, with the help of the Gershwins, George and Ira, was made into an American folk opera and produced (also by the Theatre Guild) in 1935. In 1931 his "Brass Ankle" was produced at the Masque and did fairly well.

Wife Dorothy, born in Worcester, Ohio, attended National Cathedral School at Washington, D. C., Radcliffe and the 47 Workshop at Harvard and also took courses in playwriting at Columbia and the University of Minnesota. She saw few plays in her youth but can't remember when she was not trying to write one. Her first play to be produced in New York was "Nancy Ann," with Francine Larrimore in the lead. This one had been awarded the Harvard prize in 1924. With Dorothy De Jagers she wrote "Cinderelative," which was produced in 1930.

THE SIFTONS

CLAIRE and Paul Sifton are the same age, having been born in 1898, Claire in Brazil, S. A., of Southern Baptist missionaries, and Paul in Rockford, Ill., of Canadian-American parents. Claire went to Stephens College, Paul to the School of Economics, University of London, and they both attended the University of Missouri.

Paul's first play was "The Belt," produced by the New Playwrights in 1927. His second, "Midnight," was written in collaboration with Claire and produced by the Theatre Guild in 1930. Together they wrote "1931," produced by the Group Theatre in December of 1931. In 1933 they wrote "Blood on the Moon," produced in Los Angeles. They use eight months out of every year earning enough money to write the other four.

THE NUGENTS

THE Nugents, father and son, are invariably linked as playwrights. For which linking there is good reason. Neither has ever worked independently in the living theatre—or at least hardly ever. J. C. Nugent (that would be John Charles, the father, Niles, Ohio, 1878) did write a little something called "Dream Child" in 1934, after Elliott

(Dover, Ohio, 1900) had gone over, lock, stock and type-writer, to the Metro-Goldwyn-Mayer firm of motion picture producers. Before that, beginning with "Kempy" (1922) and continuing through "Dumb-Bell" (1923), "The Rising Sun" (1924), "The Poor Nut" (1925), "Human Nature" (1925), "The Trouper" (1926), "Night-stick," with Elaine Carrington and John Wray (1927), "The Breaks" (1928) and "By Request" (1928), their productions were always jointly conceived, jointly worked out and, usually, jointly played. Usually, too, with Mrs. J. C. Nugent (Grace Mary Fertig) and Mrs. Elliott Nugent (Norma Lee) in the cast. The Nugents, in fact, have been "show folk" for several generations, reaching the legitimate theatre by way of vaudeville. Since Elliott went Hollywood the family has been represented on Broadway by "Fast Service" (1931) and, as said, by J. C. when he fathered "Dream Child" (1934). "Fast Service" had to do with a tennis champion who wooed, won and discouraged a girl by his devotion to his game. Being discouraged, she married a rich old man. Afterward the young people met again, made up, and managed to get rid of the old man. Then they continued their own romance. "Dream Child" revealed the conspiracy of a father to protect his son from the sort of hum-drum, unromantic, colorless small-town domestic life that his own had been. He arranges a New York trip for the boy, introduces him to the old theatrical boarding house where he, the father, had started his fling, and bids him make the most of his youth. Son does. He meets an artist who is seriously considering motherhood without benefit of matrimony. The next morning the young woman disappears. Years after, when the boy is married and settled, they meet again. Neither is very happy.

None of the later Nugent plays has scored a success. In fact, none that they have ever written has ever quite touched the popularity of "Kempy," the story of a plumber's helper forced into a spite marriage with a lady novelist, which had Broadway by the ears through the summer of 1922. As an actor Elliott later scored in several plays, notably in "The Poor Nut," and has played successfully in several screen productions.

THE GOODMANS

JULES ECKERT GOODMAN (Gervaise, Ore., 1876), has had little to do with the theatre since the middle nineteen-twenties. Being interested in the induction of his son, Eckert Goodman, into the playwrighting business, which the young man has hopes of following, the elder Jules came back in 1937 as co-author of "Many Mansions." This drama of the church, written by father and son, seeks to expose certain of the compromises indulged by established and accepted men of the cloth. Peter Brent, a young and liberal student of theology who hears the call of the church, is variously disillusioned and brought to trial in the end before a council of bishops that would unfrock him. He stages a stirring defense and goes out to continue his work for a true Christian church.

The Goodman years of greatest activity in the theatre saw the production of many of his plays—three the first year of his emergence, which was 1908. These were "The Test," "The Man Who Stood Still" and "The Right to Live." Blanche Walsh played the first, Louis Mann the second, and each ran a year. The third, "The Right to Live," which was the author's favorite, was a quick failure. Goodman's later work included a popular melodrama, "The Man Who Came Back," a dramatization of "Treasure Island," and a series of Potash and Perlmutter comedies with Montague Glass, author of the stories. Recent word from Mr. Goodman stresses his belief that the drama is in a sounder state today than it has been in many years, and he is frank to say that he considers the influence of Eugene O'Neill an important factor in the creation of a playwrighting medium that is far freer and more pliable in expression than any that has previously been accepted.

Leaving the public schools of Portland, Ore., Mr. Goodman took an A.B. from Harvard, an M.A. from Columbia, and was for many years prominent in the magazine field as editor and contributor.

THE HATTONS

FANNY and Frederic Hatton worked together for 29 years. Frederic was born in Peru, Ill., July 30, 1879, and was educated at Wisconsin and Princeton Universities. He became a newspaper reporter on various Illinois, Iowa and Wisconsin newspapers, eventually doing dramatic criticisms for the Chicago *Evening Post*. Mrs. Hatton, daughter of the Rev. de Witt Clinton Locke, Episcopal Dean of Chicago, was born where the Blackstone Theatre now stands and was educated in France, Germany and England. In 1912 David Belasco produced their first play, "Years of Discretion," which ran for 190 performances with Herbert Kelcey and Effie Shannon in the cast. The Hattons still like the play. There followed "The Call of Youth" (1914), "The Great Lover" written in collaboration with Leo Ditrichstein, which ran for more than a year under the management of Cohan and Harris on Broadway (1915) and for two years in London. It was revived in 1932 in an unsuccessful attempt to bring Lou Tellegen back to popularity. Their "Upstairs and Down" (1916) anticipated Scott Fitzgerald's "flapper" by four years, "The Squab Farm" (1916), "Lombardi, Ltd." (1917), "The Indestructible Wife" (1918) and many others. Early in 1930 began a series of adaptations of foreign plays including "Love, Honor and Betray" (1930), "Dancing Partner" (1930), "His Majesty's Car" (1930), "The Church Mouse" (1931), "The Stork Is Dead" (1932) and "The Red Cat" (1934). They have also written originals and screen adaptations for various picture companies.

THE STEELES

Wilbur Daniel Steele (Greensboro, N. C., 1886) was graduated from the University of Denver in 1907, returning in 1932 to receive his Litt.D. from that institution. In the meanwhile he had been studying at the Museum of Fine Arts in Boston, the Academie Julian in Paris and the Art Students League in New York. He is the first male in the Steele family for four generations who has not been in the ministry. He intended to be a painter but turned to writing instead and has had many books and short stories published. He has received innumerable awards from the O. Henry Award Committee, the Harper's Short Story Contest and others, and from the Society of Arts and

Sciences for maintaining the highest level of literary merit in the short story for over a series of years. This was a very special award, the only one of its kind. The year he went back to Denver to get his Litt.D. (1932) he was married to Mrs. Norma Mitchell Talbot, who has been co-author of two of his plays: "Post Road," successfully produced in New York in 1934, and "Penny." As "Leaning on Letty" their "Post Road" ran several seasons in the West. In 1935 Mr. Steele's "How Beautiful with Shoes," with Anthony Brown as collaborator, although well received by the drama critics, lasted only a week. Mr. Steele was one of the founders of the Provincetown Players. Norma Mitchell wrote her first play with Russell Medcraft in 1925. This was "Cradle Snatchers," which ran for 478 performances at the Music Box. The Steeles have a country place at Hamburg, Conn., called "Seven Acres."

THE HACKETTS

THE Hacketts, Albert and Frances Goodrich, are actors turned playwrights. Frances was born in Belleville, New Jersey, of good old American stock—with just a dash of Welsh, English, French and Dutch. After finishing private school she went to Vassar and later took a course at the New York School of Social Service. Started her theatre work as an actress with Henry Miller . . . "the end of the old regime, when you had no contract because it wasn't necessary . . . when you could count on fifty-two weeks work out of the year . . . because you were one of the company." She didn't consider herself much of an actress evidently and in the late twenties wrote herself a play called "Such a Lady." Her idea was to have it produced at Elitch's Gardens in Denver, where Albert Hackett helped her revamp the script. Later they wrote one called "Western Union," which was tried out in Skowhegan, Me. Lee Shubert produced their joint effort, a comedy called "Up Pops the Devil" and it ran for 148 performances, encouraging them to write "Bridal Wise," which got 128 performances in 1932. Albert Hackett was born in New York City and was educated by a private tutor. Acted with Olga Nethersole, Maude Adams and many other famous players. These collaborators were married and started writing for pictures in 1932, "trying to save enough money to afford the luxury of writing a play again."

THE EMERSONS

ANITA Loos and John Emerson have collaborated successfully as playwrights for both stage and screen. John Emerson (Sandusky, Ohio, 1874) was the son of an Episcopal minister and educated for the ministry. He took to the stage instead. He played with Mrs. Fiske for a couple of years, was long her stage manager, and later served in the same capacity for Charles Frohman, the Shuberts and many other producers. His first play was "The Conspiracy" in 1912.

Anita Loos (Sisson, Calif., 1894) contributed fiction to the newspaper press and wrote two books: "Gentlemen Prefer Blondes" and "But Gentlemen Marry Brunettes." The first of these, with the help of her husband, she made over into a play which was produced by Edgar Selwyn in 1926 and ran just one performance short of 200. They had previously worked together on "The Whole Town's Talking." Others were "The Fall of Eve," "Pair o' Fools," "Cherries Are Ripe" and "The Social Register." They spend most of their time now at the M.G.M. studios in Culver City.

THE BARKERS

E. L. AND Albert Barker form another father and son combination of playwrights. Edwin L., the father, was born in Westfield, Ind., reported for the Indianapolis *News* and Kansas City *Star*, became city editor of the Kansas City *Gazette* and finally wrote advertising copy in Chicago. Albert, the son, born in Chicago in 1900, also writes advertising and is an illustrator. Their first collaboration was "Buckaroo," written with Charles Beahan. The second was "The Man on Stilts" (1931), and the third, produced by the Federal Theatre in 1936, was called "American Holiday." This was a lively and often incisive satire of an American town entertaining with a public trial of "the crime of the century." There is such an influx of newspaper correspondents, photographers, publicity seekers, mobs of the idly curious and the curiously idle as to turn the place into a bedlam of notoriety and the trial into a circus of sensationalism. It was given twenty performances.

JULIUS J. AND PHILIP EPSTEIN

JULIUS J. and Philip Epstein are twins. Their first joint work as playwrights was produced in New York in October, 1936, by the Theatre Guild. It was called "And Stars Remain," and introduced Clifton Webb, musical comedy star, as a "legitimate" actor after a good many years of dancing and singing. Helen Gahagan was in the cast, too. "And Stars Remain" lasted out the subscription list and closed, the twin writers going back to Hollywood. The Epsteins were born in New York City. At Penn State College they took the playwriting course and eventually visited friends in Hollywood. There they began to write plays for the radio and screen and have continued at the job ever since. They hope to go on writing for the stage.

THE PERELMANS

SID and Laura Perelman wrote a play about Bohemia and a couple of Americans in Paris that brought Hope Williams back to Broadway. It was called "All Good Americans," and was produced in 1933. Sidney, who is Laura's husband, also wrote sketches for Vernon Duke's "Walk a Little Faster" in 1932, and has made other contributions to the New York theatre.

THE JOURNALISTIC TOUCH

Newspaper workers are frequently discovered in the one- and two-play group and never heard from again. Which does not mean that they are content to stop trying after having achieved a single production. They try, and often heed the grandfatherly advice to try, try again, but, being sensitive and easily discouraged, or hardened and easily angered, when their second or third play fails of production, or appreciation, they go back to their jobs nursing grievances and content to let the theatre get on as best it can. There are also several among them who have been handsomely rewarded in the theatre.

STARK YOUNG

FRIENDS of Stark Young, journalist and dramatist, are hoping that he will continue his interest in translating the plays of Anton Chekhov until he has added "The Three Sisters" and "The Cherry Orchard" to his recent translation of "The Sea Gull." This new version of "The Sea Gull" provided a stimulating theatre experience when it was used by Alfred Lunt and Lynn Fontanne in a Theatre Guild revival the season of 1937-38, being counted the clearest and most satisfying of all translations so far made of the great Russian's dramas. While Mr. Young has devoted much of his working life to journalism, his love of the drama has inspired his writing several plays as well. His first, "Guenevere," written in verse in 1906, was followed by a number of one-act plays, including "The Star in the Trees" and "Rose Windows." In the early twenties the Stage Society of London produced his "The Colonnade" and about the same time the Provincetown Players produced "The Saint" at the Greenwich Village Theatre in New York. Mr. Young then occupied his time with essays, poetry, magazine writing, editing, reviewing and lecturing. He was born in Como, Mississippi, in 1881; received his B.A. from the University of Mississippi and his M.A. from Columbia; was instructor of English at the Mississippi University and at Amherst, and of general literature at the University of Texas. He has served as drama critic of the New York *Times* and the *New Republic*.

ALEXANDER WOOLLCOTT

ALEXANDER WOOLLCOTT was for many years one of New York's most widely quoted dramatic critics, having held that position on the New York *Times*, *Herald*, *Sun* and *World*. Now he is equally noted as a story teller, wit, author, actor and radio broadcaster. His "Shouts and Murmurs" (also published as a book) in *The New Yorker* increased his reputation as a stylist; his books "While Rome Burns," "The Woollcott Reader" and "Second Reader" were best sellers and his fame has been enhanced by his "Town Crier" broadcasts. Obviously Mr. Woollcott hasn't an exalted opinion of his efforts as a playwright if the following answer to a questionnaire be taken literally: "What's all this nonsense of classifying as a playwright one who (on the most liberal of interpretations) is no more than 5/6 of a playwright? I did write half of one play (with G. S. K.) and (with G. S. K. and G. de M.) a third of another. When I recall their fate, it irks me to be called upon for enough clairvoyance to tell what I think about my first success. . . ." The plays referred to were "The Channel Road," which Mr. Woollcott wrote in collaboration with George S. Kaufman from Guy de Maupassant's "Boule de Suif," and which Arthur Hopkins produced in the Fall of 1929, and "The Dark Tower," also written with Mr. Kaufman, and produced by Sam Harris a little before Christmas in 1933. Each play ran about four weeks. Mr. Woollcott also likes to act. He made his professional debut as an actor in "Brief Moment" at the Belasco in 1931. The season of 1937-38 he was a featured member of the cast playing S. N. Behrman's "Wine of Choice" for the Theatre Guild. For the record, Mr. Woollcott was born in Phalanx, New Jersey, on the first of January in 1887 and schooled in Philadelphia, before going to Hamilton College.

GILBERT SELDES

GILBERT SELDES, one of the more brilliant of the literary and dramatic critics, and a columnist of standing today, had a satirical comedy called "The Wisecrackers" produced in 1925. Its failure discouraged him, but in 1930 he had recovered to such an appreciable extent that he furnished the Philadelphia Theatre Association with an adaptation of Aristophanes' "Lysistrata" that not only created a sensation in Philadelphia but also ran for 252 performances through a hot summer in New York. And yet, even with this encouragement, Mr. Seldes has not been represented in the theatre since then.

DAMON RUNYON

DAMON RUNYON, leading sports authority, has flirted with the drama for some years, though he has made more headway with the drama's sister of the screen, for which he has written such salable features as "Little Miss Marker" and "Lady for a Day." The only time he achieved a flesh and blood production of consequence, however, was in the staging of a farce called "A Slight Case of Murder," written in collaboration with the Howard Lindsay who also had a hand in "She Loves Me Not" and "Anything Goes." "A Slight Case of Murder" was voted extravagantly funny by the experts, but also outrageously incredible in story. A short run and a merry one was the result. Runyon is a Westerner, born in Manhattan, Kansas, in 1884. Out of the Pueblo, Colo., grammar schools he started a newspaper career as a reporter for the Pueblo *Chieftain*, moved on to the Denver *News* and the Denver *Post*, and finally into the Hearst organization in San Francisco. For some years he has been a sports columnist and special writer for Mr. Hearst's New York *American* and has contributed liberally to the *Saturday Evening Post* and other magazines.

JAMES MALLAHAN CAIN

JAMES MALLAHAN CAIN used journalism principally as a stepping stone to put him into the teaching and writing business. A novel of his composition that attracted unusual attention was a bit of bold realism called "The Postman Always Rings Twice." After it had chased the best sellers of its day practically out of the book stores, Mr. Cain decided to make it into a play. Richard Barthelmess of the movies came East to play in it. It was produced in February, 1936, and ran for seventy-two performances, the general opinion of the critics being that it was effective melodrama but a few shades too rough for wide consumption. Mr. Cain accepted the verdict and went back to California, vowing he would write another and better play. Cain was born in Annapolis, Maryland, in July, 1892, attended Washington College in Chestertown, and started newspaper work on the Baltimore *American*, going later to the *Sun*. He taught journalism in St. John's College, has written for magazines and syndicates, and edited the official newspaper of the 79th Division during the war.

ARTHUR HOPKINS

ARTHUR HOPKINS (Cleveland, Ohio, 1878) has a number of short plays, written when he was interested in vaudeville, and at least two long plays to his credit as a playwright, though he will go down in theatrical history as one of the foremost producers of his time. In 1933 his "Conquest," an exceptional drama following the "Hamlet" theme in tracing the determination of a son to avenge the father who had been sold out by an unfeeling mother, achieved no more than a *succès d'estime*. An earlier opus, however, in which he shared writing honors with George McWaters, a comedy called "Burlesque," was one of the outstanding successes of its season. Mr. Hopkins was also the author of "The Fatted Calf," a Brady production of 1910. Before he turned to the theatre Mr. Hopkins was a reporter on Cleveland and St. Paul newspapers. He turned from journalism to publicity and from publicity to production in vaudeville. Two of his early sketches were "Thunder Gods" for Blanche Walsh and "Holding a Husband" for Millie James.

BEN HECHT

BEN HECHT (New York City, 1894) was a reporter on the Chicago *Daily News* in 1912 when he wrote several short plays with Kenneth Sawyer Goodman under the title of "The Wonder Hat." Five years later the Washington Square Players in New York produced his "The Hero of Santa Maria." Five years after that "The Egoist" was played by Leo Ditrichstein. A few years later came "Front Page," written with Charles MacArthur (also an ertswhile Chicago reporter), on a theme they both knew intimately, the inside of a newspaper office. In New York "Front Page" ran for 276 performances. Another ex-newspaper reporter, Gene Fowler, helped Mr. Hecht with "The Great Magoo," which opened and closed in early December, 1932, but "20th Century," which opened right after Christmas of the same year, ran for 152 performances with Eugenie Leontovich in the cast. Charles MacArthur was again the Hecht collaborator. "Jumbo," a spectacular something tossed together with MacArthur (music and lyrics added by Rodgers and Hart) had a Hippodrome run in 1935-36, and the Theatre Guild produced the Hecht "To Quito and Back" in 1937. Mr. Hecht is a widely known novelist. He has written for the films since 1933. "The Scoundrel" and "Crime Without Passion" (screen plays) were written, directed and produced by Hecht and MacArthur.

CHARLES MacARTHUR

CHARLES MacARTHUR (Scranton, Pa., 1895), son of a Unitarian clergyman, attended theological seminary for two years. The reaction carried him into newspaper work, specifically newspaper work that eventually made him a feature writer for William Randolph Hearst in Chicago and New York. When he came back from the war, where he had served with the Rainbow Division as a private, he resumed his newspaper work and was a special writer for Hearst's *International Magazine*, whence he drifted into playwriting. All his plays have been collaborations. The first was "Lulu Belle," written with Edward Sheldon, his uncle; the second, "Salvation," written with Sidney Howard, and the third, "The Front Page," started a series of collaborations for the stage and screen which resulted in the firm of Hecht-MacArthur, Inc., writers and producers. "The Front Page" was followed by "20th Century" and "Jumbo" (see Hecht). The Spewacks, Bella and Samuel, were credited with having taken certain recorded adventures of this writing team of Hecht and MacArthur as the inspiration for their successful play of "Boy Meets Girl," also produced in 1935, though that soft impeachment has been denied. Mr. MacArthur is the husband of Helen Hayes, to whom he was married in 1928 in Washington, D. C., and the father of the little girl made famous in newspaper headlines as the "Act of God" baby.

JOHN BALDERSTON

John Lloyd Balderston took to playwriting about as soon as he was relieved from duty as a war correspondent in 1918. His first printed play was a war play entitled "The Genius of the Marne" and carried a preface by the late George Moore. It was never produced. His second play was frankly titled "A Morality Play for the Leisure Class." It was published in both New York and London in 1920, but also missed professional staging. He tried another,

"Tongo," in 1924, and finally landed with "Berkeley Square," in the writing of which he had some help from a London journalist, J. C. Squire. This play, which carried its modern hero through a dream adventure with his ancestors of the seventeenth century, was a success abroad and a great popular hit in America when, in a slightly altered version, it was produced here in 1929 by Gilbert Miller and Leslie Howard, with Mr. Howard playing the leading role. "Berkeley Square" had a run of 227 performances and is constantly being revived in some part of the world even today. Mr. Balderston is the adapter of the shudder classic called "Dracula," of another called "Frankenstein" which the pictures took, and co-author with J. H. Hoare of a quick failure known as "Red Planet." Balderston was born in Germantown, Philadelphia, in 1889, is of British ancestry and is often taken for a Britisher. His British ancestry, which was Tory, disowned his American ancestors, who were loyal Quakers, for "backsliding" into the Continental army. It was his great-great-grandmother who made the first American flag. Mr. Balderston has recently been doing a good bit of work in Hollywood.

EDWIN JUSTUS MAYER

EDWIN JUSTUS MAYER (New York City, 1897) was engaged as a reporter on New York papers, *The Call* and *The Globe*. He then became a press agent for a film company and later took up caption-writing. However, he was busy writing plays from the time he left the New York public schools. His first was "The Mountain Top," writ-

ten when he was 22. His first production was "The Fire-
brand," which ran for 261 performances before the season of 1924-25 had ended. It was six years before his next
play, "Children of Darkness," appeared on Broadway.
With Basil Sydney and Mary Ellis in the leads, it ran
for seventy-nine performances.

LOUIS WEITZENKORN

Louis Weitzenkorn was born in Wilkes-Barre, Pa., in
May, 1893, and thanks God for the Revolution of 1848
which was responsible for the migration of his forebears
from Germany. He attended the Harry Hillman Academy
in his home town, Pennsylvania Military College, at Chester, Pa., and later was graduated from Columbia University. By 1914 he was a reporter on the New York *Tribune*,
going from there to the *Times* and from the *Times* to the
Call, where he conducted a column headed "The Guillo-
tine," devoted largely to verse. Herbert Bayard Swope
discovered him there and made him a reporter and later
a feature editor of the New York *World*. From there he
went to the *Graphic*, where he was so emotionally stirred
that he had to give expression to his indignation in some
way. One of the most successful of newspaper plays, "Five
Star Final," was the result. This was produced by A. H.
Woods in 1930. It ran for 175 performances at the Cort.
Mr. Weitzenkorn's second play was a suburban tragedy
of young married life called "First Mortgage" (1929), the
tragic story of a harassed youth who tried to escape the
burden of his installments and the deadly routine of subur-

ban life. He wanted to own his own home, but he didn't want the home to own him. He has recently been busy in Hollywood.

JAMES HAGAN

JAMES HAGAN who was born in San Diego, California, was orphaned at an early age. He spent his youth, after public school in St. Louis, tramping through many states—"riding the 'rods' through Texas, the 'blinds' through Kansas," and settling down at last in St. Louis, where he landed in the newspaper business as fly-boy in the press room. Later he became a reporter on the *Post-Dispatch*. Still later on the New York *World*. He turned to acting, starting with a medicine show and proceeding through vaudeville to stock companies in Boston, Columbus, Elitch's Gardens in Denver, and Brooklyn as a comedian. He was stage manager for Henry Miller and Arthur Hopkins and played Shakespeare with Sothern and Marlowe for two seasons. His first play, "Guns," a story about rum runners in Chicago and Chinese runners along the Rio Grande, was forerunner of the gangster plays, and ran at Wallack's for about three months in 1928. His most successful comedy, "One Sunday Afternoon," opened February 15, 1933, after having been peddled for three years. The opening night President Roosevelt was shot at in Florida. The following day the banks closed and the stage hands went on strike, and that night the play closed. The author had twenty-five cents in his pocket. A week later "One Sunday Afternoon" was reopened and ran for 322 performances on Broadway. Later it took to the road with marked success and was sold to the movies for $26,000. Mr. Hagan's latest Broadway play, which lasted about three weeks in 1936 was "Mid-West," a realistic drama of the drought country.

JOSEPH PATRICK McEVOY

JOSEPH PATRICK McEVOY (New York City, 1895) was reared in Southern Illinois and started his apprenticeship in the newspaper business as a contributor to the South Bend *News* when he was fifteen. After he had finished his education in public and parochial schools, a year at Christian Brothers' College, St. Louis, and two years at the University of Notre Dame, he went to Chicago and became a reporter and feature writer for the *Tribune*, *Record-Herald* and *American*. He also sold much stuff to the syndicates. From some of his newspaper sketches he adapted "The Potters," which was produced by Richard Herndon in New York in 1923. He followed this with "The Comic Supplement," contributions to "The Ziegfeld Follies of 1925," "God Loves Us," "No Foolin'," "Allez-Oop" and "Americana" of 1926, 1927 and 1932. He has also written several books, including "Show Girl" and he once made a pretty good living writing greeting cards.

WARD MOREHOUSE

WARD MOREHOUSE (Savannah, Ga., 1898), dramatic columnist of the New York *Sun*, wrote "Gentlemen of the Press" (1928), variously advised by a corps of sympathetic collaborators. In the Spring of 1937 he did "Miss Quis,"

Peggy Wood being named as co-author as well as star. This was a pleasant comedy based on the adventure of an obscure charwoman who comes suddenly into the possession of a fortune.

JOHN ANDERSON

JOHN ANDERSON (Pensacola, Florida, 1898) drama critic for the New York *Journal*, attended the University Military School in Alabama and the University of Virginia. His contribution to the theatre includes three adaptations: "The Inspector General" (1930), from Gogol's famous play; a revision of "The Fatal Alibi" (1932), with Charles Laughton, and "Collision" (1932), a comedy from the German of Lothar and Sebesi.

FLOYD DELL, THOMAS MITCHELL

FLOYD DELL, author of novels, biographies, essays, verse, short stories and plays and Thomas Mitchell, actor-playwright, both started their careers in newspaper offices. Their output of plays is limited to two and both are collaborations. In 1928 their joint effort, "Little Accident," fashioned from one of Mr. Dell's stories, "An Unmarried Father," was produced by Crosby Gaige and ran for more than 300 performances. The other play, produced in 1931 at the same theatre, was called "Cloudy with Showers."

Floyd Dell, born in Barry, Ill., in 1887, followed a public school education by becoming a reporter on a Davenport paper. In 1905 he was working in Chicago and by

1911 he had become literary editor of the Chicago *Post*. Later, in New York, he was associate editor of *The Masses* and *The Liberator*. As a playwright he started in Greenwich Village with one-act plays: "The Angel Intrudes," "Sweet and Twenty," "King Arthur's Socks" and others.

Thomas Mitchell, well known actor and stage director, was born in Elizabeth, New Jersey, in 1895. His experience in the newspaper field must have been brief, for he was playing *Trincula* in "The Tempest" with the Ben Greet Players at Madison Square Garden Theatre in 1913. This was a good start for a young man and he continued with Charles Coburn's Shakespearean company touring the United States. Since that time he has played many parts and has staged many successful productions.

GENE FOWLER

GENE FOWLER was one of Ben Hecht's collaborators, helping him with "The Great Magoo." Gene was born forty-seven years ago in Denver, Colorado, as Eugene Devlan. He took naturally to newspaper work as soon as he was out of school, and has written several books that have attracted attention, notably his "Timber Line," the story of Tammen and Bonfils, Denver publishers; "Father Goose," a biography of Mack Sennett, and "Salute to Yesterday," a picturesque and fabulous story of the Rocky Mountain country.

JACK KIRKLAND

JACK KIRKLAND had advanced to a position of No. 1 reporter and rewrite man on New York's *Daily News* when he married Nancy Carroll, who was in the chorus of a Winter Garden show. Then, being in the profession, so to speak, his playwriting urges were whetted. He tried several subjects and several forms and finally sold a fairly bold and crudely builded melodramatic version of the "Frankie and Johnnie" lament he had heard in a variety of bagnios by a varied assortment of *femmes de nuit*. The police closed it. Kirkland, stopped for no more than a few weeks by such discouragement (he was 29 at the time), set about making a play of the rutty humors of Erskine Caldwell's "Tobacco Road." His fondness for the earth earthy and the sex sexy has long been apparent. "Tobacco Road" came to production in December, 1933, and was promptly set down by a majority of the play reviewers as an ugly and forbidding dramatic opus in which Henry Hull, playing the first Jeeter Lester, a Georgia primitive, achieved a magnificent characterization. For four weeks "Tobacco Road" languished. The playgoing regulars were not definitely impressed either for or against. Then, one by one, analysts, defenders and plain boosters began to appear. An editorial in the New York *Daily News* was loaded with attention-calling phrases pointing out the play's importance as a revealing picture of American home life as it concerned the abused tenant farmers of backward states in the South. Societies working for the alleviation of the condition of the poor and the under-privileged everywhere used the "Tobacco Road" pictures as illustrations of a democracy's sins which they hoped to correct. Little by little the play's business began to build. It is now in its fifth year of continuous performances on Broadway; has been exhibited by four or five touring companies; was banned by the mayor of Chicago and has made Mr. Kirkland a rich young man. He didn't have to write another play, but he did. Last January he and Sam H. Grisman produced "Tortilla Flat," which Mr. Kirkland had dramatized from a novel by John Steinbeck. Five performances and the play closed.

GEORGE F. HUMMEL, RUSSELL OWEN

GEORGE F. HUMMEL had been flirting with the theatre all his life, but he was past 50 when he wrote "The World Waits," in collaboration with Russell Owen, who represented the New York *Times* and a newspaper syndicate as correspondent on the last Byrd expedition to the Antarctic. "The World Waits" was pretty generally accepted as a record of certain dramatic happenings experienced by the Byrd group, though statements to that effect were promptly denied. Mr. Hummel wrote the play, it was insisted, and Mr. Owen merely helped him with certain technical features common to polar expeditions. The play was a taut drama in which fifteen men are cooped up in an ice-bound hut waiting for a relief ship which the leader of the expedition has been hesitant about summoning. Rebellion finally becomes crystallized and the chief aviator takes over the leadership of the expedition. As he does so word that the relief ship has been sighted is received. The aviator thereupon turns the command back to the deposed leader with the significant remark that he is much better equipped to handle the home reception and the publicity attached thereto. The play missed a popular success and was withdrawn in New York after thirty performances. A private production at the Repertory Theatre in London was successful. Mr. Hummel, born in Southold, L. I., 56 years ago, had his A.B. from Williams College in 1892, his M.A. from Columbia in 1903 and a Ph.D. from Columbia in 1910. He has done a good deal of teaching and has written a half dozen novels, including "After All," "Subsoil," "A Good Man" and "Summer Lightning." He feels that the theatre has never been in a more "healthful and promiseful" condition than it is today.

Russell Owen was born in Chicago (1889), was educated in public and private schools of Providence, R. I., reported for the New York *Sun* and *Times* (specializing in aviation) and received the Pulitzer prize in journalism for articles covering the first Byrd Antarctic expedition in 1929-30.

CARLTON MILES

CARLTON MILES (Fergus Falls, Minn.) was for fifteen years dramatic critic of the Minneapolis *Journal*. He started serving in that capacity as soon as he finished his education at the University of Minnesota. This was a logical step, since he had been writing plays and acting in them from the time he was nine, straight on through his high school and college dramatic activities. When he was 19 his comedy of college life called "Mose" was published. His first play to be produced was written with John Colton, called "Flitting Lady," and played by a Minneapolis stock company in 1913. The first Broadway production, "Nine Pine Street" (1933), was also co-authored by John Colton. Lillian Gish played in this mystery drama, founded on the Lizzie Borden case. Miles' "Portrait of Gilbert" was produced in 1934 and the next year "The Eldest" was written with Eugenie Courtwright. Mr. Miles says he was born "in the era of hard-tired bicycles," and is descended from New England ancestors.

CHARLES WASHBURN

CHARLES WASHBURN (Chicago, 1889) left grammar school for a copy boy job on the Chicago *Tribune* in 1904, which he left at the end of three years to loop-the-loop on a bicycle with a touring Carnival company, returning to the *Tribune* as a reporter in 1909. His ancestors were British and "Boston Irish" and his father was a Chicago Alderman. He came home from France, where he had been helping to win the war as a private, to fight for space in the newspapers as press agent for A. H. Woods (on the road), A. L. Erlanger, Weber and Fields, George M. Cohan (12 years) and George Abbott. In 1913 he collaborated with Edward E. Rose on a melodrama about white slavery called "Little Lost Sister." "All Editions," written with Clyde North, played three Broadway weeks, starting just before Christmas in 1936.

MAX MARCIN

MAX MARCIN (Posen, Germany, 1879) came to America as a child, went through the New York public schools and thence into the newspaper field. He was employed on the editorial staff of the New York *World* and later the New York *Press*. His first play was "Are You My Wife," written with Roy Atwell in 1910. Five years later Cohan and Harris produced "The House of Glass," which he had written with George M. Cohan, and which had a long run at the Candler Theatre. That same year, 1915, A. H. Woods produced his "See My Lawyer," followed the next year by "Cheating Cheaters" which also had a long run. Other Marcin collaborations included "Eyes of Youth" (with Charles Guernon), "Here Comes the Bride" (with Roy Atwell), "The Rape of Belgium" (with Louis Anspacher), an American version of "Seven Days Leave" (1918), "The Woman in Room 13" (with Sam Shipman) and "The Dancer" (with Louis Anspacher and Edward Loche). Mr. Marcin has done a good deal of doctoring and revising of plays.

BIDE DUDLEY

ALTHOUGH he doesn't want it generally known, his real name is Walter Bronson Dudley. To the newspaper and theatrical world he is and always has been "Bide." Born in Minneapolis in 1880, he was taken to Leavenworth, Kansas, at the age of one year. He was educated in the public schools, became a telegraph operator and then turned to newspaper work. Was dramatic editor of the New York *Evening World*. His first theatrical work was as co-author with Jack Norworth of "Odds and Ends of 1917." All of his plays except "Oh, Henry," "All Square" and "The Man on the End," with Fulton Oursler, have been musical. They include "The Little Whopper," "Come Along," "Sue Dear," "The Matinee Girl" and "Bye, Bye, Bonnie." For the past six or seven years he has been doing radio work for the national networks. Mr. Dudley points with pride to the fact that he is the father of Doris Dudley, actress; that he was the first to print the writings of Will Rogers, and that he started Norma Talmadge and Louise Brooks in pictures through newspaper publicity. He thinks there is definitely a revival of the living theatre both in New York and on the road.

WILLIAM JAMES McNALLY

WILLIAM JAMES McNALLY, dramatic editor, overseas correspondent and chief editorial writer for the Minneapolis *Tribune*, started writing plays upon his return from the World War. His "Good Bad Woman" was produced in 1919 with Richard Bennett directing and with a cast including Robert Edeson, Wilton Lackaye and Margaret Illington. "Ink," a satirical melodrama burlesquing a newspaper publisher, which he wrote under the pseudonym of Dana Watterson Greeley (1927), and "Prelude to Exile," produced by the Theatre Guild in 1936, were his other two plays.

NOVELISTS AND THE DRAMA

The list of novelists who have turned to the drama, either as an experiment or with the determined intention of proving their quality in this most difficult of literary fields, has been greatly enriched the last few seasons by the addition of such names as those of Thornton Wilder, John Steinbeck, Sinclair Lewis and others. Preceding the advent of these leaders there were, however, a goodly list of book authors who also had made their mark in the theatre. Outstanding among these writers are those grouped in this chapter.

EDNA FERBER

EDNA FERBER (born Kalamazoo, Mich., 1887) has maintained a most consistent record the last several years as a contributor to the literature of the theatre. She has worked mostly with collaborators, she furnishing the plot and they helping with the construction and theatre experience. Her first play was a dramatization of her own "Our Mrs. McChesney" (with George V. Hobart, 1915), which Ethel Barrymore played. She wrote "The Eldest" in 1920, and "$1,200 a Year" (with Newman Levy, 1920), but neither of these amounted to much. With "Minick" (1924), however, which she and George Kaufman dramatized from a Ferber story, she began a career as a playwright that has been substantially successful. Miss Ferber and Mr. Kaufman followed "Minick" with "The Royal Family" (1927), "Dinner at 8" (1933), and "Stage Door" (1936). "Dinner at 8" was one of the first multiple scene dramas to come after Vicki Baum's "Grand Hotel" (1930). (See George Kaufman.)

Miss Ferber took to newspaper work after she was graduated from the high schools of Appleton, Wis., and to magazine writing shortly after. Her success as a novelist followed.

SINCLAIR LEWIS

SINCLAIR LEWIS (Sauk Center, Minn., 1885), who won the Nobel prize in literature in 1930, is an internationally known novelist who is definitely theatre-conscious. He started his career, after receiving his A.B. from Yale, in a newspaper office and after a few years of reporting for the New Haven *Journal* and *Courier*, the San Francisco *Bulletin* and the Associated Press, became editor of *Transatlantic Tales, Volta Review*, Publishers Newspaper Syndicate and other publishing houses. His first play to be produced in New York, "Hobohemia," was shown at the Greenwich Village Theatre in 1919. By this time he had written five or six books and was at work on "Main Street," which Harvey O'Higgins and Harriet Ford later made into a play that was produced in 1921. His other novels which have been dramatized are "Elmer Gantry" adapted by Patrick Kearney (1928); "Dodsworth," made into a play by Sidney Howard (1934); "Jayhawker," in which Lloyd Lewis (no relation) collaborated with the author of the novel (1934); and "It Can't Happen Here," which John C. Moffitt working with Mr. Lewis, converted from the novel into a play for the WPA Federal Theatre in 1936. Although his name as collaborator in the plays fashioned from his books has appeared on only a few of the theatre programs, he undoubtedly has had a share in the creation of all of them.

MARGARET AYER BARNES

MARGARET AYER BARNES (Chicago, 1886), who received the Pulitzer prize for fiction in 1930 for her "Years of Grace," had already seen three of her plays successfully produced on Broadway. Notwithstanding, she went back to her field of fiction. "I like to write novels better than plays," she explains, "because of the comparative independence of a novelist's work. As has often been observed, the art of the theatre is a collaborative art—the manager, the producer, the star, the company, the scene designer and the costumer all have a share in the success or the failure of a play. Publishers play a role that is comparatively passive. Your book remains your own. . . . I still prefer the single responsibility of the novelist." The three Barnes plays produced on Broadway were "Age of Innocence," a dramatization of Edith Wharton's novel, played for over 200 performances by Katharine Cornell at the Empire Theatre, in November, 1928; "Jenny," written with Edward Sheldon and played at the Booth by Jane Cowl and Guy Standing for more than 100 performances in the Fall of 1929, and "Dishonored Lady," also with Mr. Sheldon as collaborator, produced at the Empire with Katharine Cornell playing 127 performances starting early in 1930. One of her later books, "Edna His Wife," was seen on Broadway when Cornelia Otis Skinner transformed it into a monodrama last year. Mrs. Barnes comes from British and New England ancestry; is a graduate of Bryn Mawr College; is married to Cecil Barnes, a Chicago lawyer, has two sons at Harvard and one at Milton Academy.

LOUIS BROMFIELD

Louis Bromfield is a novelist who, to listen to Louis Bromfield, does his best writing in France and his best rewriting in America. The confession was made the year he took to playwriting with a good deal of enthusiasm, because, he said, he loved the theatre devotedly. That was

1935, and he had two plays produced within days of each other—one, "Times Have Changed," in Philadelphia; the other "De Luxe," in Boston. "Times Have Changed" was an adaptation from a French drama by Edouard Bourdet called "Les Temps Difficiles," and had to do with the effort of the head of an aristocratic New England family to save the family mill fortunes through a variety of compromises with estranged relatives. "De Luxe" caught an interesting but unhappy group of American expatriates in Paris and shuffled their fates and their emotions into new alignments.

These plays, with a dramatization of an earlier novel, "The Green Bay Tree," called in the theatre "The House of Women," represent Mr. Bromfield's chief contributions to the drama to date, and none of them met with the success his friends and hosts of admirers had hoped for him. "The House of Women" continued for forty performances, "Times Have Changed" for thirty-two and "De Luxe" for fifteen.

Not too happy over these playwriting experiences Mr. Bromfield returned to story writing, in which he had earned his first fame, including the Pulitzer award for his "Early Autumn" as the best American novel of 1926. Before that he had written "The Green Bay Tree" and "Possession," and he followed the award with "A Good Woman" and "Twenty-four Hours."

Mr. Bromfield was born in Mansfield, Ohio; studied at both Cornell and Columbia Universities; was given an honorary B.A. because of his war work and won a Croix de Guerre with the American Ambulance Corps in France.

ARTHUR GOODRICH

ARTHUR GOODRICH (New Britain, Conn., 1878) has had no play produced on Broadway since the Spring of 1935 but it can hardly be assumed that he has gone back to novel writing exclusively. Before writing his first play, "Yes and No" (1917), he had written seven books, many short stories, articles and verse, had held editorial executive jobs on many magazines including *Outing, World's Work,* and the *American Magazine,* and had been an executive for Doubleday, Page & Co. "So This Is London," written five years after his first play, was a throw-back to a series of humorous articles he had written for London *Vanity Fair.* "The Ring of Truth," "The Joker" (with W. F. Payson) and "You Don't Understand" followed this and preceded his greatest success, "Caponsacchi," a dramatization of Browning's *The Ring and the Book* (written with Rose A. Palmer) which won the Theatre Club gold medal in 1926, ran for 269 performances in New York and was eventually made into grand opera, Mr. Goodrich writing the libretto. Other plays have included a new version of Sir Edward Bulwer-Lytton's "Richelieu," written for Walter Hampden who played the Cardinal and produced the play; a comedy called "Plutocrat," based on the Booth Tarkington novel of the same name; "The Perfect Marriage" and "A Journey by Night," adapted from the original German by Leo Perutz. Mr. Goodrich was graduated with a Ph.B. from Wesleyan University and took a year's graduate study at Columbia.

IN FORMER YEARS

HARRY LEON WILSON, born Oregon, Ill., 1867, was widely known for his authorship of books and as editor of *Puck*. He collaborated with Booth Tarkington in the following plays: "Foreign Exchange," "If I Had Money" (also known as "Mrs. Jim" and "Getting a Polish"), "Springtime," "The Man from Home," "Cameo Kirby," "Your Humble Servant," "Up from Nowhere," "Tweedles," "Hoosiers Abroad," and "How's Your Health." Many of his books have been dramatized: "Ruggles of Red Gap" (by Harrison Rhodes); "His Majesty Bunker Bean" (by Lee Wilson Dodd); "Merton of the Movies" (by George Kaufman and Marc Connelly).

Booth Tarkington (Indianapolis, 1869) went back to his story writing in the early nineteen twenties, after a playwriting career that included such favorites as "Monsieur Beaucaire" (1901); "The Man from Home," written with Harry Leon Wilson (1907); "Clarence" (1919), written for Alfred Lunt; "Penrod" (1916); "The Country Cousin" (1916), written with Julian Street, and a dozen other plays. Mr. Tarkington is still dividing his time between Indianapolis and Kennebunkport and still writing novels.

Rupert Hughes (Lancaster, Mo., 1872) went completely Hollywood early in the picture game, after an early stage success with "Excuse Me" (1911). His last New York production was "The Catbird" in 1920.

Fannie Hurst (St. Louis, 1889) withdrew from the drama after her "Humoresque" (1923) and "It Is to

Laugh" (1927), were offered with moderate success.

Mary Roberts Rinehart (Pittsburgh, 1876) after scoring a tremendous popular success with two farces, "Seven Days" and "The Bat," written with the late Avery Hopwood, dallied with several moderately successful plays, but went back to story writing some years ago.

THE RECENT PAST

It was fairly startling to discover the number of new playwrights who have moved into the theatre scene since the compilation of 1929. It was also a little depressing to discover the number of older playwrights of proved quality who have frankly withdrawn to merge their talents with those of the picture factory operatives of the West Coast, or given up playwriting for good and all. From many of these we are pretty sure to hear again. For the others, their past records entitle them to a place in any book devoted to the profession they have honored.

CHANNING POLLOCK

FROM the time he was 20, which was in 1900, until he was 48, which would be in 1928, Channing Pollock was an enthusiast in the theatre. An enthusiastic playwright, an enthusiastic playgoer, an enthusiastic play reader and an enthusiastic defender of all that the theatre, and in particular his theatre, stood for. Beginning with "The Pit," which he dramatized for William A. Brady while he was serving Grace George (Mrs. Brady) as a press agent, he wrote some thirty plays and musical comedy books, most of them singly, a few, principally those with music, in collaboration. And then, following a series of disappointments and what he came to believe was a malicious opposition on the part of certain of the professional reviewers, Mr. Pollock retired from the theatre in something closely resembling high dudgeon and has had comparatively little to do with it since. For the last six or seven years he has devoted himself to writing novels and lecturing. The earlier Pollock output included a dramatization of "In a Bishop's Carriage," "The Little Gray Lady," "Clothes" (with the late Avery Hopwood) and "Such a Little Queen." His later and more serious dramas included "The Fool," in which a clergyman hero tried with little success to live and preach as Christ might have done; "The Enemy," which proved with considerable conviction that hate, greed and ignorance are the cause of all wars, and "Mr. Moneypenny," which undertook, by allegory, to emphasize the Biblical warning that it shall profit a man little to gain the world if he lose his soul. The failure of "Mr. Moneypenny" by which he had set great store, was a crushing blow to the Pollock pride. He followed this with "The House Beautiful," a second allegorical legend in which a simple and imaginative New Jersey housewife pictured her honest and hard-working husband as a modern Sir Galahad buckling on his armor each morning to catch the 8.20 and fare forth into the wicked city to meet the Black Knight, who was his boss. Mr. Pollock's severer critics grew facetious in their reviews of "The House Beautiful" also and the playwright decided the game was not worth the distress it caused him.

Mr. Pollock was born in Washington, D. C., in 1880, and educated in the public schools of several Western cities to which his father's business took the family, and later by tutors in Europe and South America when his father became an associate of the consular service. He took up newspaper work in 1898, becoming a drama critic himself, and drifting from that job into publicity work for the Bradys, as noted.

BAYARD VEILLER

BAYARD VEILLER (Brooklyn, N. Y., 1869) is another whose ups and downs and ins and outs in the theatre, if diagrammatically outlined, would have the appearance of an agitated stock market graph. He began writing for the theatre as far back as 1907, after a considerable experience as a press agent. He wrote three plays, "The Common Law," "The Case of Mary Turner" and "The Fight" and could sell none of them. The one about Mary Turner was a

Veiller favorite, but Edgar and Arch Selwyn, who were his agents, could do nothing with it. Veiller, eager to quit press agenting and devote his time to playwrighting, offered to sell all three of his finished plays for the equivalent of a salary of $75 a week for fifty weeks, which would amount to $3,750. The Selwyns tried to explain to him that he was probably cheating himself, but he was impatient to close the deal and the agreement was signed.

"The Case of Mary Turner" was retitled "Within the Law" and William A. Brady bought it for Grace George. Miss George later decided that she did not want to play a thief, which this heroine technically confessed being, and left the play after it was in rehearsal. Emily Stevens was substituted and "Within the Law" was produced in Chicago in 1911. After four weeks it was withdrawn and Brady, losing faith in it, sold it back to the Selwyns for the $10,000 his production had cost him. The play was brought to New York and selected by A. H. Woods for the opening attraction of the new Eltinge Theatre the following season. By this time stock in the "Within the Law" enterprise had changed hands several times, but when produced the play was owned by the Selwyns, who had 50 per cent, Mr. Woods and Lee Shubert, who had split the other 50 per cent. The sensational success of "Within the Law," with Jane Cowl playing the heroine, is one of the historical highlights of Broadway history. The play ran for over a year, was played by as many as eight touring companies at one time and returned a fortune to its owners. Even Veiller profited to some extent, although he had, as stated, assigned his rights. The Selwyns voluntarily gave the author $100 a week during the run of the play in New York and $50 a week for each of the touring companies.

The "Within the Law" success was scored in 1912. Veiller did not have another hit until 1916, when "The Thirteenth Chair" ran for the better part of a season. After that Veiller went to Hollywood and was not heard of on Broadway again for many years. In 1927, however, he was back with another fairly startling melodramatic form. This one was the drama of an open courtroom during the hearing of a murder case, and was called "The Trial of Mary Dugan." This play, depicting in minute detail the trial of an ex-Follies girl who had been found staring wildly at the body of her dead patron, her hands blood smeared and her finger prints on the handle of a dagger, ran for nearly five hundred performances with Ann Harding the first and best known of its heroines. Happily for the popularity of the play the fair prisoner's younger brother, a lawyer, came to her rescue and finally forced a confession of guilt from the State's chief witness.

Mr. Veiller again went into temporary retirement following this success, but not in Hollywood. He had bought a Connecticut farm which he named "Bayard's Burden," and spent much of his time there. His next emergence was in 1929, when he helped Becky Gardiner with the writing of "Damn Your Honor." This related the love of a nineteenth century buccaneer named La Tour who stole the Governor's wife. Playgoers were chill in its reception. "Damn Your Honor" was gone in a week.

Again in 1930 Mr. Veiller made a sortie from his Connecticut acres, bringing with him another melodrama called "That's the Woman" which he sold to Charles B. Dillingham. This also was concerned with a trial for murder in which an innocent young man was about to be convicted on circumstantial evidence. He had an alibi, but he would not use it because it involved a married woman. The hero's attorney finally tricks the lady in question into stepping out and confessing that she was the prisoner's companion the night of the murder. "That's the Woman" contained many of the old Veiller tricks with melodrama, but did not sell. And again Mr. Veiller disappeared from the Rialto, returning again to Hollywood for a spell.

EDWARD SHELDON

EDWARD BREWSTER SHELDON (Chicago, 1886) unhappily has been limited in his playwrighting by an invalidism that has kept him confined to his bed for many years. To quote "American Playwrights of Today," Mr. Sheldon "was one of the first young men to draw attention to and justify the existence of Prof. George Pierce Baker's class in play construction then known as English 47 at Harvard. Sheldon came out of Harvard in 1907 with a play called 'Salvation Nell' which the Harrison Grey Fiskes bought in 1908. He followed with 'The Nigger,' which was a decade ahead of its time, 'The Boss,' 'The High Road' (with Mrs. Fiske) and other plays until in 1913 he produced 'Romance' and achieved an immediate and lasting box-office popularity." This was the author's first big box-office success, Doris Keane playing it in both England and America over a period of years. Other Sheldon plays have been "The Jest," a notable adaptation of Sam Benelli's "La Cena Delle Beffe" with John and Lionel Barrymore in the cast, and "Dishonored Lady," with Katharine Cornell.

EDGAR SELWYN

EDGAR SELWYN (born Cincinnati, 1876), who will be recalled by older playgoers for a number of hits, "The Country Boy," "Nearly Married," etc., is a Hollywood executive and apparently interested in nothing else, although last Summer he was credited with the authorship of a piece called "Possession" which he had some hope of seeing on Broadway. With his brother, Arch, and Crosby Gaige as associates, Edgar was for many years prominent in play producing, his firm having sponsored the outstanding success of "Within the Law," among others. (See Veiller.)

FRANK CRAVEN

FRANK CRAVEN (Boston, 1875) also went Hollywood in a big way, after contributing such comedy hits to the theatre as "The First Year," "Too Many Cooks" and "The Nineteenth Hole." He came back to Broadway briefly and happily in 1930 to produce and play in another typically Cravenesque comedy called "That's Gratitude." The Craven part was that of a small time theatre manager who goes to the aid of a suffering salesman in an adjoining hotel room, shares a pint of liquor with him and becomes his friend. The salesman takes the theatre man home, where he not only overstays his welcome but also becomes involved in family difficulties. He agrees to make a prima donna of the homely daughter of the family and does so, with the help of a plastic surgeon. When she is a success she jilts her benefactor and runs away with a tenor. Mr. Craven came back to Broadway as an actor the season of 1937-38 to play the role of the stage manager in "Our Town."

GEORGE MIDDLETON

GEORGE MIDDLETON (Paterson, N. J., 1880) who wrote "Adam and Eva" with Guy Bolton a long time ago, and "The Big Pond" with A. E. Thomas as recently as 1928, has been confining his attention to the printed play the last several years. A satirical number called "Siss! Boom! Blah!" was threatened with production but missed and "That Was Balzac" is still waiting for a proper actor to play it.

THOMPSON BUCHANAN

THOMPSON BUCHANAN (New York, 1877) made the leap to Hollywood at the first shake of a contract after he had scored with "A Woman's Way" (1909), "The Cub" (1910), with Douglas Fairbanks as the hero, "The Bridal Path" (1913), etc. He came back in 1919 to do "Civilian Clothes" and stayed on to try a couple of others, including one called "Sinner" (1927). He was back again in 1930 with a comedy called "As Good as New" in which a cheating husband is caught by his wife and her detectives. The wife agrees to delay divorce proceedings to avoid scandal, but the children are taken into their parents' confidence. A marriageable daughter thereupon decides she will do her sex investigations before she marries, hoping thus to avoid her parents' mistakes, and a son runs away from home to escape the humiliation of a stepmother. The estranged couple decide upon a reconciliation to save the home. "As Good as New" was given fifty-six performances. Mr. Buchanan went back to Hollywood.

EDWARD CHILDS CARPENTER

EDWARD CHILDS CARPENTER (Philadelphia, 1871) is another who does such writing for the screen as seems important at the moment, though his first and last love is the drama. He, too, has been giving a lot of time to well-paying odd jobs the last several years, following a considerable success with such remembered confections as "The Cinderella Man" (1915), "Bab" (1920), which was Helen Hayes' first starring opportunity and which Mr. Carpenter took from a Mary Roberts Rinehart story; "Connie Goes Home" (1923) and "The Bachelor Father" (1928), one of the last of the Belasco successes. Recently this playwright escaped his cinema keepers long enough to collaborate with Laurence Gross on a piece called "Whistling in the Dark" (1932). With Ernie Truex featured, this one ran for 143 performances. It presented the amusing adventure of a writer of crime fiction who wanders into a crooks' hideout and is detained until he can think up a perfect murder that will defy the police. He supplies the crooks with a plan for such a murder, and then spends torturesome hours trying to save the intended victim. In 1933 Carpenter did the book for a musical piece called "Melody," with Irving Caesar lyrics and Sigmund Romberg music, and a year later he made over a Walter

Hackett plot into a comedy called "Order, Please" (1934). This was the tale of a wild Westerner in search of a brunette in New York. He becomes tangled with a blonde and a murder mystery in the same hotel and barely escapes detention as a murder suspect. Out of trouble he takes the blonde and goes back to Wyoming. "Order, Please" was through in two weeks.

The Carpenters expected that Edward Childs would take kindly to the business of his forebears, who were in coke and steel and also in Pittsburgh, but the boy had different ideas. He wanted to write. He found himself a job as a stock company actor to give him background. Then he took to newspaper reporting to support him while he went back to studying with a tutor. With the tutor he learned a lot about writing that he thought he knew, but didn't. His first plays included "The Barber of New Orleans," "The Challenge" and "The Tongues of Men." It was "The Cinderella Man" that set him up, really. At the moment he is haunting Broadway again with a script or two salvaged from Hollywood.

ARTHUR RICHMAN

ARTHUR RICHMAN (New York, 1886) has been back from Hollywood frequently since he went to the coast in the late nineteen twenties, but only twice with plays to produce. One of these was "Heavy Traffic," which Gilbert Miller presented in the Fall of 1928, and the other "The Season Changes," produced by Robert Milton in 1935. "Heavy Traffic" told of a maturing and amorous lady, played by Mary Boland, who ran into difficulty getting a divorce until she met a certain handsome detective. It was played for eight weeks. "The Season Changes" related the experience of a problem child who was greatly dependent upon her mother but who thought to marry a married man as soon as he could divorce his wife. She is desperately interested in marriage so long as she is opposed by her mother, but once the mother agrees with her she decides to give up marriage and stay at home. Eight performances and this was all over.

Mr. Richman is a native New Yorker. He was educated by private tutors. Having refused at an early age to go to school, he miraculously made his resolution stick. He had the playwriting urge from the age of fourteen. He was 31 when the Shuberts bought "Not So Long Ago" (1920), and that practically ruined him for anything except a playwriting career. During the war he wrote "The Little Belgian," which was quickly abandoned in Philadelphia. He sold "A Serpent's Tooth" to John Golden in 1922 and "The Awful Truth" to Gilbert Miller for Charles Frohman, Inc., the same year. Ina Claire played the heroine of "The Awful Truth," a heroine who had to call in her first husband to satisfy her prospective second husband that no scandal attached to their divorce. The first husband lies like a gentleman, but also falls in love with Ina all over and ends by remarrying her. "The Far Cry" (1924), "All Dressed Up" (1925), "Antonia" (1925), an adaptation, and "A Proud Woman" (1926), preceded the jump to Hollywood, but none scored importantly.

LAURENCE STALLINGS

LAURENCE STALLINGS (Macon, Ga., 1894) was off to a fine start as a playwright of originality and promise when he collaborated with Maxwell Anderson, first on "What Price Glory?" and later on "First Flight" (1925), a biographical drama concerned with a high-lighted adventure from the life of the young Andrew Jackson, and "The Buccaneer" (1925), telling of Raider Morgan's conquest of Panama City. The promise held in the matter of workmanship but not in the selection of subject. His next two tries were with musical dramas, "Deep River" (1926), a lovely opera with a score by Frank Harding that proved a cut above popular taste in quality, and "Rainbow" (1928), a sturdy Western melodrama for which Oscar Hammerstein II wrote the score. He went back to drama with "A Farewell to Arms," which he adapted from the Ernest Hemingway best seller for A. H. Woods. Elissa Landi, making her American debut, played the romantic nurse, and Glenn Anders the vitally alive Lieutenant Henry. Judging from audience reactions there appeared to be not enough of Hemingway left to satisfy the book's readers and too little appeal in the curtailed romance to stir the interest of playgoers unfamiliar with the original. "A Farewell to Arms" was withdrawn after three weeks. Miss Landi promptly went to Hollywood and remained there until the current season (1937-38) when she came back to play in "The Lady Has a Heart."

Mr. Stallings' career has been as filled with romance and adventure as those of his stage heroes. He was a reporter in Atlanta when he was sent to get an enlistment story about the U. S. Marines in 1917. He wrote the story and then went back and joined the Marines. He saw heavy fighting in France, losing a leg and gaining a captaincy at Château-Thierry. Back in America and out of hospital after many months, he returned to newspaper work in Washington and to study at the University of Georgetown, where he earned a Master of Science degree. He previously had taken an A.B. at the Lake Forest College in North Carolina. He was a book reviewer on the *Morning World* in New York when he wrote "What Price Glory?" with Anderson, at that time an editorial writer. He went to Hollywood in 1925 and wrote scenarios for "The Big Parade" and "Old Ironsides," and some years later took up the work of editing news reels, an outstanding assignment being the Italian campaign in Ethiopia. He flirted briefly with the stage again in 1937, when he evolved a plot for "Virginia," later revised and staged at the Center Theatre in New York.

JOHN COLTON

JOHN COLTON (Minnesota, 1891) who burst suddenly into prominence with the production of the play he co-authored with Clemence Randolph called "Rain" (1922), has done a good deal of work of one kind or another in California since last we were talking about him in 1929, but nothing of consequence in the drama. In 1933 a piece called "Saint Wench," which had been tried out in San Francisco by Ruth Chatterton as "The Devil's Plum Tree," was produced in New York by Helen Menken with herself in the name part. It was a free adaptation from a Hungarian original and related the adventure of a physically weak but spiritually stalwart heroine who, being betrothed to one man, met a handsome bandit in the wood and was taken quite by surprise. Later, after she is married, the bandit returns and it is impossible for her to get him out of her thought or out of her room. Fortunately her husband, who was a churchman, understands, and the suffering lady is finally able to conquer passion and become a saint with great healing power. "Saint Wench" ran two weeks.

This same season Mr. Colton and Carleton Miles took over a play manuscript prepared by William Miles and Donald Blackwell, who had tried to chisel a proper melodrama out of the Lizzie Borden murder case that kept Fall River, Mass., agog for months forty odd years ago, and rewrote it as "Nine Pine Street." Lillian Gish played the Borden character, called Effie Holden. Mentally unbalanced by the death of her mother and the quick marriage of her father, Effie bashed in the skull of her stepmother and killed her father with a heavy walking stick. When arrested she calmly announced that she was not at home at the time of the murder, stood trial and, helped by the influence of her friends of the local church, successfully won her release. For twenty years thereafter she continued to live in the old Holden home with most of the neighbors still wondering whether she was guilty or not guilty. The play was withdrawn after twenty-eight performances.

Otherwise, Playwright Colton has failed further to capitalize his success with "Rain," which the late Jeanne Eagels played for five years, and "The Shanghai Gesture," which was written for the late Mrs. Leslie Carter, taken over by Florence Reed and played for the better part of three years.

Mr. Colton was born in Minnesota, but was a babe in arms when his parents took him to Japan. His father at that time was a collector of art objects for Vantine & Co. As a child he traveled through India, China and Japan, was educated by tutors in the Orient and in France and England. Returning to America he flunked a succession of examinations at Columbia, went West to recover, "bummed around" for two years and wound up in Minneapolis. Here he took up newspaper work and eventually had a play produced by a stock company. Afterward he wrote magazine stuff in New York, got a job in Hollywood and out there met Somerset Maugham, who gave him permission to dramatize a short story sold originally as "Miss Thompson." Coming back to New York he asked Miss Randolph to help with the dramatization and "Rain" was the result. Recently he has been working on a new "Mary Stuart" play for Jane Cowl.

LULA VOLLMER

LULA VOLLMER (Keyser, N. C., 1898) is not a one-play woman. She has written a half dozen dramas for the living theatre, perhaps a dozen scenarios and a long list of radio plays linked together under the title of "Moonlight and Honeysuckle." Her one play to achieve conspicuous success, however, is the "Sun-up" that started late in 1923, ran through the season of 1923-24 in New York and was later played successfully in many American cities and in London. Wherever the play was seen Lucille La Verne, the original Widow Cagle, repeated her success as the homely, pipe-smoking, loyal mountain woman who set out to avenge the killing of her son in the war and was stopped by his voice calling upon her to do her part in banishing hatred, the cause of all wars, from the thoughts of men.

In 1930 Miss Vollmer tried an adaptation of a Hungarian play written by Imre Fazekas called "Troyka." This was a fairly confused story of an orphan girl who was adopted by a Siberian prisoner. She later became the object of two men's desires and was finally forced to run away with a third as a solution to her expanding problem. It ran but two weeks. The season following an original Vollmer play called "Sentinels" was produced at Christmas time. It related the loyalty of a colored servant who was willing to sacrifice her own son to save a son of the family for which she had worked all her life. In the crisis the white boy confessed. "Sentinels" also proved a failure, and Miss Vollmer continued with her radio and scenario work.

Miss Vollmer (who was christened Louisa Smith Vollmer) spent many years of her childhood in the lumber camps of the South, lumber being her father's business. She came to New York in 1918, after graduating from the Normal and Collegiate Institute of Asheville, N. C., and for a time was associated with the business offices of the Theatre Guild. She wrote "Sun-up" in two weeks, and then spent five years trying to get it produced.

It was obscurely played first at the Provincetown Theatre. She followed "Sun-up" with two other plays having to do with Southern mountain characters, "The Dunce Boy" (1925), and "Trigger" (1927). In 1937 she came back briefly with another Southern play, "The Hill Between," which just missed popular endorsement.

VINCENT LAWRENCE

VINCENT LAWRENCE, like so many of the playwrighting guild, has stuck pretty close to Hollywood since he first went there in the late nineteen-twenties. He has made but two bids for Broadway favor since 1928, when he had three plays produced, "A Distant Drum" in January, a revival of his "In Love with Love" in May and a musical comedy, for which he wrote the book with Fred Thompson, called "Treasure Girl," in November. The musical play got sixty-four performances, but the others had short engagements. In September, 1931, Lawrence, backed by Philip Goodman, dashed in briefly with an unhappy exhibit called "Washington Heights," and dashed right out again after seven performances. This was the story of an unhappy genius who, falling under the influence of a sex-crazed neighbor, attacked a visiting niece, who jumped from a fire escape to save her honor. Action at least.

Lawrence came within hailing distance of success on several occasions previous to his defection. Once with "In Love with Love," originally produced the season of 1923-24; again with "Spring Fever" (1925), which James Rennie and Marion Coakley played for sixty performances, and again with "Sour Grapes" (1926), which got forty performances with Alice Brady and John Halliday. The playwright was born in Roxbury, Mass., in 1890, went from the public schools to Andover and thence to Yale. Eight years ago he confessed that he had never been able to fool either the critics or his audiences.

GILBERT EMERY

GILBERT EMERY (né Gilbert Emery Bensley Pottle, Naples, N. Y., 1875) has also had the experience of many playwrights who have taken to pictures. Finding a plot or story that seems better suited to the living theatre than to the screen theatre he has shipped it to Broadway and hopefully awaited results. In many instances such plays are carelessly written. Frequently the author has been unable to give rehearsals and production his personal aid, and quick failure has resulted. Emery, whose promise was high when his first plays, "The Hero" (1921), and "Tarnish" (1923), were staged, suffered two quick failures with "Housewarming" in 1932 and "Far-Away Horses," written with Michael Birmingham, in 1933. The first told of a pair of Yankees who were married in Paris and who returned to their old home town in New England. At home they ran into a good deal of in-law trouble. The spunky bride finally burned down their house to get rid of unwelcome wedding presents. "Far-Away Horses" was a sordid tale of a messy Irish family that went through everything it could lay hands on in the way of income and gifts and was still hopeless at the play's end. These two got four performances each. Mr. Emery wisely stayed on in pictures.

The playwright's first success, "The Hero," was produced just after the war, in 1921, first at special matinees and later, following a blast of critical approval, as a regular attraction. Richard Bennett played the chief role. The play told of an irresponsible lad who was a hero in the war but a good deal of a rotter at home and ran for ten weeks. "Tarnish" (1923) ran the better part of a season. Mr. Emery, working with the author, later made a dramatization of Amelie Rives' "Love in a Mist," which had a run of seventy-four performances, with Madge Kennedy and Sidney Blackmer playing the leads.

Mr. Gilbert attended the Oneonta Normal School and Amherst College and, using the other half of his name, Emery Pottle, had a novel, "Handicapped," and many short stories to his credit before he turned to the stage.

PATRICK KEARNEY

PATRICK KEARNEY (Delaware, Ohio, 1895) is another of the younger playwrights who made a promising start and ran into an open switch with a Hollywood terminus. His "A Man's Man" in 1925 was accepted as a forerunner of greater plays to come. His dramatization of Theodore Dreiser's "An American Tragedy" in 1926 seemed a confirmation of expectations, and when he made a play from Sinclair Lewis' "Elmer Gantry," the ways were cleared for him and his career. Little has happened, so far as Mr. Kearney and the living theatre are concerned, since then. "Elmer Gantry," produced in August, 1928, ran for six weeks with Edward Pawley in the name part. It introduced Elmer to the "religious racket" in Kansas, where he seduces the daughter of Deacon Bains. Moving eastward Elmer is saved again by the revivalist, Sharon Falconer. Sharon and her Atlantic City tabernacle are destroyed by fire and Elmer moves on to undertake the purification of Zenith.

In 1931 Mr. Kearney worked with Harry Wagstaffe Gribble on an Irish comedy, "Old Man Murphy," which got a four-week run. He is a 1915 graduate of Ohio State University, was a newspaper reporter and magazine story contributor in New York for many years and has been fussing with the films since 1917.

JANE COWL

PLAYWRITING has been a sort of interesting side line for Jane Cowl. She has not done a great deal of it, but what she has done has attracted attention—enough attention, at least, to force her out of the anonymity she at first tried to protect with pen names, or by giving her collaborators all the credit. With Jane Murfin she wrote "Lilac Time," one of the first of the war plays, in 1916. It told of the French girl who was loved and left by the handsome English officer. With Miss Murfin again she wrote "Daybreak," in 1917. This was an emotional drama about an unhappy wife who sought to conceal her motherhood from a beast of a husband. The same collaborators wrote a third play in 1919 called "Smilin' Through," and this proved their greatest popular success. It was a story of spirit guidance which brought heaven pretty close to a lot of people who had suffered losses in the Great War.

Miss Cowl and Miss Murfin produced a fourth opus called "Information, Please," with which the then new Selwyn Theatre was opened in 1918. In this Miss Cowl played the flighty wife of a British member of parliament who conducted a sort of fake elopement from England to America. She got on the boat with the man, but locked herself in her stateroom. When they arrived in America she shooed him into a men's club and was shortly reconciled with her pursuing husband. There was a ten-year lapse then during which Miss Cowl devoted herself to her stage career. In 1929 she helped Theodore Charles with a dream play about an unhappy Pierrot and Columbine. And in 1935 she wrote a play with Reginald Lawrence called "Hervey House" which has had a London hearing but has not been seen in America.

Miss Cowl is a Boston girl by birth, but she has spent most of her life in New York. She went to school in Brooklyn, and later to the Columbia University. She began her stage career with David Belasco and achieved her first starring triumph in 1912 when she played the heroine of "Within the Law." Since then she has played many parts and is still a country-wide favorite.

JOHN GOLDEN

JOHN GOLDEN has been fairly secretive about his activities as a playwright. He has worked on many scripts and with dozens of authors, but has been entirely satisfied to permit the man or woman who first submitted to him the idea for a play to have the credit for whatever happened to the idea after it had been put into work at the Golden play factory.

On one or two scripts, however, the authors themselves have insisted on sharing the credit or dividing the blame. Thus, with Kenyon Nicholson Mr. Golden wrote the comedy called "Eva the Fifth," which had a run of sixty-three performances in 1928. He wrote "After Tomorrow" with Hugh Stangé, and this comedy ran for seventy-seven performances in 1931. It is not written in the record that the producer was also co-author of a comedy Dan Jarrett wrote called "Salt Water," which Frank Craven played for eighty-three performances in 1929, but it so stands in the Golden files. He also was part author of "A Divine Drudge," written with Vicki Baum and produced in 1933.

It is rather as a writer of lyrics, however, and of musical comedy librettos that the Golden record bulks largest in American theatre history. He was writing songs for the late Marie Dressler as far back as her Koster and Bial days, and did the book for her first Broadway play, a piece called "Miss Print." He was responsible for the book and lyrics of several of the Hippodrome's biggest productions in the early nineteen hundreds. Song hits that included "Poor Butterfly" and "Good-by Girls, I'm Through" were among his earlier contributions to the nation's joy. He was also the author of a comic song famous in its day called "I Can Dance with Everybody but My Wife," sung for a season or two by the then popular comedian, Joseph Cawthorne.

Mr. Golden was born in New York City in 1874. Much of his youth was spent in Wauseon, Ohio, where the parental Joseph Golden was in business, and also in the local band as a clarinet player, and the maternal Amelia Tyreler Golden sang in the village choir. His return to New York as a young man was followed by a course of study at the New York University and jobs in Poole's Theatre and Niblo's Garden.

The Golden career as a producer began when he and the late Winchell Smith produced "Turn to the Right," which was an immediate and long-lasting success. There followed a succession of other hits, including "Lightnin'," "The First Year," "Seventh Heaven" and the like, building a considerable fortune for the producer.

JOHN B. HYMER

JOHN B. HYMER (Bowling Green, Ky., 1873) had a run of luck and activity as a dramatist during and after the World War. He had long been associated with vaudeville bills and had written innumerable sketches when he produced a piece called "Petticoats" in 1915, and another on which he collaborated with Mabel Pierpont in 1918 called "Realization." His first hit was earned in collaboration with the late Samuel Shipman and was the long-running "East Is West" (1918), followed by three written with LeRoy Clemens, "Aloma" (1925), "The Deacon" (1925) and "Weeds" (1925). With Shipman he wrote "Crime" (1927), "Fast Life" (1928), and "Scarlet Pages" (1929). His last three plays have been "Zoom" (1932), with W. E. Barry, "Happy Landing" (1932), also with Barry, and "The Lady Detained" (1935), with Shipman. Since then Mr. Hymer has been working in Hollywood where his son, Warren Hymer, is active in pictures.

WALTER FERRIS

INSTRUCTOR in English at Yale from 1911 to 1917 and headmaster at Roxbury School from 1917 to 1924, Walter Ferris obviously started out to make education his vocation. His early playwriting was an avocation. He writes that he "knew little of the theatre until my first conversion in 1924 or 1925; my second and complete conversion when I married Violet Kemble Cooper in 1929." His best known achievement was "Death Takes a Holiday" adapted from an Italian comedy by Alberto Cassella. The original version, a robust and fairly rollicking comedy was turned over to Mr. Ferris for revision and the play straightway began to assume a new form and character. The Professional Players Group presented it in Washington, Pittsburgh and Philadelphia and later, December of 1929, to be exact, it was produced in New York. The reception was friendly but not enthusiastic. However, interest steadily increased until the fantastic drama had been presented 180 times. Prior to this success Mr. Ferris had had two plays produced in New York: "The First Stone," based on Mary Heaton Vorse's story with a Cape Cod setting, and included in Eva Le Gallienne's repertory at the Civic Theatre in January, 1928, and "Judas," written with Basil Rathbone and produced at the Longacre by Dwight Deere Wiman and the late William A. Brady, Jr. Mr. Ferris was born in Green Bay, Wisconsin, and educated at Beloit College and Yale Graduate School. He has been active in Hollywood.

HARRY WAGSTAFF GRIBBLE

HARRY WAGSTAFF GRIBBLE is one who, as playwright, helps others with their plays more frequently than he helps himself. He has specialized in direction for a number of seasons. This has served to keep him in New York and probably accounts for the infrequent mention of him as a Hollywood possibility. His first claim to theatre fame was his writing of the comedy "March Hares" in 1921. There followed a long series of musical comedy and revue librettos, a drama, "Stella Dallas," with Gertrude Purcell; a farce, "Oh, Mama," with Wilton Lackaye; a piece called "Mister Romeo," written with W. A. Mannheimer, and a stirring religious drama, "Revolt."

Of recent seasons Mr. Gribble has been no less busy. In 1930 he made a modern version of "The Earl of Essex," basing his text on an older play John Banks wrote in 1682, as well as two 18th century versions. The season of 1930-31 he collaborated with Patrick Kearney on the comedy, "Old Man Murphy," and made an adaptation of the musical play, "Meet My Sister," which, with Bettina Hall and Walter Slezak singing the leads, ran for 167 performances. With Shirley Warde and Vivian Crosby he wrote a mystery play, "Trick for Trick," in 1932 and "The Perfumed Lady," a farce, in 1934. Last season he did some work on "Virginia" at the Rockefeller Center Theatre.

Gribble is an Englishman, born in Kent, but he has been long in America. His schools included Emmanuel College and Cambridge University. He had some thought of being an organist when a boy. It was, however, a clerkship he gave up for the theatre.

AND OTHERS

WHILE most of those playwrights of achievement and promise whose records were included in the first volume of "American Playwrights of Today" have maintained some contact with the living theatre in recent years, there are many who have gone to Hollywood and have not returned.

These would include James Gleason (born New York, 1886) whose comedies, "The Fall Guy" (with George Abbott), "Is Zat So?" (with Richard Taber) and "The Shannons of Broadway" were popular in the middle nineteen twenties; William Hurlbut (Belvidere, Ill., 1883), whose early plays included "The Fighting Hope" (1908) for Blanche Bates and "The Writing on the Wall" (1909) for Olga Nethersole, and whose "The Bride of the Lamb" (1926) was one of Alice Brady's last starring ventures in New York; Lewis Beach (Saginaw, Mich.), who started well with a one-acter called "The Clod," which the Washington Square Players did, and later scored a popular success with "The Goose Hangs High"; Maurine Watkins (Louisville, Ky., 1900) whose "Chicago" was a sensational Broadway success in 1926, and who, by the record has added but one play to it, an adaptation of Samuel Hopkins Adams' "Revelry," the alleged Harding exposure of 1927, which failed; Philip Bartholomae (Chicago, 1882), who, consistently enough, scored an overnight hit with a farce called "Over Night" (1912), and who wrote many plays the next several years, including "Little Miss Brown," "Very Good Eddie," etc., but never was quite able to duplicate his first success; Dr. Louis Anspacher (Paducah, Ky., 1879), who, after a notable success with "The Unchastened Woman" (1926), returned to magazine writing and lecturing; and Beulah Marie Dix (Kingston, Mass., 1876), who wrote many plays in the old days, achieved fame with "The Road to Yesterday," written in collabora-

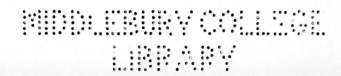

tion with Evelyn Greenleaf Sutherland, in 1906, came back to Broadway briefly with "Ragged Army," written with Bertram Millhauser in 1933, but who has been "intensively devoted to the art of the Cinema since the season of 1919-20."

THESE ALSO SERVE

There are thousands of entries and a large field in the annual Playwrights' Handicap. Some, if we continue the racetrack terminology, run but a single race and are withdrawn. Some are named for a second event, and not a few are left at the post. It would be impossible to name all these entries, but herein are contained the names and skeletonized records of those who have made a definite showing in this field.

SINCE NINETEEN HUNDRED AND NINETEEN

The appended list includes only those playwrights who have had two or more plays produced professionally since the season of 1919-20. Such omissions as may have occurred were due to accident or to a lack of co-operation on the part of uninterested contributors.

Adler, Hyman. Born Austria 1890; educated in Austria and Germany; came to New York aged 19; with Yiddish theatre until 1912. First play in English, co-authored by Philip Bartholomae, "The Open Book," later called "Neighbors" (1919); other plays "The Street Wolf" (1928) co-authored by Edward Paulton, "Challenge of Youth" (1930) with Ashley Miller, "Tomorrow's Harvest" (1934) with Hans Rastede, and "Lady Luck" (1936) with R. L. Hill.

Andrews, Charlton. Born Connersville, Ind., 1878; attended Indianapolis classical school; took a Ph.B. degree at De Pauw University; did newspaper work in Chicago and Indianapolis. Wrote "State Line," "His Majesty the Fool," and "The Torches"; decided to go commercial and wrote "Ladies Night"; after Avery Hopwood and A. H. Woods finished with its staging, it ran for forty-seven weeks in New York; done as a picture by Jack Mulhall and Dorothy Mackail; wrote "Bluebeard's Eighth Wife," "The Dollar Daddy," "Sam Abramovitch," "The Golden Age" (1928) written with Lester Lonergan and "Get Me in the Movies" (1928) with Philip Dunning. Adapted "Fioretta" in 1929.

Ballard, Fred (John Frederick). Born Grafton, Neb.; ancestors fought in the American Revolution; attended George Pierce Baker's classes at Harvard; won the John Craig prize with "Believe Me Xantippe," first produced in the Castle Square Theatre in Boston in 1912 and subsequently at the 39th Street Theatre in New York; John Barrymore, Katherine Harris, Henry Hull, in the principal parts; wrote "Ladies of the Jury," which A. L. Erlanger and George Tyler produced for Mrs. Fiske; other plays include "Young America" (1915) with Otto Kruger and Peggy Wood; "The Cyclone Lover" (1928), written with Charles A. Bickford, and "Henry's Harem" (1926).

Barry, William Edwin. Born Woonsocket, R. I., 1897; Irish parentage;

graduated from Fordham University. First play dramatization of "The Jade God" (1929), from a novel of the same name by Alan Sullivan; "Happy Landing" (1931), written with John B. Mayer, produced by the Shuberts.

Basshe, Em Jo. Born Russia 1900; left Russia at the age of eleven; educated in high school, Valparaiso, Columbia and Chicago Universities. First play "The Copy Cat's Holiday"; first production "The Bitter Fantasy." His "Doomsday Circus" produced in Germany, 1932, and at Orange Grove Theatre, Los Angeles, 1933; "Snickering Horses" and "John One Hundred," short plays, produced at the Civic Repertory and Daly's Theatre, New York, 1936.

Beahan, Charles. Born Clearfield, Pa., of Irish-German parents, 1904; educated at St. Francis Parochial School and Columbia University. "Jarnegan" (1928), dramatization of Jim Tully's novel, starring Richard Bennett, followed by "Buckaroo," written with A. W. and E. L. Barker; "Little Orchid Annie" (1930), with Hadley Waters; "Hold Your Horses," musical comedy by Russel Crouse and Corey Ford (1933), based on a play they had written with Mr. Beahan.

Bein, Albert. Born Kishineff, Rumania, 1903. Family settled in Chicago in 1905. First produced play "Little Ol' Boy" (1933); "Let Freedom Ring" (1935), based on Grace Lumpkin's novel "To Make My Bread," produced by the author and Jack Goldsmith, had a short run, was revived and continued for total of 108 performances; both plays caused spirited discussion. Mr. Bein has been granted a fellowship by the Guggenheim Foundation.

Bennett, Dorothy. Born Anderson, Indiana (English-Irish-French ancestry), 1906; finished public school in Detroit; studied playwriting in the New School of Social Research in New York City. In 1935 her first play (written with Irving White), "Fly Away Home," ran for two hundred performances. Miss Bennett is now in Hollywood.

Berkeley, Martin. Born Brooklyn, N. Y., 35 years ago; attended Dickinson College and Johns Hopkins; did some acting and was active in the Little Theatre movement. First play, "Obsession," produced at Ogunquit summer theatre; in 1936 D. A. Doran produced "Seen But Not Heard," written in collaboration with Marie Baumer; 1937 his "Roosty" had a week's run.

Black, Jean Ferguson. Born New York 1900. First play dramatization of Christopher Morley's "Thunder on the Left"; followed by "Penny Wise" (1937), with Kenneth MacKenna and Linda Watkins in cast.

Blankfort, Michael. Born New York 1907; went to University of Pennsylvania, after finishing high school at De Witt Clinton, New York;

took post-graduate course at Princeton; taught psychology at Bowdoin and Princeton. First play, "Sailors of Cattaro," an adaptation from the German of Friedrich Wolf, translated by Keene Wallis; produced at the Civic Repertory Theatre by the Theatre Union, Inc.; ran for several months in 1934. In 1936 his "Battle Hymn," written with Michael Gold, one of the widely discussed Federal Theatre productions; ran 72 performances at the Experimental Theatre; in 1937 Current Theatre Players presented his "The Brave and the Blind" at the Artef Theatre.

Bloch, Bertram. Born New York 1893; educated public schools and New York Law School; director of a Little Theatre in Washington just before the war. First production "Third Shot"; next "Glory Hallelujah," written with Thomas Mitchell; John Golden produced his "Joseph" (1929), starring George Jessel, George Kaufman directing; ran two weeks; "Jewel Robbery," translation from the Hungarian of Lazlo Fodor, produced by Paul Steger 1932; late in 1934 "Dark Victory," written in collaboration with George Brewer, produced at the Plymouth with Tallulah Bankhead the star; continued for 52 performances.

Bolton, Guy Reginald. Born England. First play, "The Drone," produced New York, 1911; Douglas Wood collaborator; has written and helped to write 50 plays and musical comedies, including "Hit-the-Trail Halliday," by Bolton and George Middleton; "Have a Heart" (with P. G. Wodehouse); "Adam and Eva," "The Light of the World," and "The Cave Girl" (with George Middleton), "Oh, Kay," "Rio Rita" (with Fred Thompson), "Rosalie" (with Wm. Anthony McGuire), "Polly" (with George Middleton), "Top Speed" (with Bert Kalmar and Harry Ruby), "Simple Simon" (with Ed Wynn), "Girl Crazy" (with John McGowan, Ira and George Gershwin), "Anything Goes," written with P. G. Wodehouse, revised by Howard Lindsay and Russel Crouse, Cole Porter providing music and lyrics; ran for four hundred performances.

Booth, John Hunter. Born New Orleans 1887. First production was "The Masquerader" in which Guy Bates Post appeared; other produced works have been "Keep Her Smiling," "Rolling Home," "The Hurricane," "No Trespassing," "The Winged Messenger," "Brass Buttons" and "Wolves." Has been in Hollywood since 1928.

Brentano, Lowell. Born New York City 1895; attended Friends Seminary, public schools of Orange, New Jersey, and Harvard, where was awarded his A.B. in 1918. First play "The Spider" (1927), (written with Fulton Oursler), produced by Sam H. Harris and Albert Lewis, ran 100 performances. "Zeppelin" (1928), written with Earle

Crooker and McElbert Moore; "Family Affairs" (with Earle Crooker); "Danger, Men Working" (1936), with Ellery Niden.

Brooks, George S. Born February, 1895, on a farm at Pearl Creek, New York; educated at Middlebury Academy, Salt Lake Collegiate Institute, Warsaw High School, the University of Rochester, and, while in the army, the University of Poitiers, France. Co-author of "Spread Eagle" with Walter Lister; of "Celebrity," with Willard Keefe, and of "The Whip Hand," with Marjorie Chase.

Brown, Martin (Meredith Gibson Brown); born Montreal, Canada, 1888. First play and production "A Very Good Young Man" (1918); other plays, "The Exciters," "The Love Child" (an adaptation), "The Lady," "Great Music," "Cobra," "The Dark," "The Strawberry Blonde," "Praying Curve" and "Paris." Wrote "The Idol" (1929); Elsie Ferguson played his "Amber" in San Francisco in 1933.

Brownell, John Charles. Born Burlington, Vermont, of Scotch mother and Yankee father sixty years ago. First play "The Nut Farm" (1929); "Brain Sweat" (1934), failed and was transformed from a Negro to an Irish play, renamed "The Impossible Mr. Clancy"; Federal Theatre did it as "Mississippi Rainbow" in original color; in 1935 two of his plays were produced: "Her Majesty the Widow" with Pauline Frederick and "A Woman of the Soil"; lives in Larchmont, N. Y.

Buchanan, Thompson. Born New York 1877. Educated in the public schools of Jamestown, Knoxville and Louisville, emerging as a reporter on the Louisville *Courier-Journal;* later drama critic on the Louisville *Herald;* also reporter on New York papers; lieutenant of Field Artillery during war. Before the war he had written a dozen plays; since that time his plays produced in New York have been "Civilian Clothes" (1919), "The Sporting Thing to Do" (1923), "Pride" (1923), "Bluffing Bluffers" (with John Meehan) (1924), "Sinner" (1927), "Star of Bengal" (1929), and "As Good as New" (1930).

Burns, Bernard K. Born Johnstown, New York, 1881. Educated Colgate Academy, Hamilton, New York; served in the Philippines in the regular army. First play "The Woman on the Jury"; wrote "Tread of Men."

Caesar, Arthur. Born in Rumania 1892; came to this country at an early age; educated New York public schools and at New York University. First play and production "Out of the Seven Seas"; others "Off Key," "The Maker of Images," "Madame Judas" and "When the Dead Get Gay."

Campbell, Lawton. Born Montgomery, Ala., 1896; graduated from Sidney Lanier High School, Montgomery, and Princeton, 1916. Wrote plays for High School, the Triangle Club of Princeton; first full length play to be produced a comedy called "Madam Melissa"; next "Immoral Isabelle," with Frances Starr, and "Solid South" with Richard Bennett (1930). Is vice-president of General Foods Corporation; ancestors include Robert Morris, signer of the Declaration of Independence, and Dr. Tisdale, Chief Surgeon on the U. S. Frigate *Constitution*.

Carb, David. Born Fort Worth, Texas, 1892; educated there and at Harvard. "The Voice of the People" his first production; among others "Immodest Violet," "A Very Proper Lady," "Face Value," "The First Lady," "The Kiss," "A Way with Women," "Queen Victoria" (with Walter Prichard Eaton), and "Long Ago Ladies" (Boston) 1934.

Carroll, Earl. Born Pittsburgh, Pa., 1892. Dramatic plays include "Lady of the Lamp" (1920), "Daddy Dumplins," with George Barr McCutcheon (1920), and "Bavu" (1922); has written book and lyrics for seven editions of Carroll Vanities; also for "Fioretta" (1929), adapted by Charlton Andrews; in 1933, with Rufus King, wrote a musical mystery play, "Murder at the Vanities."

Caspary, Vera. Born Chicago of Portuguese and German parentage 1903; educated in Chicago. First Broadway play "Blind Mice," written with Winifred Lenihan (1930); "Geraniums in My Window" (1934), written with Samuel Ornitz.

Chapin, Anne Morrison. Born Shoals, Indiana; educated high school and normal college. First play "The Wild Wescotts" (1923); first success "Pigs" (1924), (written with Patterson McNitt); wrote "Jonesy" (1929), with John Peter Toohey; "No Questions Asked" (1934).

Chodorov, Edward. Born New York City 1904. Educated at Erasmus Hall, Brooklyn, and Brown University. First play "Wonder Boy" (with Arthur Barton), produced in 1931; in Spring of 1935 Potter and Haight produced his "Kind Lady," a drama adapted from a Hugh Walpole story, with Grace George the star.

Clemens, Le Roy LaRue. Born Brooklyn, N. Y., 1889; attended Rock Ridge Hall School in Massachusetts; entered the theatre as an actor. Among plays and collaborations are "Watch Your Neighbor," "Love on Account," "Young Mr. Dudley," "After the Rain," "The Poppy God," "Aloma of the South Seas," "Alias the Deacon," "The World Loves a Winner"; first production "Watch Your Neighbor" with Leon Gordon; his first success "Aloma of the South Seas"; last Broadway play, "Cortez," written with Ralph Murphy.

Collison, Wilson. Born Glouster, Ohio, 1892. Has written many plays, including "Kitty Comes Home," "The Girl with Carmine Lips," "Up in Mabel's Room," "A Bachelor's Night," "The Girl in the Limousine," "Getting Gertie's Garter," "Red Dust," and worked with many collaborators.

Crump, John Gray. Born Eureka Springs, Arkansas, 1898. Educated at the Missouri Military Academy; student at the American Academy of Dramatic Art. Has had produced on Broadway "Hipper's Holiday" and "Don't Look Now."

Cullinan, Ralph. Born Ennis, County Clare, Ireland, 1887; came to America 1908; was a bar-tender when America went into the war; enlisted with Ninth Infantry, Second Division, regular army; twice wounded; turned to writing plays; first Broadway production "Loggerheads"; other plays "Magpies," "Black Waters," "You Can't Win"; collaborated in "The Banshee," "Terror," "The Winding Road" and "Caravan."

Cunningham, Leon Max. Born Leslie, Michigan, 1899; educated public schools and University of Michigan. Among his works "Mr. Mundy," "Courage, Camille," "Neighbors," "Sweetheart" and "Hospitality."

Cushing, Catherine Chisholm. Born Ohio; educated private schools Washington, D. C.; editor *Harper's Bazaar*. First play "Miss Ananias"; others include "The Real Thing," "Kitty MacKaye," "Jerry," "Widow by Proxy" (for May Irwin): "Pollyanna," "Lassie," "Glorianna," "Marjolaine," an adaptation of "Pomander Walk": "Topsy and Eva," (for the Duncan sisters): "Edgar Allan Poe," and "Master of the Inn," an adaptation.

Cushing, Tom. Born New Haven, Conn., 1879. Went to Westminster School, Simsbury and Yale University; graduated 1902. With Percy Heath wrote the English book and lyrics for the adaptation of "Sari," an operetta, which ran for a year; adapted "Blood and Sand" from an Ibañez novel for Otis Skinner; other plays "Thank You" (with Winchell Smith), "Laugh, Clown, Laugh!" (with David Belasco), adapted from the Italian of Faurto Martini; "The Devil in the Cheese" and "La Gringa." Working in Hollywood for several years.

Damrosch, Gretchen (Finletter). Born Augusta, Me., 1901. Daughter of Walter Damrosch, granddaughter of James G. Blaine. First play "The Runaway Road," produced in Chicago under the auspices of Mrs. Samuel Insull, 1926; other plays "The Life Line" (1930), "The Passing Present" (1931), "If and When" (1933), and "Picnic" (1934).

Davies, Valentine. Born New York City 1905; went to Horace Mann School, New York College and the University of Michigan; graduated 1927; studied with George P. Baker Yale Drama School. First play "Three Times the Hour" (1931), produced by Brock Pemberton; also a dramatization of a Charlie Chan story by Earl Derr Biggers, "Keeper of the Keys" (1933); Arthur Hopkins produced his "Blow Ye Winds"

(1937), with the screen idol, Henry Fonda, in the cast.

Davis, Irving Kaye. Born New York City 1900; attended public and high schools; produced plays "The Right to Dream," "Veils," "Diana," "Courtesan," "All Rights Reserved" and "So Many Paths."

De Costa, Leon Pablo. Born Barcelona, Spain, 1886; educated at the Royal College, Leipzig, the Academy of Music, Danzig, and the Royal Academy of Music, Berlin. First American work lyrics and music for "Fifty-fifty Ltd."; author of "Page Miss Venus," "Inn Mates," "Kosher Kitty Kelly" and "The Blonde Sinner."

Delf, Harry. Born New York City 1893. Educated in public schools, College of the City of New York and Columbia; appeared in vaudeville with his sister, Miss Juliet. His plays are "The Family Upstairs," "Atlas and Eva," "The Unsophisticates," and "She Lived Next to the Firehouse" (with William A. Grew). His most successful play was "The Family Upstairs," which ran two and a half months on Broadway, was played successfully in stock (one week in sixty theatres) and for 14 consecutive months in Australia; revived on Broadway in 1933.

Dorfman, Nat N. Born New York City 1894; educated Townsend Harris High School and Columbia University. Wrote "The International Revue" with Lew Leslie, 1930; also "Rhapsody in Black," 1931; author of "Take My Tip," "Errant Lady" and "Blackbirds of 1933."

Du Bois, William. Born St. Augustine, Florida, 1906; studied at the University of Florida and took a degree in the Columbia School of Journalism, 1925; for eight years on the New York *Times*. Plays produced on Broadway are "Pagan Lady" (1930), "I Loved You Wednesday" (written with Molly Ricardel) (1932), and "Haiti," drama about the Black Napoleon, produced by the WPA Federal Theatre in 1938.

Ellis, Edith. Born Coldwater, Mich., a region colonized by her maternal ancestors; her father, Edward C. Ellis and her mother, Ruth McCarthy, were of the stage; their daughter was a member of their company. In early nineties wrote "Mrs. B. O'Shaughnessy" for George Monroe; 1904 wrote and produced "The Point of View," "Man and His Mate," and "Mary Jane's Pa," in which both Henry Dixey and Max Figman starred. Has written some thirty plays including a dramatization of "Anna Karenina," "He Fell in Love with His Wife," "Seven Sisters," "The Man Higher Up," "The Devil's Garden," "Sonya," "White Collars," "The Love Thief," and "The Last Chapter," written with her brother Edward Ellis in 1930.

Entrikin, Knowles. Born Moline, Ill., 1891; educated Moline public schools and Beloit College; an authority on marionettes, having staged Tony Sarg shows. Plays include "The Small Timers," and "Seed of the Brute," produced in New York.

Ernst, Jessie. Born New York City 1893; educated Hunter College. First play "Storm Center" (1927), second, "The Red Cat" (1935), later made into a movie.

Erskin, Chester. Born Austria. Educated Hudson, N. Y.; abandoned law for the stage. Adapted Lazlo Fodor's "I Love an Actress" and Alfred Savior's "He," both produced in 1931; "The Puritan," he dramatized from Liam O'Flaherty's novel, and produced in January, 1936.

Eyre, Laurence. Born Chester, Pa., 1881; privately educated. Among his plays are "The Things That Count," his first success; "Driftwood," "Miss Nelly o' N'Orleans," "Martinique," "The Merry Wives of Gotham," "The Steam Roller," "Gala Night" and "Mayfair."

Fagan, Myron C. Graduate of Cornell University; began writing as reporter for Chicago *Tribune*. Plays include "Hawthorne U.S.A." (starring Douglas Fairbanks), "The Higher Law," "The White Rose" (starring Mrs. Leslie Carter), "The Little Spitfire," "Indiscretion," "Nancy's Private Affair," "Peter Flies High" and "Memory."

Flexner, Anne Crawford. Born Georgetown, Kentucky, 1874. Dramatization of Alice Hegan Rice's "Mrs. Wiggs of the Cabbage Patch" first play to attract attention; others were "A Lucky Star" (1910), dramatized from "The Motor Chaperon," a story by the Williamsons; "The Marriage Game" (1913), "The Blue Pearl" (1918), "All Soul's Eve" (1920), and "Aged 26" (a play about the poet Keats), which narrowly missed success in December, 1936.

Flint, Eva Kay. Born Russia 1902; to the United States in 1906; educated Brooklyn public schools; met Martha Madison and collaborated with her on four plays; their fifth, "Subway Express," ran through the season of 1929-30; "The Up and Up" (1930), and "Under Glass" (1933), she wrote with George Bradshaw.

Flournoy, Richard F. Born Pine Bluff, Arkansas, 1901. First play "Fly By Night," which did, the third night; Hal Skelly produced the next one, "Come What May," in 1934; later the same year Courtney Burr produced his "Ladies' Money."

Ford, Harriet French. Born Seymour, Conn., 1878. Drawn to stage early; studied with David Belasco at American Academy of Dramatic Art; an actress for six years. First play "The Greatest Thing in the World" (1900), written with Beatrice de Mille, produced successfully with Sarah Cowell LeMoyne as star; dramatization of "A Gentleman of France" for Kyrle Bellew and Eleanor Robson, and another of "Audrey" for Miss Robson followed; helped Joseph Medill Patterson with "The Little Brother of the Rich" and "The Fourth Estate," first of modern newspaper plays; with the late Harvey O'Higgins wrote "The

Argyle Case," "The Dummy," "Polygamy," "The Dickey Bird," "Mr. Lazarus," "On the Hiring Line," "Main Street," a dramatization of the Sinclair Lewis novel, and "Sweet Seventeen"; wrote "In the Next Room" (1923), with Eleanor Robson Belmont; "Christopher Rand" (1929), most recent opus.

Forrest, Sam. Born Richmond, Virginia, 1871. First play "Word of Honor." Others included "Paid" produced in Boston, "Sigh XYZ" in Chicago, "Redlight Annie" (with Norman Houston), "Thoroughbreds" (with Lewis B. Ely) and "The O'Neil Woman" written with his wife, Mary Ryan; associated with Sam H. Harris and George M. Cohan for a quarter of a century. "I think we have more fine minds writing plays than at any time in my life time in the theatre covering a period of 47 years," declares Mr. Forrest. "The danger to these fine minds is Hollywood."

Fox, Paul Hervey. Wrote "Soldiers of Fortune" with George Tilton; "The Great Man," "Foreign Affairs" (1932), (with George Tilton), and "If I Were You" (1938), with Benn Levy.

Franklin, Pearl (Mrs. Wallace Clark). Born Bedford, Iowa, 1888. Attended Lewis Institute and George Pierce Baker's class at Radcliffe. First play "Young America," with Fred Ballard; other plays "Thunder," with Elia Peattie (also known as "Howdy, Folks"), "Following Father" and "Cowboy Crazy" (with George Abbott).

George, Grace. Born New York 1879. Educated at Notre Dame Convent, N. J.; was student at American Academy of Dramatic Art; internationally known as an actress. Her plays include "The Nest," adapted from "Les Noces d'Argent"; "To Love," adapted from "Aimer"; "She Had to Know," "Domino," "Mademoiselle" and "Matrimony Pfd," all adaptations from the French; last written in collaboration with James Forbes.

Gilbert, Edwin L. Born 28 years ago in New York; attended Universities of Michigan and Florida; wrote "This Thing Success" (1930), prize winner in a Miami Little Theatre Tournament; wrote "The Golden Journey," which opened in Boston as "Days of Grace" (1936).

Gold, Michael. Born New York City 1895, of Rumanian-Hungarian parents; special courses at New York University and Harvard. First play "Money" a one-acter presented at the Provincetown Theatre in 1920; "Hoboken Blues" (1928), produced at the New Playwrights Theatre; "Fiesta" (1929), produced by Experimental Theatre, Inc.; "Battle Hymn" (1936), written with Michael Blankfort, produced by WPA Federal Theatre, had 72 performances.

Golden, I. J. Born New York; law course at the New York University;

practiced in St. Louis; studied Mooney-Billings case and wrote "Precedent" (1931), which had a run of 184 performances; also played in San Francisco and Los Angeles; "Re-Echo" (1934), produced in New York.

Golding, Samuel Ruskin. Born Ozery, Russia, 1891; brought to Rhode Island at the age of ten months; educated at Brown University and New York Law School. First play a dramatization of "The Silver Horde," Rex Beach's novel; other plays "Open House," "Pyramids," "The Black Cockatoo," "New York," and "Divorce A La Carte"; co-author of "The Bronx Express," "The Unknown Woman," and "Through the Night"; "Puppet Show" and "On Location" (1937).

Goodhue, Willis Maxwell. Born Akron, Ohio, April, 1880; first play "A Battle Scarred Hero," afterward known as "Hello, Bill"; other plays include "Dust," "Myrtie," "All Wet," "Head First," "Katy Did," "Oh, Johnny," "Mr. Betty," "Love 'Em All"; produced on the West Coast, "Pop Goes the Weasel" and "Chickens Come Home." Went Hollywood in 1932.

Gordon, Kilbourn. Born Washington, D. C., 1890. A drama reviewer in that city, later actor, manager and press agent. Co-author "Enemies Within," "The Man Outside" and "Big Game"; co-author, with the late Chester DeVonde, of "Kongo" and "Tia Juana"; with Willard Robertson of "The Proper Spirit" and "Open All Night"; with Arthur Caesar of "Out of the Seven Seas."

Gordon, Leon. Born Sussex, England, 1894; comes from a theatrical family long associated with Drury Lane Theatre, London; was educated at St. John's, England, and Cherbourg University, France. First plays, "The Gentleman Ranker" (1912), "Drummed Out" and "Leave the Woman Out" (1913), were produced in England; in 1918 appeared in New York in "Watch Your Neighbor," which he had written with Le Roy Clemens; plays in which he has had a writing part include "White Cargo," "The Man Upstairs," "Garden of Weeds," "The Piker," and "Undesirable Lady" (1933).

Grew, William. Born Philadelphia 1887. Early plays include "The Sap," "The Mating Season," "The Smart Alec," "My Girl Friday," "Nice Women," "Jerry-for-Short," and "She Lived Next to the Firehouse" (with Harry Delf), have been produced in the past decade.

Gropper, Milton Herbert. Born New York 1897. Attended Erasmus Hall High School and Columbia University. Work includes "Gypsy Jim" and "New Toys," both with Oscar Hammerstein II, "Ladies of the Evening," "We Americans," "Mirrors," "The Big Fight" (with Max Marcin), "Inspector Kennedy" (with Edna Sherry), "Bulls, Bears and

Asses" and "Sing and Whistle" (for Ernie Truex).

Gross, Laurence. Born Evansville, Indiana, 47 years ago; graduate Evansville High School. First play "The Conquering Male," produced by Arch Selwyn with Ernest Lawford and Madge Evans in the cast; first success, "Whistling in the Dark," which ran for 265 performances in 1932.

Gross, Stephen Gage. Born Oakland, California; educated at Columbia, University of California and Cambridge; worked in radio. First effort as a playwright revision of a play called "Bottled." "The Hook-Up," written with Jack Lait, followed in 1935. "One Good Year," written with Lin S. Root, lasted 215 performances. Thence to Hollywood.

Harbach, Otto Abels. Born Salt Lake City 1873. Attended Knox College and Columbia University. First work to be produced "Three Twins"; among his books and adaptations have been "Madame Sherry," "The Wall Street Girl," "The Firefly," "High Jinks," "Katinka," "Going Up," "The O'Brien Girl," "Kid Boots," "No, No, Nanette," "Rose-Marie," "Golden Dawn," "Nina Rosa," "The Cat and the Fiddle," "Roberta," adapted from a novel by Alice Duer Miller, and "Forbidden Melody." Many long runs included with scores by Jerome Kern, Sigmund Romberg and Rudolf Friml.

Hargrave, Roy. Born New York City, July 16, 1908. Educated Barnard School for boys, Cutler, Mackenzie, and briefly, Williams College. First play "Houseparty," written with Kenneth Phillips Britton; with Ruth Welty wrote "With Privileges" (1930), and "A Room in Red and White" (1936), with Laura Adair and Thomas Schofield.

Harris, Elmer Blaney. Started writing plays back in 1908 with "The Offenders;" wrote "The Great Necker," "Stepping Out," "Young Sinners," "Ladies All" (with Prince Bibesco), "A Modern Virgin" and "Marriage for Three."

Hobart, Doty. Born September 29, 1886, in Brattleboro, Vermont. At 28 began writing scenarios; after the war gave 14 years to pictures both in New York and Hollywood, with more than 200 scripts to his credit. First play "Sadie" (1927), produced in Philadelphia; New York productions "Thoroughbred" (1933), "Every Thursday" (1934), "Double Dummy" (1936).

Housum, Robert. Born Cleveland, Ohio, 1887. Graduated from Yale in 1908 and took his M.A. degree in 1911. First play "In Glass Houses," written in collaboration with Charles Hopkins; others include "Sylvia Runs Away," "Winding Stairs," "Persons Unknown," and "Maid Errant"; his first success, "The Gypsy Trail."

Jackson, Fred. Took kindly to the writing of farce in 1915, producing

"A Full House." Followed with "The Naughty Wife," "La, La Lucille," "The Hole in the Wall," "Two Little Girls in Blue," and "Cold Feet" (with Pierre Gendron). "Wife Insurance" was produced at the Ethel Barrymore Theatre in 1934 but was a quick failure. "The Bishop Misbehaves" (1935), produced by John Golden, ran for several months. Mr. Jackson has interrupted his Hollywood work with summer stock productions.

Kallesser, Michael. Born Freeland, Pa., 1889. First play was "The Ingrate" produced on the road with Lillian Foster; has had New York productions of "One Man's Woman," "Trial Marriage," "Marriage on Approval," "He Understood Women" (written with Frances Lynch) and "Rockbound" with Amy Wales as collaborator.

Kaye, Benjamin M. Born New York City 54 years ago. Went to Horace Mann High School and Columbia College as holder of a Pulitzer Scholarship; received his A.B.; added an LL.B. at Columbia Law School. First play "She Couldn't Say No" (1926); ran nine weeks; "I Want My Wife" (1926), "The Curtain Rises" (1926), and "On Stage" (1935), produced by Laurence Rivers, Inc., with the late Osgood Perkins and Selena Royle in the cast.

Keefe, Willard. Born Morton, Minn., March 7, 1898; "fruit of the Irish-American homesteaders of the Sixties." First play, written with George S. Brooks, "Celebrity"; Edward J. Foran collaborated with him on "Privilege Car" (1931).

Kennedy, Aubrey. Born Winnipeg, Canada, 1888; educated Winnipeg schools and St. Mary's College, Dayton, Ohio; written or collaborated upon "Seeing Things," "Loving Ladies" and "Behold This Dreamer"; "Nude with Pineapple" (1936), by Mr. Kennedy and Fulton Oursler, produced at Pasadena Community Theatre.

Kennedy, Charles Rann. Born Derby, England, 1871. Educated Saltley College School, Saltley, Warwickshire, England. Best known for "The Servant in the House"; other plays include "The Winterfeast," "The Idol-Breaker," "The Terrible Meek," and "The Chastening"; appeared in several of these with his wife, Edith Wynne Matthison with whom he conducts the drama department of the Bennett Junior College at Millbrook, New York. Recent "Crumbs" (1931), "Flaming Ministers" (1932), "Face of God," and "Beggar's Gift" (1935), none of which has appeared in New York.

Kennedy, Mary. Born in Claxton, Georgia; educated public schools and convents in Jacksonville, Fla., and at St. Mary's in Augusta, Ga. First production "Mrs. Partridge Presents" (1925), written with Ruth Hawthorne; co-author "Captain Fury," which Otis Skinner tried out.

Author of "Jordan" and "Question the Night," a novel (1938).

King, Rufus. Born Rouses Point, New York, 44 years ago; educated Cutler Military Academy and Yale University; wrote "Murder at the Vanities" (1934), with Earl Carroll; "Invitation to a Murder" (1935), and "I Want a Policeman" (1936), with Milton Lazarus.

Kirkpatrick, John. Born Montgomery, Alabama, 1896; educated Montgomery schools and University of Alabama. First success "The Book of Charm" (1925), later shortened to "Charm," produced by Rachel Crothers at the Comedy in 1925; wrote "The Love Expert" (1929), and "Ada Beats the Drum" (1930).

Kling, Saxon. Born Paulding, Ohio, 41 years ago; graduated from Ohio State University and the American Academy of Dramatic Art. First play "Crashing Through" (1928); wrote "Tomorrow" (1928), with Hull Gould; "The Lady Refuses" (1933), and "Room Without Walls," which Charles Hopkins tried out at Huntington, L. I.

Knoblock, Edward. Born New York 1874; educated at Harvard. First play "The Club Baby"; attracted attention with "The Shulamite" (1906); did a translation of "Sister Beatrice" (1910); wrote "The Faun," "Kismet" and "Milestones" (with Arnold Bennett); "My Lady's Dress," "Marie Odile," "Paginini" (for George Arliss); "Tiger! Tiger!" (for Frances Starr); "The Lullaby" (Florence Reed); "Simon Called Peter" (with Jules Eckert Goodman); "Speak Easy" (with George Rosener); "The Mulberry Bush"; helped J. B. Priestley adapt "The Good Companions" (1931); "Evensong" (1933), and "If a Body" (1935), (with George Rosener).

Koch, Howard. Born Central Park West, New York City; received A.B. at Bard College and LL.B. at Columbia University. First play "Great Scott"; wrote "Give Us This Day" (1933).

Krasna, Norman. Born Long Island, New York, 1909. Attended New York University and Brooklyn Law School. First play "Louder Please" (1931); wrote "Small Miracle" (1934), which ran for 117 performances. Thence to Hollywood.

Kummer, Frederic Arnold. Born Catonsville, Md., near Baltimore, 1873; educated Baltimore Schools, Baltimore City College and Rensselaer Polytechnic. First play "Mr. Buttles" (1907); other plays "The Other Woman," "The Brute," "The Painted Woman," "The Magic Melody" (with Sigmund Romberg): "My Golden Girl" (with Victor Herbert): "The Bonehead," "The Voice," "Julie" and a play with music by Harry Tierney, "Song of Omar" (1935).

Kusell, Daniel. Born Virginia, Ill., 1894. First play "The Gingham Girl" (1922); dramatized "The River's End" (1924); collaborated with James

P. Judge on "Square Crooks" (1926), which ran for 150 performances; adapted "Piggy" (with Alfred Jackson) from "The Rich Mr. Hoggenheimer"; wrote the book for "Cross My Heart," and "The Party's Over" (1933).

Le Baron, William. Born Elgin, Ill., 1884; educated University of Chicago and New York University; wrote annual college show with Deems Taylor; also "The Echo" (1910), "The Very Idea," first play; others "Back to Earth," "Nobody's Money," "The Scarlet Woman," "I Love You"; wrote "Her Regiment" (with Victor Herbert): "Apple Blossoms" (with Fritz Kreisler and Victor Jacobi): "The Love Letter" and "The Half Moon" (with Victor Jacobi); has been in Hollywood for some time; director of Cosmopolitan Film Productions, supervisor for Famous Players, vice president Film Booking Studios, and vice president Radio Picture Corporation.

Lauren, Samuel K. Graduated from University of Chicago; did some tinkering on "Coquette"; wrote "Those We Love" (1930), and "Men Must Fight" (1932), with Reginald Lawrence.

Lawrence, Reginald. Comes from New Jersey, was educated at Princeton. First Broadway play "Men Must Fight" (1932), with Samuel K. Lauren; collaborated with John Haynes Holmes on "If This Be Treason" (1935), produced by the Theatre Guild.

Lazarus, Milton. Born Boston, Mass., 1898. First play "American Plan" (1933), with Manuel Seff; wrote "Whatever Goes Up" (1935), "I Want a Policeman" (1935), with Rufus King.

Lester, Elliott. Born Hoboken, N. J., 1893. Educated University of Pennsylvania, elected to Phi Beta Kappa; taught English literature in Philadelphia. Plays include "The Mud Turtle," "Take My Advice," "The Medicine Man" and "Two Seconds." Then to Hollywood.

Levy, Melvin. Wrote "Gold Eagle Guy" (1934); produced by the Group Theater; wrote "A House in the Country" (1937).

Linder, Mark. Born New York City. Converted his vaudeville sketch, "The Frame-Up," into full length play, "Chatham Square"; Mae West liked the idea but not the play which she rewrote as "Diamond Lil" (1928); got 176 performances; wrote "The Squealer," and had a hand in "Room 349," "The Honor Code," "Triplets" and "Summer Wives" (1936).

Lipman, Clara (Mrs. Louis Mann). Born Chicago, Ill. Wrote "Julie Bon Bon," played in it with Louis Mann; wrote "The Lady from Westchester," "His Protégé," "The Temperamental Girl," "Billy with a Punch"; with Samuel Shipman wrote "Elevating a Husband," "It Depends on the Woman," "Children of Today," and "The Head of the

House."

Locke, Edward. Born England 1869; settled in America 1882. First successful play "The Climax"; wrote "The Case of Becky," "The Land of the Free," "The Dancer" (with Louis Anspacher and Max Marcin), "The Woman Who Laughed," "Mike Angelo," for Leo Carillo, the book for "The Love Call," "57 Bowery" and "The Studio Girl."

Madison, Martha. Born New York City; studied at American Academy of Dramatic Arts. Wrote "Subway Express" (1929), (270 performances), and "The Up and Up" (1930), with Eva Kay Flint; "The Night Remembers" (1934), by herself.

Maibaum, Richard. Born New York City 1909. Graduated from New York University and the University of Ohio with the privilege of adding B.A., M.A. and Phi Beta Kappa to his name. Wrote "The Tree" (1932), "Birthright" (1933); with Michael Wallach and George Haight wrote "Sweet Mystery of Life" (1935). Then Hollywood.

Maltz, Albert. Born Brooklyn, N. Y., 1908. Educated at Columbia University and Yale School of Drama; ancestry Lithuanian and Polish. Wrote "Merry-Go-Round" (1932) and "Peace on Earth" (1933), with George Sklar; "Black Pit" (1935) and "Private Hicks" (1936). "Peace on Earth" ran for 144 performances.

Mandel, Frank. Born San Francisco 1884; graduated from University of California. First play "Our Wives" (1912), written with Helen Kraft; others included "The High Cost of Living," adapted from the German; "Sherman Was Right" (1916); "The Sky Pilot" (1918); "The Five Million" with Guy Bolton (1919); "My Lady Friends" with Emil Nyitray (1919). Began to write musical comedies with Oscar Hammerstein and Otto Harbach; "Jimmie" (1920); "Mary" (1920); "The O'Brien Girl" (1921); "Queen of Hearts." Back to straight comedy with Guy Bolton with "Nobody's Business" (1923) and a farce called "The Lady Killer" written with his wife Alice Mandel (1923). "No, No, Nanette" with Otto Harbach, ran a year in Chicago and for 321 performances in New York; has written "The Desert Song" with Hammerstein (1926), "The New Moon" with Lawrence Schwab and Hammerstein (1927), and "Follow Through" with Schwab (1929). "May Wine," adapted from "The Happy Alienist" by Eric von Stroheim and Wallace Smith, music by Sigmund Romberg, ran for 213 performances in 1935-36.

Mannheimer, Wallace. Born New York City 1887. Received B.S. at College of the City of New York and A.M. and Ph.D. at Columbia University. In 1932, with Isaac Paul, he wrote "Broadway Boy." Prior to this he had written "Mister Romeo" (1927), with Harry Gribble.

Mankiewicz, Herman J. Born New York 1898. Educated Harry Hillman Academy, Wilkes-Barre, Pa., and Columbia University. First play and production, "The Good Fellow" (with George S. Kaufman): also "The Wild Man of Borneo" (with Marc Connelly) and "We, the People" (not, however, to be confused with play of same title produced by Elmer Rice in 1933). Been in Hollywood where writing dialogue for some time.

Marks, Maurice. Born New York; graduate College City of New York. First play "A Muddled Model"; wrote "Double Harness" (with Edward A. Paulton); wrote lyrics for "Bringing Up Father" (1913) and "Rain or Shine" (1928), (with James Gleason).

Marlow, Brian. With Herman Bernstein adapted "The Command to Love" (1927) from a comedy by Rudolph Lothar and Fritz Gottwald; ran for 247 performances; adapted "Napi" (1931) from the German of Julius Berstl; wrote "Good Men and True" (1935), with Frank Merlin.

Matthews, Adelaide. Born Kenduskeag, Me., 1886. Wrote "Hearts Desire" and "Just Married" with Anne Nichols, who later wrote "Abie's Irish Rose"; wrote "Nightie Night," "Scrambled Wives," "The Teaser," "Puppy Love" and "The Wasp's Nest" with Martha Stanley.

Mayo, Margaret. Born Illinois; educated Stanford University, California; actress until 1903; adapted "Under Two Flags," "The Jungle" and "The Marriage of William Ashe" from the novels bearing the same titles; wrote "The Winding Way," "Polly of the Circus," "Baby Mine," "Twin Beds" (with Salisbury Field), and "His Bridal Night"; "Seeing Things" and "Loving Ladies" with Aubrey Kennedy.

McCormick, Arthur Langdon. Born Port Huron, Mich.; educated at Albion College; wrote melodramas for his own use, including "The Western Girl" and "Money and the Woman"; attracted attention with "Out of the Fold" and "Wanted by the Police"; specialized in startling scenic effects, a fire scene in "When the World Sleeps," a forest fire in "The Storm," a wreck in "Shipwrecked."

McGowan, John Wesley. Born Muskegon, Mich., 1894. First play "A Well Kept Man"; first production "Mama Loves Papa"; others "Tenth Avenue," "Excess Baggage," and "Middle West"; co-author of "Hold Everything" (1928), "Heads Up" (1929), "Flying High" (1930), "Girl Crazy" (1930), "Singin' the Blues" (1931), and "Heigh-Ho Everybody" (1932); "Nigger Rich" (1929), last straight comedy.

McGuire, William Anthony. Born Chicago 1889. Educated Notre Dame, Ind. "The Heights" first New York production, followed by "Six Cylinder Love," "Everyman's Castle," "It's a Boy," "Kid Boots," "12

Miles Out," "If I Was Rich," "Rosalie" and "Three Musketeers"; his "Divorce" ran for nearly a season in Chicago; "Whoopee" ran for a year in New York; "Smiles" (1930), and then to Hollywood.

McOwen, Bernard J. First play "The Uninvited Guest" (1927); "The Skull" (1928), (written with Harry E. Humphrey) and "The Blue Ghost" (1930), (with J. P. Riewerts); "The Scorpion" (1933) and "Slightly Delirious" (1934), (with R. Adkins).

Mearson, Lyon. Born Montreal, Canada, 1889. Came to New York City at the age of four and attended New York University. Has had two plays produced on Broadway: "People Don't Do Such Things" (1927), written with Edgar M. Schoenberg, and "Our Wife" (1933) with Lillian Day.

Merlin, Frank. Born Cork, Ireland, 1893; to America in 1910. First three produced plays were "And Then What" (1924), "The Brown Derby" (1925), (a musical comedy), and "The New Gallantry" (1925), all written in collaboration with Brian Marlow; others "The King Can Do No Wrong" (1927), "Triple Crossed" (1927), and "Hobo" (1931); "Good Men and True" (1935), also with Brian Marlow.

Middlemass, Robert Middlemass. Born New Britain, Conn., of Scotch-English parentage, 1886. Educated Harvard, where he obtained his A.B. and studied with George Pierce Baker. Broadway productions include "Americans All" (1926), "The Clutching Claw" (1928), and "The Budget" (1932); wrote a one-acter called "Valiant" (1920), produced first by The Lambs, which has since been played 5,000 times in vaudeville (several years by Bert Lytell), in Little Theatres and by schools and colleges; made by Paul Muni into one of the first talkies and also heard on the radio. Mr. Middlemass is now in Hollywood.

Miele, Elizabeth. Born New Jersey 1900, Italian parentage; attended New York University Law School, passed the bar examinations. First play "City Haul" (1929); wrote "Did I Say No" (1931).

Moore, McElbert. Born Boston 1895; educated Mass. Agricultural College and Harvard. First play "The Petulant Princess"; others "Hanky Panky Land," "Spice of 1922," "Hello, Everybody," "Plain Jane," "Innocent Eyes," "The Matinee Girl," "A Night in Paris" and "Happy," all musical; last play on Broadway was "Zeppelin," written with Earle Crooker and Lowell Brentano; written many plays for amateurs, published by Samuel French.

Murphy, Ralph. Was graduated from Syracuse University with the idea that he would practice law; wrote four musical plays in college; tried acting, stage managing and directing with companies in Baltimore, Syracuse, Washington, San Francisco and Rochester; wrote "Sure

Fire" in 1926, "Sh, the Octopus" (with Donald Gallaher) in 1928, "Cortez" (with Le Roy Clemens) in 1929 and "Black Tower" (with Lora Baxter) in 1932, the last a melodrama based on a short story, "The Wine of Anubis" by Crittenden Marriott.

Nichols, Anne. Started writing plays just after the Great War; in collaboration with Adelaide Matthews wrote "Hearts Desire" and "Just Married" (1921); wrote "Abie's Irish Rose" (1922), which started on a baffling and amazing career; ran continuously for 2,532 performances until 1927; said to hold the record for the longest consecutive run of all time; "Pre-Honeymoon" (1936), written with Alford van Ronkel, got 52 performances.

North, Clyde. Born Indianapolis, Ind., 1889, with the "smell of grease paint" in his nostrils; played kid parts with Nance O'Neill and McKee Rankin; in cast of "The Deluge"; a musical play, "Yours Truly," written with Anne Caldwell, was his first; got 129 performances; "Remote Control" (with Albert C. Fuller and Jack Nelson) next; "In Times Square" written with Dodson Mitchell and "All Editions," with Charles Washburn, followed. Mr. North says his first success was "The Curse of Gold," a travesty on melodrama, produced at a Lamb's Gambol in 1922. Ziegfeld bought it for the "Frolic."

Oppenheimer, George. Born New York 1900 of German-American parentage; educated at Franklin School, N. Y. C., Tome Preparatory School in Maryland, Williams College, M.A. and Harvard University, with a Post Graduate course including Baker's Workshop. His first play was a musical revue called "The Manhatters" (1927), with music by Alfred Nathan; "Here Today" (1932) and an adaptation of Jacques Deval's "Etienne" (1934), called "Another Love," followed. Then Hollywood.

Oursler, Charles Fulton. Born Baltimore 1893. Two years in law, seven years on the staff of the Baltimore *American;* has written novels, among them "Behold This Dreamer," and "Sandalwood"; first play "The Spider," with Lowell Brentano; later plays "Behold This Dreamer," "All the King's Horses," "Nowadays"; since 1929, "All the King's Men" in New York; "Nude with Pineapple," written with Aubrey Kennedy, produced in Pasadena. Mr. Oursler is editor of *Liberty* magazine and general editorial adviser for all Bernarr Macfadden magazines. He spends most of his time at home in West Falmouth, Mass., doing his editing by teletype communication.

Page, Mann. Born Denver, Col., 1889. Educated Alexandria public schools and Episcopal High School, Alexandria, Va. First play, "The American Boy," produced at Elitch's Gardens, Denver, when he was thirteen; other plays, "Lights Out" and "The Backslapper" (with Paul Dickey), "Mama Loves Papa" (with John McGowan), "Hush Money" (with Alfred E. Jackson) and "House Afire" produced at the Little Theatre in March of 1930. Then Hollywood.

Park, Samuel John. Born Alabama 1892 of Scotch-English parentage. Wrote "Lilly White" and "Black Water," neither of which reached Broadway; his "Philadelphia" (1929) and "Black Widow" (1936) both produced.

Pascal, Ernest. Born in London, England, in 1896; brought to America in 1903; educated public schools. His first play "The Charlatan" (1922), in collaboration with Leonard Praskins; "The Amorous Antic" (1929) and "The Marriage Bed" (1929), a dramatization of one of his own novels. With Edwin Harvey Blum wrote "I Am My Youth" (1938), dealing with the loves of Percy Bysshe Shelley, produced by Alfred de Liagre.

Perlman, William Jacob. Born Prenin, Lithuania, 1886; came to America as a child; attended public schools, College of the City of New York, School of Mines, Columbia University. First play to be produced "My Country"; second "The Bottom of the Cup," a collaboration with John Tucker Battle; others "The Broken Chain" (1929), "House of Remsen" (1934), written with Nicholas Soussanin and Marie Baumer.

Perkins, Kenneth. Son of a missionary; born Kodai Kanal, South India, 1890; educated Towers Boarding School in the Far East, and Lowell High School, San Francisco, later getting his B.S. and M.A. at the University of California. First play "Bagdad" (1913), in California; "Creoles" (1927), written with Sam Shipman, got 104 performances; "Desire" (1930) in Philadelphia; "Dance with Your Gods" (1934), New York. Mr. Perkin's has had 21 novels published here and in England.

Peters, Paul. An organizer of the Theatre Union, which produced two of his three plays, "Stevedore" (1934), written with George Sklar and got 111 performances; "Mother" (1935), translated from a German version of the Gorky play, and "Parade" (1935), produced by The Theatre Guild, written with George Sklar, Frank Gabrielson, David Lesan and Kyle Crichton.

Pezet, A. W. Born Lima, Peru, Feb. 22, 1889; great grandfather once President of Peru; father represented his country at Washington; educated in Washington and at Harvard where he studied drama under Professor Baker. First play "Remaking the Raleighs" (1913), produced in Washington; "Marrying Money" (1914), in Syracuse; "Schoolgirl" (1930), written with Carman Barnes; "Hotel Alimony" (1934), adapted from a play by Adolf Philipp and Max Simon; "In Heaven and Earth" (1936), written with Arthur Goodman, produced by Federal Theatre.

Powell, Dawn. Born Mt. Gilead, Ohio, 1900, of American parents with a strain of Dutch, English and some Indian; educated public schools, B.A. from Lake Erie College. First Broadway play produced by The Group Theatre, 1933, called "Big Night"; "Jig Saw" (1934), produced by The Theatre Guild; "Walking Down Broadway" (1931), sold directly to films.

Rapp, William Jourdan. Born New York City 1895; educated at Cornell University and the University of Paris; became a bacteriologist in Department of Health. First play "Harlem" (1929), written with Wallace Thurman, and getting 93 performances; others "Whirlpool" (1929), written with Walter Marquiss; "Hilda Cassidy" (1933), written with Henry and Sylvia Lieferant; "Substitute for Murder" (1936), co-authored by Leonardo Bercovici; "The Holmeses of Baker Street" (1936), adapted by Messrs. Rapp and Bercovici from a comedy by Basil Mitchell. Mr. Rapp is editor of *True Story* magazine and was once a feature writer for the New York *Times*.

Rath, Frederick. Wrote "First Night" which intrigued New York theatregoers for three months in 1930; two others were "Solitaire" (1929), written with Koby Kohn, and "Her Tin Soldier" (1933), produced by William Brady.

Reed, Daniel. Associated with Maurice Browne at the Chicago Little Theatre, a founder of the Town Theatre, Columbia, S. C. Adapted "Scarlet Sister Mary" (1930), for Ethel Barrymore from Julia Peterkin's novel.

Reed, Luther. Born Berlin, Wisconsin, 1888; educated public schools of Beloit, Wis., and New York, and Columbia University; wrote "Dear Me" with Hale Hamilton, "The Scarlet Man" with William LeBaron; went to Hollywood.

Robertson, Willard. Born Runnels, Texas, 1886; educated public schools of Texas and Washington, D. C., honor man at National University Law School, Washington. First play "Big Game" (with Kilbourn Gordon); has also written "The Sea Woman," "Black Velvet" and "This Man's Town" (1930).

Robinson, Bertrand. Came from Denver; apprenticeship in vaudeville and stock. First play "Tommy," written with Howard Lindsay, ran 192 performances at the Gaiety in New York in 1927; "Your Uncle Dudley" (1929) and "O Promise Me" (1930), had fair runs; wrote "Crime Marches On" (1935), with Maxwell Hawkins.

Robinson, Charles. Attended drama classes at Columbia where he met

Kenyon Nicholson; together they wrote "Sailor Beware" (1936), which had a run of 500 performances, and "Swing Your Lady" (1937), 100 performances; "Mahogany Hall" (1934), first solo work.

Rogers, Merrill. Born Worcester, Massachusetts, 1892; educated at Harvard. First play "Her First Affair" (1927), taken to London in 1930; "A Thousand Summers" (1932), produced with Jane Cowl, Osgood Perkins and Franchot Tone in the cast.

Rosendahl, Henry Augustus. Born Chicago 1907; German and Dutch parentage; Military school, then University of California. First play "A Lady in Pawn" (1931), produced in Chicago; "Yesterday's Orchids" (1934), and "Strip Girl" (1935), in New York.

Rosener, George. Has written two plays with Edward Knoblock as co-author, "Speak Easy" (1927) and "If a Body" (1935). Another play, without a collaborator, "She Got What She Wanted" (1929), ran for 120 performances.

Rouverol, Aurania. Born in Salt Lake City of English and Scotch ancestry; graduated from Stanford University, studied drama at Harvard Workshop, Washington University and the University of California. First play, "Skidding" (1928), ran for 448 performances; has grossed about $70,000 in the amateur market in six years; others include "It Never Rains" (1929), got 185 performances; "Growing Pains" (1933), and "Places Please" (1937).

Royle, Edwin Milton. Born Lexington, Mo., 1862. Crossed the plains in a coach; attended a Presbyterian school, the Salt Lake Collegiate Institute, and Princeton, thence to the Edinburgh University and finally to Columbia law school. First New York production "Friends"; wrote "Capt. Impudence," "The Squaw Man," "The Struggle Everlasting," "These Are My People" and "Her Way Out."

Rubin, Daniel N. First two plays, "Night Duel" and "Devils," both produced in 1926, were failures, the third, "Women Go On Forever" (1927), with Mary Boland, was a success. Other plays were "Claire Adams" (1929), "Riddle Me This" (1932), which played 170 performances; and "Move On Sister" (1936), which failed.

Savage, Courtenay. Born New York City 1891; English, Irish and French ancestry; private and public schools and Columbia. First play, "Don't Bother Mother" (1925), second, "They All Want Something," made out of E. J. Rath's book, "The Dark Chapter," a success; others produced on Broadway include "The Buzzard," "Virtue's Bed," "The Queen at Home" (with Shirley Warde and Vivian Cosby) and "Loose Moments" (1935). "The Little Dog Laughed" written with Jean Ferguson from Leonard Merrick's story, "Nelly Was a Lady" and "Forever and Forever" have been tried out in summer theatres.

Scarborough, George Moore. Born Mt. Carmel, Tex., 1875. Studied at Baylor University; graduated from the University of Texas with an LL.B. in 1897. In Texas a lawyer. In New York a reporter on the *American;* worked with the U. S. Department of Justice. First play "The Lure"; others "At Bay," "What Is Love?" "The Heart of Wetona," and "The Son Daughter," both revised by Mr. Belasco; late plays, "From Hell Came a Lady," produced in Los Angeles; "Bad Babies" and three written with Anna Westbay: "The Heaven Tappers," "The Girl I Loved" and "The Moon of Honey."

Schoenfeld, Bernard C. Born New York City. Went to both Harvard and Yale. First play "Shooting Star" written with Noel Pierce; second, "Hitch Your Wagon" (1937), tried in New York. Mr. Schoenfeld lives in Washington where he is an officer on the Educational Radio Project of the government.

Scott, Allan. Wrote "Good-bye Again" with George Haight which Arthur Beckhard produced in December, 1932, with Osgood Perkins and Sally Bates playing the leads; ran 200 performances; his "In Clover" (1937), previously called "Midsummer Night," did not do so well.

Sklar, George. Born Meriden, Conn., of Russian-Jewish parents, 1908; went to Yale, 1929; drama school course, 1931. First play written with Albert Maltz, called "Merry-Go-Round"; others "Peace on Earth," "Stevedore" (1934), written with Paul Peters, and "Parade" (1935), produced by Theatre Guild.

Stangé, Hugh. Born New York City 1894; Irish and French; attended Loyola School and New York Military Academy; member combat unit of the 27th Division, A.E.F. First produced play a dramatization of Booth Tarkington's "Seventeen" with Stannard Means as collaborator; produced Chicago, 1917, New York 1918; others include "You Know Me, Al," a 27th Division show that grossed $60,000 in ten days; "Fog-Bound," "Tin Pan Alley," "Headquarters," "False Dreams, Farewell," "After Tomorrow" (1931), written with John Golden; "The Long Road" (1930), "Veneer," and "Mother Sings."

Stanley, Martha. Born Cape Cod, Mass., 1879. Educated high schools, Summer training schools and Boston school of Journalism. First play "My Son"; also has written in collaboration with Adelaide Matthews "Nightie Night" (played around the world), "Scrambled Wives," "The Teaser," "Puppy Love," "The Wasp's Nest" and "Let and Sublet" (1930).

Starling, Lynn. Born Hopkinsville, Ky., 1893. Educated in public schools and at Centre College. Taught at Lawrenceville School for Boys, on stage for ten years. First play "Meet the Wife"; also is author of "In His Arms," "Weak Sisters," "Skin Deep," "A Cup of Sugar" (1931), "The First Apple" (1933). Now in Hollywood.

Stewart, Donald Ogden. Born Columbus, Ohio, 1894. Attended Phillips Exeter and Yale; joined the Navy to see the war; became an actor in Philip Barry's "Holiday" in 1928; played a part in his own play, "Rebound," in 1929; wrote "Fine and Dandy," a musical comedy, and "Los Angeles," with Max Marcin.

Stillman, Henry. Born in Brooklyn. Educated in the public schools. First play "Prince Vagabond"; others were "Nightshade," "Nocturne" (from Swinnerton's novel) and "Lally." Two were produced out of New York: "As Others See Us" and "The Other Side."

Stone, Sydney. Born Yorkshire, England, 1884; educated at St. George's and by tutors; writing for the American stage for more than a decade. First play "Love Scandal" (1923), followed by "Their First Baby," "Restless Woman," "The Barrister," "Jerry Decides" and "Over the Wire."

Sturges, Preston. Born Chicago, Ill., 1898, of Irish-English-American ancestry; educated in France, Switzerland, Germany, and America; attended Dr. Coulter's School in Chicago, Irving School, New York City. First play, "The Guinea Pig" (1929), produced first at the Provincetown Wharf Theatre, Cape Cod, later in New York; next play, "Strictly Dishonorable" (1929), was produced by Brock Pemberton and ran continuously for 557 performances. "Recapture" (1930), "The Well of Romance" (1930), and "Child of Manhattan" (1932), followed. Then Hollywood.

Thompson, Julian. Wrote "The Warrior's Husband" (1932), in which Katharine Hepburn made an early hit. Ran for three months in New York in 1932; adapted Walter Hasenclever's German comedy, "Her Man of Wax" (1933).

Toler, Sidney. Born Warrensburg, Mo., 1874. First play "The Belle of Richmond"; other plays "The Exile," "Playthings," "The Man They Left Behind," "The Dancing Master," "Miss Efficiency," "Golden Days" (written with Marion Short), "House on the Sands" and "Ritzy" (1930), with Viva Tattersall.

Totten, Joe Byron. Born Brooklyn, New York, of Scotch-Irish parentage in 1875; educated at St. Francis Xavier and St. Francis of Assisium Colleges in New York; has been actor, director and playwright; has written half a hundred plays, among them: "Alibi Bill," "The Cowboy and the Squaw," which toured for three years; "Spook House"

(1930); many adaptations, including "House of Bondage" (by Reginald Wright Kauffman), which had a long tour; "Arms and the Woman" (by Harold McGrath); "Riders of the Purple Sage" (by Zona Gale); "John Barleycorn" (by Jack London); "Valiants of Virginia" (by Hallie Erminie Rives).

Treadwell, Sophie. Born in California of pioneer stock—Spanish and English; protégée of Madame Modjeska; helped write that actress's memoirs. First Broadway production "Gringo" (1922). Others "Oh, Nightingale" (1925), "Machinal" (1929), which later played at the Kamerny Theatre in Moscow for a year; "Ladies Leave" (1929), "Lone Valley" (1933), "Plumes in the Dust" (1936), a biographical drama about Edgar Allan Poe.

Tully, Richard Walton. Born Nevada City, Cal., 1877. Educated at University of California. Started writing at the turn of the century with "A Strenuous Life" and "Rose of the Rancho." "The Bird of Paradise," produced by Oliver Morosco at Daly's, was his most successful play and has been making money or trouble for him ever since its 112 performances on Broadway back in 1912. The trouble consisted of a long and bitter law suit brought by Grace A. Fendler, author of "In Hawaii," claiming plagiarism. The Court of Appeals of New York upheld Mr. Tully's claim of authorship after six years of litigation in 1932. In 1930 the play was adapted into a musical comedy by Howard Emmet Rogers (music by Rudolph Friml) and produced by Arthur Hammerstein.

Unger, Gladys. Born San Francisco, Cal., settled in London, England; wrote a couple of hundred plays, including "Henry of Lancaster," which Ellen Terry played, and later "The Son and Heir"; wrote musical comedy books, "The Nightbirds," "Marriage Market" and "Betty"; after the war she returned to America and did a series of adaptations for Lee Shubert, including "The Goldfish" for Marjorie Rambeau, "The Business Widow" for Leo Ditrichstein, "The Love Habit," "The Werewolf," "Stolen Fruit," "The Monkey Talks," "Lovely Lady," "The Madcap," "Starlight," for Doris Keane, and "Two Girls Wanted," which played for forty-two weeks. Recent plays have been "Ladies of Creation," "Nona," "$25 an Hour" (with Leyla Georgie), "Private Beach" (with Jesse Lasky) and an adaptation from the German of Wilhelm Sterck called "Experience Unnecessary."

Waters, Hadley. Born New York City 1896. First production in New York "The Ghost Parade" (1929); wrote "Little Orchid Annie" (1930), which had had its première in Los Angeles, where Ruth Taylor and Betty Bronson played the leads in different revivals.

Waters, Marianne. Born Worcester, Mass., 1906. First play to be produced in New York "Only Human" (1933). Others included "The Blue Widow" (1933) with Queenie Smith and "Right This Way" (1938), which had previously been called "Hitch Your Wagon."

Webb, Kenneth. Born New York 1892. Educated Collegiate School and Columbia University; nephew of Digby Bell, comedian. First long play, "One of the Family," ran over 200 performances in New York. "The Houseboat on the Styx," written with John E. Hazzard, had a long run and "Gay Divorcee," a musical adaptation by Mr. Webb and Samuel Hoffenstein of a comedy written by Dwight Taylor and based on a play by the late J. Hartley Manners, made a record of 250 performances in late 1932. Other Webb plays are "Zombie" and "Birdie."

Weiman, Rita. Born Philadelphia; attended Friends' Central School in Philadelphia, Art Students' League in New York; wanted to be an actress, took it out in writing. Collaborated with Alice Pollock and produced "The Co-respondent"; afterward wrote "The Acquittal" and "Moon Magic." In December of 1937 "The King's Breakfast," written by Miss Weiman and Maurice Marks, was produced at the Repertory Theatre in London.

West, Mae. Born Brooklyn 1892. Mother an actress; started her stage career at a tender age; switched from stock to vaudeville and then to musical shows. Her first play was "Sex," written under the pseudonym of Jane Mast; "The Wicked Age" (1927) appeared under the alleged authorship of Anton Scibilia; "The Drag" faded out under the frown of censorship; "Diamond Lil" (1928), had a run and brought Miss West to the attention of the public; "The Constant Sinner" (1931) followed, after which Miss West left for Hollywood.

Wilbur, Crane. Born Athens, New York, 1889. Started in the theatre as an actor in 1904; connected with the movies for some years. His first plays were "The Common Cause" (1918), and "The Love Liar" (1918). Others followed: "The Ouija Board" (1920), "The Monster" (1922), "Easy Terms" (1925), "The Song Writer" (1928), "Halfway to Hell" (1934), and "Are You Decent" (1934), which had a run of 188 performances.

Willard, John. Born San Francisco 1888; educated in Paris and at the University of California; an aviator during the war; an actor later. First play "Eunice," a Greek tragedy in blank verse; others "The Blue Flame," "The Green Beetle," "The Red Hate," "The Cat and the Canary," "Sisters," "Fog," "Adventure" and "Twelve Hours," produced by Reginald Bach at the Comedy Theatre, London, in December, 1930.

Wilmurt, Arthur. Born New York City 1906. Received B.A. at Amherst 1928; spent three years at Yale under George P. Baker. First play "Guest Room" tried out at Yale and arriving on Broadway in October of 1931. His adaptation of André Obey's "Noah" (1935), was produced with Pierre Fresnay in the leading role.

Wilson, Frank. Born New York City 1891; attended American Academy of Dramatic Art for three years after finishing Grammar School; one of the best known of the Negro playwrights; has written about 20 Negro playlets on Negro life; leads in "In Abraham's Bosom" and "Porgy." His first play, "Pa Williams Gal" (1923), played by the late Richard B. Harrison of "Green Pastures" and the late Rose McClendon; other plays "Brother Jones" and "Meek Mose"; his "Walk Together Chillun" (1936) produced by the WPA Federal Theatre.

Young, Howard Irving. Born Jersey City 1893; educated New York University and at the Sorbonne; scenario writer and production manager for the motion pictures. First play "March On!" (1925), "Not Herbert," "Camera," "The Star Gazer," "Hawk Island" and "The Drums Begin."

INDEX OF PLAYWRIGHTS

329

INDEX OF PLAYS